FOUNDATIONS OF
EDUCATION:
DISSENTING VIEWS

Foundations of Education:
Dissenting Views

Edited by

James J. Shields, Jr.
Associate Professor
City College
The City University of New York

Colin Greer
Executive Editor
Social Policy Magazine

JOHN WILEY & SONS, INC.
New York • London • Sydney • Toronto

Copyright © 1974, by John Wiley & Sons, Inc.

All rights reserved.

No part of this book may be reproduced by any means, nor transmitted, nor translated into a machine language without the written permission of the publisher.

Library of Congress Cataloging in Publication Data:

Shields, James J   comp.
  Foundations of education: dissenting views.

  Bibliography: p.
  1. Education—United States—Addresses, essays, lectures.   I. Greer, Colin, joint comp.   II. Title.

LA205.S47 1974   370'.973   73-16438
ISBN 0-471-78634-9
ISBN 0-471-78635-7 (pbk.)

Printed in the United States of America

10 9 8 7 6 5 4 3 2 1

contents

One   The Functions and Purposes of Schools: Philosophical
   Foundations   1
   James Herndon, *Find a Good School and Send Your Kid There*   8
   Paulo Freire, *The Banking Concept of Education*   14
   Paul Goodman, *Education: Incidental and Scholastic*   23

Two   An Historical Perspective on the Functions and Purposes
   of Schools   29
   Colin Greer, *Public Schools: The Myth of the Melting Pot*   29
   Joel H. Spring, *Anarchism and Education—The Dissenting
      Tradition*   36
   Clarence J. Karier, *Elite Views on American Education*   44

Three   The Social and Cultural Dimension: Family
   Background and Educational Opportunity   55
   Peter Schrag, *End of the Impossible Dream*   55
   S. M. Miller and Pamela Roby, *Education and Social Mobility*   65

Four   How Schools are Financed: The Economic Foundations
   of Education   75
   John E. Coons, William H. Clune, and Stephen Sugarman,
   School Financing: Its Uses as an Apparatus of Privilege.   75

Five   Who Controls Education: The Politics of Education   89
   Christopher Jencks, *Who Should Control Education?*   90
   James Ridgeway, *Universities as Big Business*   101
   Alan Wolfe, *Reform Without Reform*   107

Six   Education in International and Comparative Perspective   115
   Brian Jackson and Denis Marsden, *Eighty-Eight Working Class
      Children Who Succeeded in School*   116

Seven   Educational Alternatives: Reforming the School
   System   137
   John Bremer and Michael von Moschzisker, *The School
      Without Walls: Philadelphia's Parkway Program*   138
   Judith Areen and Christopher Jencks, *Educational Vouchers:
      A Proposal for Diversity and Choice*   148

Eight   Educational Alternatives: Free Schools and No
    Schools   157
    Jonathan Kozol, *Free Schools*   158
    George Dennison, *The Lives of Children: The Story of the First
      Street School*   163
    Paul Goodman, *The Present Moment in Education*   169
    Ivan Illich, *After Deschooling, What?*   173

Nine
    James J. Shields, Jr., *A Postscript: Social Reform as Educational*   187
      Policy.

Ten   Bibliography   197

introduction

The subtitle, "Dissenting Views on American Public Education," was chosen carefully. Even though educational dissent has served as a useful vehicle for centering the attention of a large segment of the public on educational questions, it has, more often than not, severely distorted the important issues that lie at the base of significant reform. The distortion is largely a result of the failure to come to terms with the relationship between schooling and social inequality. Expressions of dissent rarely come to grips with the ways in which schools function to serve society. Indeed, this is why the last decade of highly charged declarations on the school crisis has generated so little change either within schools or outside.

The tide of disssent rides, with a certain degree of regularity, between progressive and conservative. Currently, the thrust seems to be moving toward a form of conservatism that stresses institutional efficiency and rests on the assumption that schools succeed when they achieve safety and security for the well-positioned individuals in society. In progressive periods, personal freedom and matters related to social justice and public schooling are emphasized. However, in practice, progressives and conservatives are similar in that, finally, both support reforms that reflect a very narrow definition of education. Education is treated as if it were synonymous with schooling, and the relationship of schooling to the other sources of education is largely ignored.

Beneath the different vocabularies of the conservatives and the progressives lies a traditional faith that school reform will somehow bring about social mobility and the good life. The reality is that after all manner of school reform, stratification and immobility continue to be reflected and reinforced by schools, most notably in the ways in which intelligence is defined. School process has successfully socialized children into widely unequal positions in society and has conditioned the mass of society into a state of impotence, fear, dependence, and irresponsibility that prepares them to accept an assembly-line adult life.

The contradiction between reform rhetoric and the educational reform that it generates is considerable. Students, whether educated by those who define education in conventional academic terms or by those who value feelings and personal relations above all else, find their education serves the existing socioeconomic pattern. Whether IQ or peer grouping or creative expression are used, the same children win

1

and the same children lose, perennially reflecting abilities acquired through social class position in the world outside the school.

Even though various periods of progressive reform—the Progressive era at the turn of the century, the New Deal era of Depression days, and the New Frontier era of the 1960s—have contributed a great deal to the possibilities for educational change, the results rarely were open-ended either in process or in outcome. Innovations such as child-centered schooling, desegregation, community control and decentralization, and now free and affective education have been narrowly translated into school practice. Often, these innovations have served as little more than mechanisms for the old hierarchies of privilege to buy time to reassemble their position in periods of changing needs and consciousness.

While most educators have some sense of the movement of educational practices to the tune of the societal drummer, few of them permit this awareness to impinge on their workaday lives. The general subservience of public schooling to outside forces has yet to be explicitly acknowledged in anything but the most superficial ways. For this reason, most efforts to reform schools operate within a framework that limits their long-range significance.

The time has come when we must dig below surface issues and expose for public debate the ways in which schools in America freeze children into widely unequal social classes and treat them like so many silly geese being stuffed for a kind of corporate *fois gras*. The scope of action allowed to pupils extends only as far as receiving, filing, and storing teacher deposits. What appear to be teacher questions on the surface really turn out, under analysis, to be statements. Teachers tend to ask a "question" and then move from student to student, disregarding perfectly reasonable answers, until someone gives the answer desired.

The result is that in all classrooms—"open" and "closed"—students instinctively develop strategies for conning teachers. In the process, thinking is obliterated, real questions are thwarted, and curiosity is inhibited. Typically, the well-educated person is an adapted man whose capacity to think, to feel, and to act has been schooled out of him.

None of this is new. C. Wright Mills' description of the well-schooled and well-placed person of the 1950s still provides a good base for definition:

"He has no projects of his own; he fulfills the routines that exist. He is not truly aware of his daily experience and its actual standards; he drifts, he fulfills habits . . . . He loses his independence, and more importantly he loses the desire to be independent; in fact, he does not

*have hold of the idea of being an independent individual with his own
mind and his own worked-out way of life."*

School is a desperate competition where everyone loses, although
some lose more than others. Students are thrown out on their own and
pitted against each other in such a way that it becomes an accepted
fact that survival depends upon cheating in examinations, plagiarizing
other people's work, and conning teachers and administrators.

The fear of losing is great; it is a fear that colors every school
experience without exception. James Herndon, imaginative educator
and sensitive parent, was touched by this fear through his son and
deals with the experience in *How to Survive in Your Native Land.* One
day as he accompanied his son, Jack, to his first-grade class in what
everyone agreed is a good school run by good people, Jack burst into
tears. Herndon's efforts to console his son were in vain; Jack was too
frightened. Why? Jack had forgotten his homework.

Jack was only in first grade, but he was already aware that in school
there are winners and losers, and that winners succeed at the expense
of losers. As Herndon points out, the median on the bell curve is not a
median, nor is it an average, nor is it a norm. It is a losing sign, a
failure, a hex. To succeed, you must be out on the right-hand edge
where the curve approaches the base line. Unfortunately, it is the
nature of bell curves that only a few can be there.

Some people defend competition as a legitimate method of teaching.
No one, however, would defend the rigged competition we have in
schools. Practically everyone knows about the "school fix" except the
poor, who have been manipulated into believing that schooling offers
them possibilities for their own ascent. The reality is that schooling
does not make it easier for the poor to earn the credentials required for
good jobs. Schooling is an institutionalized obstacle course designed to
keep the poor on the bottom and to make them think that is where they
deserve to be.

When the Fleishmann Commission reported, in 1972, that the biggest
problem in New York State is the high correlation between student
socioeconomic and racial origin and school success or failure, it was
simply stating afresh what school studies since the late nineteenth
century had revealed. As several of the selections that follow indicate,
the statistics on the role that social-class position plays in school
grades, academic achievement, IQ scores, and college attendance is
overwhelming.

Nowhere is the effort to maintain unequal schooling for the various
social classes more evident than in the way in which schools are financed. This is well-illustrated in the case of two New York school dis-

tricts within 10 miles of each other, Great Neck and Levittown. While the local property tax in each community in 1969 was the same, school property taxes in Great Neck generated four times as much money per student as they did in Levittown. Thus the Levittown student had $1189 spent on his education, while $2077 was spent on each Great Neck student.

Since the typical household income in Levittown is considerably less than in Great Neck, families in Levittown paid a greater proportion of their income on school property taxes and received substantially fewer dollars in return for education. Families in poor school districts often pay higher taxes for an inferior education for their children. This is as true in most of the other 50 states as it is in New York.

The problem is that the schools mirror a society that is consciously unjust and unequal. School is the dependent variable in the school-society relationship. On all grade levels, and in all classes, the public school favors the children of the rich and the established. Schools are used by the middle and upper classes to start their children on the road to the limited number of good positions in society. They know that much of their children's success depends on their ability to acquire more and better schooling than the mass of society. Of course, others are aware of the importance of schooling as well. Much of the conflict we witness in education centers around the struggle of well-placed individuals in society to maintain the competitive advantage of their children. John Holt, in *Freedom and Beyond,* notes that the comfortable, pleasant, and powerful places in society are occupied, and that the people in those places are not going to move out of them and down in society so that the poor can move up and in. He points out that as long as the overall shape of the job pyramid remains the same, and as long as the number of good, fair, and bad jobs remains what it is, any poor person who moves up to a better job is going to move up at someone's expense.

Schools, no less than other institutions in our society, reflect the dominant values of that society. Ours is a world of coordination, scheduling, and programming, a world where the watchwords have become maximization and optimization, and virtue is defined in terms of efficiency. Organizations are run like machines and men function as machinelike men. Daniel Bell once remarked that the modern corporation is archetypical of these contemporary rhythms. And the school, as he said, reflects this. Hence, the current reform fad, for example, to make education goals "competency" or "proficiency" based.

The competency-based education movement continues what is now a rather well-established tradition in American education of drawing upon the industrial corporation for educational philosophy, methods, and organization. Raymond Callahan's decade-old *Education and the Cult of Efficiency* traces the history of the introduction of business values and practices into schools between 1900 and 1930. He points out that in the first decade of this century reformers extolled modern business methods and saw in them the solution to educational problems. Schools, they felt, should be organized and operated in a businesslike way.

The reformers were so successful that school administrators soon began to adopt the businessman as their model. And so three generations of school reformers succeeded in making the schools more businesslike. The direction of education in America between 1900 and 1930, as Callahan records it, is one in which educational questions are subordinated to business considerations.

But schools are not just managed as if they are business operations; they function to promote business values, too. One of the most important business values taught is consumerism. On no other matter—religious, political, or moral—are individuals so elaborately and skillfully instructed.

One of the most widely accepted principles in our society is the more we produce and sell, the better things are. Annual increase in the Gross National Product (GNP) is used as a test of social success. Consumption, and its corollary "growth," are the *sine qua non* in strategies of development and definitions of progress. As a result, our schools maintain, with an almost religious fervor, winning and losing, having and not having as the dominant framework out of which they operate.

Paul Goodman recognized this years ago when he wrote that in this society we grow up absurd. It may even be that absurd is too mild an invective to describe a world in which objects are more important than people, and in which the corporate superstructure, public and private, influences all social relationships. It is a matter for invective, but it is a matter for awe as well. As John Kenneth Galbraith writes, "It is the genius of the industrial system that it makes the goals that reflect its needs coordinate with social virtue and human enlightenment."

Faced with the charge that there is something terribly wrong with the schools, professional educators usually fall back on the consumption syndrome as a defense. Inevitably, the cause and the proposed solutions offered for educational problems can be reduced simply to the word *more*. The sky could be completely papered with the articles written by educators about the need for more. Spokesmen for the AFL-CIO-affiliated teachers union, for example, argue that the solution to the problem of how to educate the last third of the students in our schools is ". . . more teachers . . . better physical facilities . . . (and) new devices which increase the productivity of educational workers. . . ." Theodore Sizer, historian and former dean of the Harvard Graduate School of Education, provides another example in a statement he made to a *New York Times* reporter. Sizer said, ". . . the public schools are, at the bottom, sound and effective, and that most of their ills can be cured by *more* money."

It is common knowledge that more money and more schooling within the context of our existing society is not the answer. Yet, most school reform efforts fail to face this reality. The answer is not to be found in new ways for schools to do their job better; instead, the task is to reorient schools away from an exploitative social structure and turn them around so that they function to promote tension in their relationship with other societal institutions.

ONE

The Functions and Purposes of Schools: Philosophical Foundations

Few analyze in depth the meaning of schooling in their lives. When faced with the question of what school means to them, some respond matter of factly: It means nothing; it is a frightful waste of time. Most, however, see school as the place where they acquire basic skills, especially skills related to reading and writing and a smattering of knowledge about man and his world. Schooling is largely seen as something that is done at a certain age, simply a path that must be followed while waiting for adulthood.

Schooling does more for us than we realize; the school as a social institution is immensely successful. But, unfortunately, the school succeeds in ways that are destructive to those it theoretically exists to serve. Along with lessons in reading, health education, auto mechanics, algebra, and social studies, students are given more indirect lessons in their own worthlessness, the virtues of inequality and social exploitation, and the standardization of thought, feelings, and behavior for the sake of technical and corporate efficiency.

Whatever the original purpose of schooling was, whether it was to transform Irish shepherds into clerics, as Goodman claims, or to prepare men to participate in a democracy, as Jefferson argued, schools have evolved into institutions that destroy much of what is wholesome in man. Through competitive exercises, schools label children as winners and losers, rob them of their ability to feel, to think and act, and teach them to accept and adapt to the world as it is. In all these functions, the schools serve the well-placed and established in society. Obviously, the schools are a long way from where they started and a long way from achieving the humanistic ideals of freedom, equality, and justice that they were created to support.

FIND A GOOD SCHOOL
AND SEND YOUR KID THERE

James Herndon

If Excelsior! School deals with really disadvantaged kids then Tierra Firma Elementary deals with advantage. Its kids come from Tierra Firma itself, the first suburb of San Francisco, discovered or invented for the reason all suburbs are discovered or invented—its people hope to drop out of the problems of America and enjoy its promise.

The people of Tierra Firma are the advantaged of America. They make enough money to afford cheap developer-built houses, cars, boats, bowling balls and plenty of Sta-Prest pants, but, since that is true of many other groups of people in America, including the rich, that is not the source of their advantage. They are advantaged because they believe in the promise of America and are actually satisfied by it when they get it and by the striving which they must constantly do to keep getting and believing in it. They believe, for instance, that as long as you are free to buy things on credit then you can keep going to work in order to pay those payments and that the one justifies the other and makes it meaningful. They know what you are supposed to do and by and large make an effort to do it and see the results and they are not cynical about the results. They have perhaps moved from big old Mission Street or North Beach wooden carpenter-Gothic houses and flats, where the plumbing is always going out of whack and streetcars run past the door, to three-bedroom tract houses with a back yard and a palm tree in the front and a garage and streets where the kids can ride bikes, and they are glad they did so. Middle-class and rich people disdain Tierra Firma and move into those same old wooden houses and pay $40,000 and another $20,000 to fix them up good because they are not satisfied with America, just like the poor who have to stay in them without fixing them up. The advantaged move to Tierra Firma. They are advantaged because, I repeat, America still holds promise for them; if you do right, you can really get all this that Tierra Firma affords, and since that is exactly what they do want, and since they can get it, they are satisfied. No doubt many of them understand the political and economic manipulations necessary in order for Tierra Firma to exist; no doubt they have gripes about property tax and this and that; no doubt they know the poor exist and something perhaps ought to be done about it; no doubt many are against the war; no doubt they are

Source. James Herndon, *How To Survive In Your Native Land.* Copyright © 1971 by James Herndon. Used with permission of Simon & Schuster, Inc.

not all racists; and no doubt they know the TV ads are phony . . . but they are cast in the present right image of the country and know that they can and will make it in America *because they are really satisfied* with what they have got out of it. I know that if you hang around with liberal intellectuals or with militant Third World people or with poor people or with radical college students or, simply, if you hang around with people who are dissatisfied with the state of affairs, you will get the idea, and hope it is true, that most people in America are dissatisfied and then you will predict major changes in the country. To correct that mistaken state of mind, I hope you will go to work in Tierra Firma someday.

The fact remains that Tierra Firma Elementary School is one of the best public schools I have ever seen, and that is why I took Jay out there to school, and why, when Jack decided he'd like to go out there too, I took both my boys. It is a good school because of the principal, and because of the teachers whom he collected together over the rather long period of time that he has been principal there. It is a good school because for a few years there was a district superintendent who tried to get intelligent, serious people to come to work in the district and, once they did, allowed them to work. I have a good deal of respect for all the people involved in Tierra Firma School; they are, by and large, exactly the kinds of people that educational writers are always saying ought to be working with kids in school. They are bright, serious, hardworking, confident, innovative, humorous, well-read, creative, with-it. They are not repressive, narrow, grade-oriented, vain, afraid, hung-up on testing, conventional, or chicken-shit. They have guts; they like and respect the kids. The school itself is O.K. In modern one-story motel style, all the rooms open directly to the outdoors. There is plenty of space—a large asphalt play area for basketball, bikes and four-square, a big grass area, a little-kid's playground with swings and slides and monkey bars and tanbark, and a huge upper field of grass which is what convinced Jay to go there. He could see himself running free on that big grass field, looking like a whooping crane about to take off.

All right. But see, this is the same school that Fran visited and all the kids were running around on that really pleasant playground yelling about murder and MR and fuck you. That is what the kids are supposed to be doing in them no-good schools, in them ghetto schools, in them big-city pore schools, in them rich hippie dope-smoking schools, in them terrible repressive tracked grade-mad bureaucratic lesson-planned honky colonialist Fascist pig Cossack San Francisco schools with Irish or Italian old ladies who ought to have been nuns or ex-Navy disappointed commanders for principals. That is not what, in theory and on principle, kids are supposed to be doing in what few good schools there are in existence, for in fact the very reason for making the effort to have any good schools is so that the kids won't be in this bad shape. So why, if it's really a good school ain't it doing any good? Why is it that in this good school with these good people that Jack, in the first grade, who is really what everyone agrees is an excellent student—he can read, as far as I can see, anything, he can write, and not only that but he likes to draw and write and read a good deal of the time, he can in short do everything that the school, any school, wants him to be able to do and not only that but he is wise enough to be reasonably well behaved and polite when it counts . . . why is it that if one day on the way to this good school he realizes that in his urgency to get up to Mr. Ling's corner store and buy some fake wax teeth to show off and later chew, he has forgotten to bring along his homework in writing or math . . . why is it that then he bursts into tears? Why is it that then no effort of mine will console him? Why is he frightened? He, of all kids going to that good school, has the least reason to be frightened.

There is one reason, and only one, and it is crucial. That is that an American public school must have winners and losers. It does not matter in this respect what kind of school it is. In Berkeley, now that Mr. Sullivan has integrated the schools, it is the black kids who sit in Remedial Reading and the white kids who sit in Enriched this or that. When they are together in some general course the well-dressed sharp clean-and-pressed shoe-shined poor black kid sits in class next to the Salvation-army-surplus-store-ugly-dressed white rich kid and the beautiful poor black kid doesn't know what the teacher is talking about and the white ugly rich kid knows everything and can read or even has read everything the teacher can, even if that surplus-store white kid disdains the whole thing and won't answer or discuss or even attend class, even if he goes and smokes shit across the street or heads for the communal hills . . . try as he may to become an outcast the school knows that he is a winner even if he rejects winning. The intelligent hip young teacher will be copying his ugly clothes while pretending to try and straighten him out, get him off drugs, interest him in Egypt, which the teacher probably don't know nothing about. Or the intelligent old conservative teacher will be talking in the teachers' room about how bright the long-haired-ugly-clothes kid is even if a pain in the ass and that the school must find a way to motivate him, or force him, the country needs him, and so on. After class the black kid finds eight other black kids who have just had the same classroom experience and they link arms and walk jiving down the hall, covering the passageway wall to wall, forcing every one of them ugly know-it-all white play-poor winning motherfuckers with professor-fathers to change direction, go around the other way, shrink up against the wall. This phenomenon is then called racial unrest.

But over in Oakland there will be an all-black school, Mr. Sullivan not having passed through that town yet. It may be that the school would prefer to have some ugly white kids to be winners, but they in fact ain't got any. Does that mean a school full of losers? Not at all. That school has got to have winners too, and so some sharp pore beautiful black kids wind up in the A group and some others in the H group. It may be that if the kids in the Oakland A winner's group transferred over to Berkeley they would end up being losing kids, or it may be not. It doesn't make any difference. In Oakland they are winners. The H kids find the A kids in line at the cafeteria and hit them in they mouths.

In Tierra Firma, up until recently, all the kids have been these same advantaged lower-middle-class kids (white, black and brown) I've already mentioned. They ain't by and large ugly rich Army-Navy-store whites nor lime-green-creased pore beautiful blacks. So therefore the school only has winners? Certainly not. What kind of school would that be? Some of them advantaged kids have got to lose. It may be that if the losers of Tierra Firma transferred to Berkeley or Oakland then they would be winners. Or it may not be. The students who end up in a place like M.I.T. are certainly the winners of the Western world, the smartest, most with-it, craftiest Western technological human beings ever produced but even then all of them cannot be winners. Some of them must flunk out, because M.I.T. being a school in America has also got to have losers. Would those M.I.T. losers be winners at S.F. State? Maybe so and maybe not.

That is why Jack, my beloved son of seven years, bursts into tears and cannot be consoled. That is why some students of M.I.T. are throwing dodge balls at each other's heads, and a large group of physicists stands around the outskirts of the school grounds crying, and why nothing can console them even if someone hits them or doesn't hit them in they mouths.

They cry because the losers are going to get some revenge some way. But they also cry because the winning is never permanent. You may be a winner in the first grade, but by the fourth you may be losing. The rites of passage of the school go on and on. Each year it is circumcision time all over again; obviously you may weep for what has been hacked off by the time you are thirty-five and have a PhD.

How does the school make certain that it will have winners and losers? Well, obviously by giving grades. If you give A's, you must also give F's. Without the rest of the grades, the A is meaningless. Even a B is less good than an A—in short, every kid who does not get an A is failing and losing to some extent. The median on the bell curve is not a median, it is not an average, it is not a norm, not to the school and not to the kids in the school. It is a losing sign, a failure and a hex. You must be way out there on the right-hand edge where the curve approaches the base line. But it is the nature of bell curves that most everyone cannot be there.

But even if the school abandons grades and IQ and achievement testing it will still produce losers aplenty and winners. The fundamental act of the American public school is to deal with children in groups. Once it has a group of children of any age, it decides what those children will be expected to do, and then the teacher, as representative of the school, tells the children all at once. The children hear it, and when they hear it they know whether they can do it or not. Some of the children will already know how to do it. They will win. The teacher comes into the teachers' room the first day and says I already know who the good students are. I can predict the grades of almost every kid. Sure enough, the prediction works with minimum variation.

You deal with the children in groups. You teach first graders to read. You write *ch* on the board, and ask Who knows how this sounds? Some kids already know and raise their hands with tremendous relief. They are going to make it this year. Others think they know, but aren't sure. (Maybe *ch* has changed since their mamas told them.) Others never heard of it. They might be happy to know what it sounds like (why not?) but at the same time they see that a lot of other smart kids already know.

Whatever class, age group, grade, section it is, in a public school the subject matter is carefully arranged so that some of the kids will already know it before they get there. Then, for a little while in the primary grades, the school will try to teach those who didn't know it already. But it doesn't really work. It doesn't work because the winners keep intruding, raising their hands in advance of the question, or because while the teacher works with the losers on what the winners already know the winners are free to read or draw or talk to one another and therefore learn other stuff and when the loser gets into the second grade, having learned what the school demanded that he knew before he entered the first grade, the second grade will have assessed what the winners know and the losers don't know and produce that as the subject matter for the year. Later on, of course, the school will refuse to teach the losers at all. *In all public schools in the United States* the percentage of kids who cannot really read the social studies textbook or the science textbook or the directions in the New Math book or the explanations in the transformational grammar book is extraordinarily high. Half the kids. The school tells everyone that reading is the key to success in school, and no doubt it is, a certain kind of reading anyway. Does the school then spend time and effort teaching those kids who can't read the texts how to read the texts? Shit no, man. Why mess up a situation made to order for failure? At Spanish Main Intermediate School there are some eleven hundred students, at least half of whom can't read the books they lose and have to pay money for at the end of the year. The school hires one remedial reading teacher, who will only deal with about forty students per year. Even then, this teacher will not really teach the kids to read, but of course will review some complicated and nutty system which (again) some of the remedial reading students already know (although they can't read) and the others don't, for the remedial reading class is part of the school too. Well of course the school says it ain't got money enough for all them remedial reading teachers, otherwise it would love to teach everyone to read. But it does have money enough for a million social studies teachers to teach Egypt to groups of kids, a small percentage of whom already know everything about it, a large percentage of whom know enough to copy the encyclopedia, the text, or other kid's homework, and another large percentage of whom can't do anything but sit there, get in trouble, provide jobs for counselors and disciplinary vice-principals and consultants and psychologists (all of whom get paid to deal with problems the school causes every day) and become an unending supply of failure for the school.

So Jack does not misinterpret the school. Were you thinking that the homework was given to see if he could do it? To see if he had learned what was taught? You haven't learned your lesson. The homework was given to the winners to see if they would do it that night and bring it the next day. (It was given to the losers to show them they couldn't do it.) If they forget or refuse, they may have to stop being winners. For the fate of winners in a school is that they must do, over and over again, exercises and reviews and practices and assignments that they already know how to do, over and over again for twelve years, then four more, then four more . . . just as Jack has got to stop reading his books every morning in order to get ready to go to school in order to spend time doing workbooks and exercises so that he'll learn to read his books.

The school's purpose is not teaching. The school's purpose is to separate sheep from goats. You can find a very good school with lots of grass where the teachers don't yell at you. It separates. By all means send your kid there.

THE BANKING CONCEPT OF EDUCATION

Paulo Freire

A careful analysis of the teacher-student relationship at any level, inside or outside the school, reveals its fundamentally *narrative* character. This relationship involves a narrating Subject (the teacher) and patient, listening objects (the students). The contents, whether values or empirical dimensions of reality, tend in the process of being narrated to become lifeless and petrified. Education is suffering from narration sickness.

The teacher talks about reality as if it were motionless, static, compartmentalized, and predictable. Or else he expounds on a topic completely alien to the existential experience of the students. His task is to "fill" the students with the contents of his narration—contents which are detached from reality, disconnected from the totality that engendered them and could give them significance. Words are emptied of their concreteness and become a hollow, alienated, and alienating verbosity.

The outstanding characteristic of this narrative education, then, is the sonority of words, not their transforming power. "Four times four is sixteen; the capital of Pará is Belém." The student records, memorizes, and repeats these phrases without perceiving what four times four really means, or realizing the true significance of "capital" in the affirmation "the capital of Pará is Belém," that is, what Belém means for Pará and what Pará means for Brazil.

Narration (with the teacher as narrator) leads the students to memorize mechanically the narrated content. Worse yet, it turns them into "containers," into "receptacles" to be "filled" by the teacher. The more completely he fills the receptacles, the better a teacher he is. The more meekly the receptacles permit themselves to be filled, the better students they are.

Education thus becomes an art of depositing, in which the students are the depositories and the teacher is the depositor. Instead of communicating, the teacher issues communiqués and makes deposits which the students patiently receive, memorize, and repeat. This is the "banking" concept of education, in which the scope of action allowed to the students extends only as far as receiving, filing, and storing the deposits. They do, it is true, have the opportunity to become collectors or cataloguers of the things they store. But in the last analysis, it is men

Source. From *Pedagogy of the Oppressed,* by Paulo Freire. Copyright © 1970 Herder and Herder, Inc. Used by permission of the Seabury Press, New York.

themselves who are filed away through the lack of creativity, transformation, and knowledge in this (at best) misguided system. For apart from inquiry, apart from the praxis, men cannot be truly human.[1] Knowledge emerges only through invention and re-invention, through the restless, impatient, continuing, hopeful inquiry men pursue in the world, with the world, and with each other.

In the banking concept of education, knowledge is a gift bestowed by those who consider themselves knowledgeable upon those whom they consider to know nothing. Projecting an absolute ignorance onto others, a characteristic of the ideology of oppression, negates education and knowledge as processes of inquiry. The teacher presents himself to his students as their necessary opposite; by considering their ignorance absolute, he justifies his own existence. The students, alienated like the slave in the Hegelian dialectic, accept their ignorance as justifying the teacher's existence—but, unlike the slave, they never discover that they educate the teacher.

The *raison d'être* of libertarian education, on the other hand, lies in its drive towards reconciliation. Education must begin with the solution of the teacher-student contradiction, by reconciling the poles of the contradiction so that both are simultaneously teachers *and* students.

This solution is not (nor can it be) found in the banking concept. On the contrary, banking education maintains and even stimulates the contradiction through the following attitudes and practices, which mirror oppressive society as a whole:

(a) The teacher teaches and the students are taught.
(b) The teacher knows everything and the students know nothing.
(c) The teacher thinks and the students are thought about.
(d) The teacher talks and the students listen—meekly.
(e) The teacher disciplines and the students are disciplined.
(f) The teacher chooses and enforces his choice, and the students comply.
(g) The teacher acts and the students have the illusion of acting through the action of the teacher.
(h) The teacher chooses the program content, and the students (who were not consulted) adapt to it.
(i) The teacher confuses the authority of knowledge with his own authority, which he sets in opposition to the freedom of the students.
(j) The student is the Subject of the learning process, while the pupils are mere objects.

It is not surprising that the banking concept of education regards men

---

[1] *Praxis* means reflection and action upon the world in order to change it.

as adaptable, manageable beings. The more students work at storing the deposits entrusted to them, the less they develop the critical consciousness which would result from their intervention in the world as transformers of that world. The more completely they accept the passive role imposed on them, the more they tend simply to adapt to the world as it is and to the fragmented view of reality deposited in them.

The capability of banking education to minimize or annul the students' creative power and to stimulate their credulity serves the interests of the oppressors, who care neither to have the world revealed nor to see it transformed. The oppressors use their "humanitarianism" to preserve a profitable situation. Thus they react almost instinctively against any experiment in education which stimulates the critical faculties and is not content with a partial view of reality but always seeks out the ties which link one point to another and one problem to another.

Indeed, the interests of the oppressors lie in "changing the consciousness of the oppressed, not the situation which oppresses them";[2] for the more the oppressed can be led to adapt to that situation, the more easily they can be dominated. To achieve this end, the oppressors use the banking concept of education in conjunction with a paternalistic social action apparatus, within which the oppressed receive the euphemistic title of "welfare recipients." They are treated as individual cases, as marginal men who deviate from the general configuration of a "good, organized, and just" society. The oppressed are regarded as the pathology of the healthy society, which must therefore adjust these "incompetent and lazy" folk to its own patterns by changing their mentality. These marginals need to be "integrated," "incorporated" into the healthy society that they have "forsaken."

The truth is, however, that the oppressed are not "marginals," are not men living "outside" society. They have always been "inside"—inside the structure which made them "beings for others." The solution is not to "integrate" them into the structure of oppression, but to transform that structure so that they can become "beings for themselves." Such transformation, of course, would undermine the oppressors' purposes; hence their utilization of the banking concept of education to avoid the threat of student *conscientização*.[3]

The banking approach to adult education, for example, will never propose to students that they critically consider reality. It will deal instead with such vital questions as whether Roger gave green grass to the goat, and insist upon the importance of learning that, on the contrary,

---

[2] Simone de Beauvoir, *La Pensée de Droite, Aujord'hui* (Paris); ST, *El Pensamiento politico de la Derecha* (Buenos Aires, 1963), p. 34.

[3] The term *conscientização* refers to learning to perceive social, political and economic contradictions and to take action against the oppressive elements of reality.

Roger gave green grass to the rabbit. The "humanism" of the banking approach masks the effort to turn men into automatons—the very negation of their ontological vocation to be more fully human.

Those who use the banking approach, knowingly or unknowingly (for there are innumerable well-intentioned bank-clerk teachers who do not realize that they are serving only to dehumanize), fail to perceive that the deposits themselves contain contradictions about reality. But, sooner or later, these contradictions may lead formerly passive students to turn against their domestication and the attempt to domesticate reality. They may discover through existential experience that their present way of life is irreconcilable with their vocation to become fully human. They may perceive through their relations with reality that reality is really a *process*, undergoing constant transformation. If men are searchers and their ontological vocation is humanization, sooner or later they may perceive the contradiction in which banking education seeks to maintain them, and then engage themselves in the struggle for their liberation.

But the humanist, revolutionary educator cannot wait for this possibility to materialize. From the outset, his efforts must coincide with those of the students to engage in critical thinking and the quest for mutual humanization. His efforts must be imbued with a profound trust in men and their creative power. To achieve this, he must be a partner of the students in his relations with them.

The banking concept does not admit to such partnership—and necessarily so. To resolve the teacher-student contradiction, to exchange the role of depositor, prescriber, domesticator, for the role of student among students would be to undermine the power of oppression and serve the cause of liberation. . . .

It follows logically from the banking notion of consciousness that the educator's role is to regulate the way the world "enters into" the students. His task is to organize a process which already occurs spontaneously, to "fill" the students by making deposits of information which he considers to constitute true knowledge.[4] And since men "receive" the world as passive entities, education should make them more passive still, and adapt them to the world. The educated man is the adapted man, because he is better "fit" for the world. Translated into practice, this concept is well suited to the purposes of the oppressors, whose tranquility rests on how well men fit the world the oppressors have created, and how little they question it.

The more completely the majority adapt to the purposes which the

[4] This concept corresponds to what Satre calls the "digestive" or "nutritive" concept of education, in which knowledge is "fed" by the teacher to the students to "fill them out." See Jean-Paul Sartre, "Une idée fundamentale de la phénomenologie de Husserl: L'intentionalité," *Situations I* (Paris, 1947).

dominant minority prescribe for them (thereby depriving them of the right to their own purposes), the more easily the minority can continue to prescribe. The theory and practice of banking education serve this end quite efficiently. Verbalistic lessons, reading requirements,[5] the methods for evaluating "knowledge," the distance between the teacher and the taught, the criteria for promotion: everything in this ready-to-wear approach serves to obviate thinking.

The bank-clerk educator does not realize that there is no true security in his hypertrophied role, that one must seek to live *with* others in solidarity. One cannot impose oneself, nor even merely co-exist with one's students. Solidarity requires true communication, and the concept by which such an educator is guided fears and proscribes communication.

Yet only through communication can human life hold meaning. The teacher's thinking is authenticated only by the authenticity of the students' thinking. The teacher cannot think for his students, nor can he impose his thought on them. Authentic thinking, thinking that is concerned about *reality*, does not take place in ivory tower isolation, but only in communication. If it is true that thought has meaning only when generated by action upon the world, the subordination of students to teachers becomes impossible.

Because banking education begins with a false understanding of men as objects, it cannot promote the development of what Fromm calls "biophily," but instead produces its opposite: "necrophily."

"While life is characterized by growth in a structured, functional manner, the necrophilous person loves all that does not grow, all that is mechanical. The necrophilous person is driven by the desire to transform the organic into the inorganic, to approach life mechanically, as if all living persons were things... Memory, rather than experience; having, rather than being, is what counts. The necrophilous person can relate to an object—a flower or a person—only if he possesses it; hence a threat to his possession is a threat to himself; if he loses possession he loses contact with the world... He loves control, and in the act of controlling he kills life." [6]

Oppression—overwhelming control— is necrophilic; it is nourished by love of death, not life. The banking concept of education, which serves the interests of oppression, is also necrophilic. Based on a mechanistic, static, naturalistic, spatialized view of consciousness, it transforms students into receiving objects. It attempts to control thinking and

[5] For example, some professors specify in their reading lists that a book should be read from pages 10 to 15—and do this to "help" their students!

[6] Eric Fromm, *The Heart of Man,* New York, Harper and Row, 1966, p. 41.

action, leads men to adjust to the world, and inhibits their creative power. . . .

Education as the exercise of domination stimulates the credulity of students, with the ideological intent (often not perceived by educators) of indoctrinating them to adapt to the world of oppression. This accusation is not made in the naïve hope that the dominant elites will thereby simply abandon the practice. Its objective is to call the attention of true humanists to the fact that they cannot use banking educational methods in the pursuit of liberation, for they would only negate that very pursuit. Nor may a revolutionary society inherit these methods from an oppressor society. The revolutionary society which practices banking education is either misguided or mistrusting of men. In either event, it is threatened by the specter of reaction. . . .

Those truly committed to liberation must reject the banking concept in its entirety, adopting instead a concept of men as conscious beings, and consciousness as consciousness intent upon the world. They must abandon the educational goal of deposit-making and replace it with the posing of the problems of men in their relations with the world . . . .

Through dialogue, the teacher-of-the-students and the students-of-the-teacher cease to exist and a new term emerges: teacher-student with students-teachers. The teacher is no longer merely the-one-who-teaches, but one who is himself taught in dialogue with the students, who in turn while being taught also teach. They become jointly responsible for a process in which all grow. In this process, arguments based on "authority" are no longer valid; in order to function, authority must be *on the side of* freedom, not *against* it. Here, no one teaches another, nor is anyone self-taught. Men teach each other, mediated by the world, by the cognizable objects which in banking education are "owned" by the teacher.

The banking concept (with its tendency to dichotomize everything) distinguishes two stages in the action of the educator. During the first, he cognizes a cognizable object while he prepares his lessons in his study or his laboratory; during the second, he expounds to his students about that object. The students are not called upon to know, but to memorize the contents narrated by the teacher. Nor do the students practice any act of cognition, since the object towards which that act should be directed is the property of the teacher rather than a medium evoking the critical reflection of both teacher and students. Hence in the name of the "preservation of culture and knowledge" we have a system which achieves neither true knowledge nor true culture.

The problem-posing method does not dichotomize the activity of the teacher-student: he is not "cognitive" at one point and "narrative" at another. He is always "cognitive," whether preparing a project or engaging in dialogue with the students. He does not regard cognizable objects as his private property, but as the object of reflection by himself and the students. In this way, the problem-posing educator constantly re-forms his reflections in the reflection of the students. The students— no longer docile listeners— are now critical co-investigators in dialogue with the teacher. The teacher presents the material to the students for their consideration, and re-considers his earlier considerations as the students express their own. The role of the problem-posing educator is to create, together with the students, the conditions under which knowledge at the level of the *doxa* is superseded by true knowledge at the level of the *logos*.

Whereas banking education anesthetizes and inhibits creative power, problem-posing education involves a constant unveiling of reality. The former attempts to maintain the *submersion* of consciousness; the latter strives for the *emergence* of consciousness and *critical intervention* in reality.

Students, as they are increasingly posed with problems relating to themselves in the world and with the world, will feel increasingly challenged and obliged to respond to that challenge. Because they apprehend the challenge as interrelated to other problems within a total context, not as theoretical question, the resulting comprehension tends to be increasingly critical and thus constantly less alienated. Their response to the challenge evokes new challenges, followed by new understandings; and gradually the students come to regard themselves as committed.

Education as the practice of freedom—as opposed to education as the practice of domination—denies that man is abstract, isolated, independent, and unattached to the world; it also denies that the world exists as a reality apart from men. Authentic reflection considers neither abstract man nor the world without men, but men in their relations with the world. In these relations consciousness and world are simultaneous; consciousness neither precedes the world nor follows it. . . .

In problem-posing education, men develop their power to perceive critically *the way they exist* in the world *with which* and *in which* they find themselves; they come to see the world not as a static reality, but as a reality in process, in transformation. Although the dialectical relations of men with the world exist independently of how these relations are perceived (or whether or not they are perceived at all), it is also true that the form of action men adopt is to a large extent a function of how they perceive themselves in the world. Hence, the teacher-student and the students-teachers reflect simultaneously on themselves and the world without dichotomizing this reflection from action, and thus establish an authentic form of thought and action.

Once again, the two educational concepts and practices under analysis come into conflict. Banking education (for obvious reasons) attempts, by mythicizing reality, to conceal certain facts which explain the way men exist in the world; problem-posing education sets itself the task of demythologizing. Banking education resists dialogue; problem-posing education regards dialogue as indispensable to the act of cognition which unveils reality. Banking education treats students as objects of assistance; problem-posing education makes them critical thinkers. Banking education inhibits creativity and domesticates (although it cannot completely destroy) the *intentionality* of consciousness by isolating consciousness from the world, thereby denying men their ontological and historical vocation of becoming more fully human. Problem-posing education bases itself on creativity and stimulates true reflection and action upon reality, thereby responding to the vocation of men as beings who are authentic only when engaged in inquiry and creative transformation. In sum: banking theory and practice, as immobilizing and fixating forces, fail to acknowledge men as historical beings; problem-posing theory and practice take man's historicity as their starting point.

Problem-posing education affirms men as beings in the process of *becoming*—as unfinished, uncompleted beings in and with a likewise unfinished reality. Indeed, in contrast to other animals who are unfinished, but not historical, men know themselves to be unfinished; they are aware of their incompletion. In this incompletion and this awareness lie the very roots of education as an exclusively human manifestation. The unfinished character of men and the transformational character of reality necessitate that education be an ongoing activity.

Education is thus constantly remade in the praxis. In order to *be,* it must *become.* Its "duration" (in the Bergsonian meaning of the word) is found in the interplay of the opposites *permanence* and *change.* The banking method emphasizes permanence and becomes reactionary; problem-posing education—which accepts neither a "well-behaved" present nor a predetermined future—roots itself in the dynamic present and becomes revolutionary.

Problem-posing education is revolutionary futurity. Hence, it is prophetic (and, as such, hopeful). Hence, it corresponds to the historical nature of man. Hence, it affirms men as beings who transcend themselves, who move forward and look ahead, for whom immobility represents a fatal threat, for whom looking at the past must only be a means of understanding more clearly what and who they are so that they can more wisely build the future. Hence, it identifies with the movement which engages men as beings aware of their incompletion—an historical movement which has its point of departure, its Subjects and its objective.

The point of departure of the movement lies in men themselves. But since men do not exist apart from the world, apart from reality, the movement must begin with the men-world relationship. Accordingly, the point of departure must always be with men in the "here and now," which constitutes the situation within which they are submerged, from which they emerge, and in which they intervene. Only by starting from this situation—which determines their perception of it—can they begin to move. To do this authentically they must perceive their state not as fated and unalterable, but merely as limiting—and therefore challenging.

Whereas the banking method directly or indirectly reinforces men's fatalistic perception of their situation, the problem-posing method presents this very situation to them as a problem. As the situation becomes the object of their cognition, the naïve or magical perception which produced their fatalism gives way to perception which is able to perceive itself even as it perceives reality, and can thus be critically objective about that reality.

A deepened consciousness of their situation leads men to apprehend that situation as an historical reality susceptible of transformation. Resignation gives way to the drive for transformation and inquiry, over which men feel themselves to be in control. If men, as historical beings necessarily engaged with other men in a movement of inquiry, did not control that movement, it would be (and is) a violation of men's humanity. Any situation in which some men prevent others from engaging in the process of inquiry is one of violence. The means used are not important; to alienate men from their own decision-making is to change them into objects.

This movement of inquiry must be directed towards humanization— man's historical vocation. The pursuit of full humanity, however, cannot be carried out in isolation or individualism, but only in fellowship and solidarity; therefore it cannot unfold in the antagonistic relations between oppressors and oppressed. No one can be authentically human while he prevents others from being so. . . .

Problem-posing education, as a humanist and liberating praxis, posits as fundamental that men subjected to domination must fight for their emancipation. To that end, it enables teachers and students to become Subjects of the educational process by overcoming authoritarianism and an alienating intellectualism; it also enables men to overcome their false perception of reality. The world—no longer something to be described with deceptive words—becomes the object of that transforming action by men which results in their humanization.

EDUCATION:
INCIDENTAL AND SCHOLASTIC

Paul Goodman

INCIDENTAL EDUCATION AND PEDAGOGY

To be educated well or badly, to learn by a long process how to cope with the physical environment and the culture of one's society, is part of the human condition. In every society the education of the children is of the first importance. But in all societies, both primitive and highly civilized, until quite recently most education of most children has occurred incidentally. Adults do their work and other social tasks; children are not excluded, are paid attention to, and learn to be included. The children are not "taught." In many adult institutions, incidental education is taken for granted as part of the function: families and age-statuses, community labor, master-apprentice arrangements, games and plays, prostitution and other sexual initiation, religious rites and churches. In Greek *paideia*, the entire network of institutions, the *polis*, was thought of as importantly an educator.

Generally speaking, this incidental process suits the nature of learning better than direct teaching. The young see real causes and effects, rather than pedagogic exercises. Reality is often complex, but the young can take it by their own handle, at their own times, according to their own interest and initiative. Most important, they can imitate, identify, be approved or disapproved, cooperate and compete, without the anxiety of being the center of attention; there is socialization with less resentment, fear, or submission. The archetype of successful education is infants learning to speak, a formidable intellectual achievement that is universally accomplished. We do not know how it is done, but the main conditions seem to be what we have been describing: adult activity is going on, involving speaking; the infants are only incidental yet they participate, are attended to and spoken to; they play freely with their speech sounds; it is advantageous to them to make themselves understood. Finally, according to Jespersen, children pick up their accent and style from the gang of other children; it is their uniform, the way they appoint themselves.

Along with incidental education, however, most societies also have

Source. Paul Goodman, "The Present Moment in Education: A Dissenting View," as it appeared in the *N.Y. Review of Books.* From NEW REFORMATION: NOTES OF A NEOLITHIC CONSERVATIVE. Copyright © 1969 by Paul Goodman. Reprinted by permission of Random House, Inc.

institutions specifically devoted to teaching the young. Such are identity rites, catechism, nurses and pedagogues, youth houses, formal schooling. I think there is a peculiar aspect to what is learned by such means rather than picked up incidentally. But let me emphasize strongly and repeatedly that it is only in the last century in industrialized countries that the majority of children have gotten much direct teaching at all, and it is only in the past few decades that formal schooling has been extended into adolescence and further. E.g., in the United States in 1900 only 6 percent went through high school and 1/4 percent through college. Yet now formal schooling has taken over, well or badly, very much of the more natural incidental education of most other institutions.

This may or may not be necessary, but it has consequences: these institutions, and the adults in them, have correspondingly lost touch with the young, and the young do not know the adults in their chief activities. Like the jails and insane asylums, schools isolate society from its problems, whether preventing crime, curing mental disease, or bringing up the young. And to a remarkable degree vital functions of growing up have become hermetically re-defined in school terms: community service means doing homework, apprenticeship is passing tests for jobs in the distant future, sexual initiation is high school dating, and rites of passage are getting diplomas. Crime is breaking school windows, and rebellion is sitting-in on the Dean. In the absence of adult culture, there develops a youth sub-culture.

Usually there has been a rough distinction in content, in what is learned, between incidental education and direct pedagogy. Ordinary social activities that do not exclude children tend to be matter-of-fact, and children taking part without anxiety can be objective, if not critical. But pedagogy, whether directed by elders, priests, or academics, deals with what is not evident in ordinary affairs; it aims to teach what is more abstract, intangible, or mysterious, and the learner, as the center of attention, is under personal pressure. All social activity socializes its participants, but pedagogy socializes deliberately, according to principles, instilling the morals and habits which are the social bonds.

There are, of course, two opposite interpretations of why pedagogy wants to indoctrinate, and in my opinion both are correct. On the one hand, the elders, priests, and schoolteachers are instilling an ideology to support their system of exploitation, including the domination of the old over the young, and they have to make a special effort to confuse and mystify because the system does not recommend itself to common sense. At present, when formal education swallows up so much time of life and pretends to be practical preparation for every activity, ideological processing is especially deadly. Those who succumb to it have no wits of their own left and are robots.

On the other hand, there perhaps *are* vague but important wisdom and abstractions that must be passed on, which do not appear on the surface in ordinary occasions and which require personal attention, special pointing, repetition, and cloistered reflection. Thus, champions of liberal arts colleges say that, one way or other, the young will pick up contemporary know-how and mores, but the greatness of Mankind—Hippocrates and Beethoven, Enlightenment, Civil Liberties, the Sense of the Tragic—will lapse without a trace unless the scholars work at it. I sympathize with the problem as they state it; but in fact I have not heard of any method whatever, scholastic or otherwise, to *teach* the humanities without killing them. Myself, I remember how at age twelve, browsing in the library, I read *Macbeth* with excitement, but in class I could not understand a word of *Julius Caesar* and hated it; and I think this was the usual experience of people who read and write well. The survival of the humanities has seemed to depend on random miracles, which are becoming less frequent.

Finally, unlike incidental learning, which is natural and inevitable, formal schooling is a deliberate intervention and must justify itself. We must ask not only is it well done, but is it worth doing and *can* it be well done? Is teaching possible at all? There is a line of critics from Lao-tse and Socrates to Carl Rogers who assert that there is no such thing as teaching, of either science or virtue; and there is strong empirical evidence that schooling has little effect on either vocational ability or citizenship—e.g., Donald Hoyt, for American College Testing, 1965, found that college grades have no correlation with life achievement in any profession. At the other extreme, Dr. Skinner and the operant-conditioners claim that they can "instruct" for every kind of performance, they can control and shape human behavior, as they can do with animals sealed off from the ordinary environment; but they are careful to say they do not "educate" in the sense of developing persons (whatever that might mean). It is disputable whether human children are good subjects for this kind of instruction in any society we like to envisage.

In the middle, the main line of educators, from Confucious and Aristotle to John Dewey, held that, starting from the natural motives of the young, one can teach them good habits of morals, arts, and sciences by practice; the learners take on a "second nature" which they can then use by themselves, they are not simply programmed. And on various theories, Froebel, Herbart, Steiner, or Piaget have held that such teaching is possible if it addresses the child's powers in the right order at the right moments. But sociologists like Comte or Marx seem to say that the background social institutions and their vicissitudes overwhelmingly determine what is learned, so it is not worthwhile to think about pedagogy, at least as yet. I will not pursue this discussion here—my bias is that "teaching" is largely a delusion—but we must bear in mind that such fundamental disagreements exist.

THE SCHOLASTIC

Turn now to actual formal schooling in the United States, the country most technologically advanced (but the story is not very different in other developed and developing countries, including China and Cuba). The school system, expanding and increasingly tightly integrated, has taken over a vast part of the educational functions of society, designing school-preparatory toys from age two and training for every occupation as well as citizenship, sexuality, and the humanities. Yet with trivial exceptions, what we mean by School—namely, curriculum generalized from the activities of life, and divided into departments, texts, lessons, scheduled periods marked by bells, specialist teachers, examinations, and graded promotion to the next step—is a sociological invention of some Irish monks in the seventh century to bring a bit of Rome to wild shepherds. It is an amazing success-story, probably more important than the Industrial Revolution.

At first, no doubt it was a good thing for wild shepherds to have to sit still for a couple of hours and pay strict attention to penmanship and spelling. And mostly it was only aspiring clerics who were schooled. By an historical accident, the same academic method later became the way of teaching the bookish part of a couple of learned professions. There is no essential reason why law and medicine are not better learned by apprenticeship, but the bookish was clerical and therefore scholastic, and (perhaps) any special education containing abstract principles was part of the system of mysteries, therefore clerical, and therefore scholastic.

This monkish rule of scheduled hours, texts, and lessons is also not an implausible method for giving a quick background briefing to large numbers, who then embark on their real business. Thus Jefferson insisted on universal compulsory schooling, for short terms in predominately rural communities, so children could read the newspapers and be catechized in libertarian political history, in order to be citizens in a democracy. Later, in compulsory urban schools, the children of polyglot immigrants were socialized and taught standard English, a peculiar dialect, so they could then try to make good in an economy which indeed proved to be fairly open to them in the long run. The curriculum was the penmanship, spelling, and arithmetic needed for the business world. Naturally, forced socialization involved drastic cultural disruption and family fragmentation, but perhaps it was a good solution—we have yet to see how it works out.

The context of schooling at present, however, is entirely different. The monkish invention is now used as universal social engineering. Society is conceived as a controlled system of personnel and transactions—with various national goals, depending on the nation—and the schools are the teaching machine for all personnel. There is no other way of entry for the young. And teaching tries to give psychological preparation in depth. Schooling for one's role, in graded steps, takes up to twenty years and more and is the chief activity of growing up; any other interest may be interrupted. The real motivation for a five-year-old's behavior, thus, is geared fifteen years in the future.

In highly productive technologies like ours, of course, which do not need manpower, a more realistic interpretation is that the social function of long schooling is to keep the useless and obstreperous young *away* from the delicate social machine, to baby-sit and police them. Yet it comes to the same thing. Whether by accident or design, the schools are not like playgrounds or reservations; rather, the texture of school experience is similar to adult experience. There is little break between playing with educational toys and watching ETV, being in grade school and the Little League, being in high school and dating, being in college and drafted, being personnel of a corporation and watching NBC. It is a curious historical question whether the schools have been transformed to the model of business organization, or the adult world has become scholastic, with corresponding arrested maturation. The evidence is that up to about 1920, business methods had a preponderant influence; but since 1945, the school monks have increasingly determined the social style and adults have become puerile.

Since the trend has been to eliminate incidental education and prepare the young deliberately for every aspect of ordinary life, we would expect pedagogy to become secularized and functional. Yet radical students complain that the schooling is ideological through and through. The simplest, and not altogether superficial, explanation of this paradox is that scholastic mystery has transformed ordinary adult business. Society is run by mandarins, the New Class.

Even on its own terms, this is not working well. Schooling costs more than armaments. It does not in fact prepare for jobs and professions— e.g., evidence compiled by Ivar Berg of Columbia shows that dropouts do as well as high-school graduates on that level of jobs. It does not provide peaceful baby-sitting and policing. Instead of an efficient gearing between the teaching machine and the rest of the social machine, the schools seem to run for their own sakes, accumulating bluebooks; there is a generation gap; many of the young fail or drop out and others picket. Predictably, the response of school administrators is to refine the processing, to make the curriculum still more relevant, to enrich the curriculum, to add remedial steps, to study developmental psychology for points of manipulation, to start earlier, to use new teaching technology, to eliminate friction by admitting students to administrative functions.

But social engineering is uneducational in principle. It pre-structures behavior and can become discriminating, graceful, and energetic only if the organism creates its own structures as it goes along.

In the long run, human powers are the chief resources. In the short run, unused powers assert themselves anyway and make trouble, and cramped powers produce distorted or labile effects. If we set up a structure that strictly channels energy, directs attention, and regulates movement (which are "good things"), we may temporarily inhibit impulse, wishing, daydreaming, and randomness (which are "bad things"); but we also thereby jeopardize initiative, intrinsic motivation, imagination, invention, self-reliance, freedom from inhibition, and finally even health and common sense. It is frequently said that human beings use only a small part—"2 percent"—of their abilities; so some educators propose much more demanding and intellectual tasks at a much earlier age. And there is no doubt that most children can think and learn far more than they are challenged to. Yet it is likely that by far the greatest waste of ability, including intellectual and creative ability, occurs because a playful, hunting, sexy, dreamy, combative, passionate, artistic, manipulative and destructive, jealous and magnanimous, selfish and disinterested animal is continually thwarted by social organization and perhaps especially by schooling. If so, *the main purpose of pedagogy at present is to counter-act and delay socialization as long as possible.* Our situation is the opposite of the seventh century; since the world has become scholastic, we must protect the wild shepherds.

TWO

An Historical Perspective on the Functions and Purposes of Schools

The history of education has played a crucial role in maintaining a conventional wisdom about public schools that promises economic mobility and democratic process. These myths are used to rationalize existing inequalities, suggesting the belief that the disadvantaged will make it in good time as most others have done, or that there is something irremediably wrong with the motivation and ability of the people themselves. This history has allowed schools to take credit for "success" and blame its clients for "failure." Meanwhile, the serious questions at the heart of inequality in America and the viability of democratic process, as they exist in the relation of schools to society in particular, have gone unasked.

The three selections in this chapter view public education as a class-based institution in the service of the corporate state. Greer shows how schools have not helped the poor to "make it" in America; Joel Spring examines a longstanding alternative tradition in formal education; and Clarence Karier looks at the privileged model of public education that reflects and reinforces the hierarchical rigidities of the social order.

PUBLIC SCHOOLS:
THE MYTH OF THE MELTING POT

Colin Greer

It is fashionable these days to point to the decline of the public school, as if there were a time in some golden past when the schools really served all of the people all of the time. Legend tells of the Little

Source. Excerpts from "Public Schools: The Myth of the Melting Pot," by Colin Greer. Copyright © 1969 by *Saturday Review.* First appeared November 15, 1969 in *Saturday Review,* used with permission.

Red Schoolhouse that made equal opportunity available to children of every economic and social class, and, a little later in the nation's history, functioned as the primary instrument of the melting pot that offered poor immigrant children access to the fullness of American life. Today the schools are criticized for their failure to provide equality of opportunity to poor black children. The charge is true, but it is by no means the whole truth, nor is it new. The public schools have always failed the lower classes-both white and black. Current educational problems stem not from the fact that the schools have changed, but from the fact that they continue to do precisely the job they have always done.

What we are witnessing, in our current panic over urban education, is no more than an escalation of the criticisms made by school reformers since the turn of the century. The many innovations introduced over the past fifty years have made it easier for school systems to handle the high numbers of students brought into the schools by compulsory attendance legislation and a job market requiring increasingly sophisticated talents, but they have not changed the basic function of the schools as the primary selector of the winners and losers in society.

The very fact that we can look with pride at more and more students going on to secondary and higher education reveals a system that with increasing efficiency benefits some and denies others in the bosom of its material prosperity. Public schooling cannot be understood, nor the current problems manifest in it, apart from a consideration of the predominant influence of social and economic class. For at least the last eighty years, socio-economic class, as signified by employment rates and levels, has determined scholastic achievement, as measured by dropout and failure rates.

From 1890, at least, the schools failed to perform according to their own as well as the popular definition of their role. In virtually every study undertaken since that of Chicago schools made in 1898, more children have failed in school than have succeeded, both in absolute and in relative numbers. The educators who collaborated on the Chicago study found an exceedingly high incidence of poor school performance. They were quick to look to foreign birth as an explanation, but immigrants spawned Americans and still, with each passing decade, no more than 60 per cent of Chicago's public school pupils were recorded at "normal age" (grade level); the rest were either "overage" (one to two years behind), or "retarded" (three to five years behind). In Boston, Chicago, Detroit, Philadelphia, Pittsburgh, New York, and Minneapolis, failure rates were so high that in no one of these systems did the so-called normal group exceed 60 per cent, while in several instances it fell even lower—to 49 per cent in Pittsburgh, and to 35 per cent in Minneapolis.

The truth is that the mobility of white lower classes was never as rapid nor as sure as it has become traditional to think. The 1920 census, for example, showed that even the favored English and Welsh migrants found half their number tied to the terrifying vulnerability of unskilled labor occupations. Americans of English stock (dominating national language, customs, and institutions), had 40 per cent of their number working in coal mines and cotton factories.

And what of the school in all this? Clearly, according to the same body of data, a close relationship obtained between various group designations (native-born with and without foreign parents, and foreign-born), which revealed that levels of school retention in any given group coincided with that group's adult employment rate. Dropout rates for all groups, including the Negro, were in direct proportion to rates of adult unemployment. Further, the high degree of school achievement among Jews, which has confirmed our expectation of public schools, did not mean success for all Jews. Otherwise, why the remedial classes and dropout panic in several of the schools on New York's Lower East Side with as much as 99 per cent "Hebrew" registration? Where the family was poor enough to take in boarders to cover rental costs, and desperate enough to join the city's welfare roles, then delinquency, prostitution, and child labor were as much the burden of Jewish families, for whom such characteristics were real if not typical.

With rising industrial unemployment and an expanded technological economy, the school-leaving age increased so that the problem of caring for all grades of ability on the elementary school level escalated to the high school level. Vocational instruction programs were an inevitable corollary to the academic program and quickly became a symbol of the school's stratification role. Today, the junior college serves as the junior high school had served earlier, operating to a large extent as an extension of secondary education, with back-seat status justified by the democratic rationale of monumental numbers to be catered to.

The pattern of school failure has been perennially uniform, but concern for it was by no means as great as the concern on the part of educators to get more pupils into school. In 1917, and again in 1925, federal compulsory education legislation put added strength behind various state actions to this effect. Compulsory school-leaving age moved from twelve to fourteen and then to sixteen, but always with the proviso that the two years at the top were dispensable for those who either achieved a minimal grade proficiency determined by the classroom teacher or, more importantly, could prove that they had a job to go to.

In 1919 Chicago gave 10,000 such work permits, in 1930 only 987. Between 1924 and 1930 the allocation of work permits in a number of cities was reduced by more than two-thirds. The school had not suddenly become essential to mobility, but a shrinking unskilled job market required fewer men less early, and so the schools were expected to fill the gap.

The assumption that extended schooling promotes greater academic achievement or social mobility is, however, entirely fallacious. School performance seems consistently dependent upon the socio-economic position of the pupil's family. For example, of high school graduates who rank in the top fifth in ability among their classmates, those whose parents are in the top socio-economic status quartile are five times more likely to enter graduate or professional schools than those of comparable ability whose parents fall in the bottom quartile. Similarly, while American males born after 1900 spend more years in school than their nineteenth-century predecessors, federal and other estimates indicate no concomitant redistribution of economic and social rewards.

The factory, the union, the political machine were agents of mobility and Americanization before the school. Local stability for an ethnic group preceded its entry into the more prosperous reaches of society. The establishment of an ethnic middle class was basic to entry onto a wider middle-class stage via public education. It was the nation's demand for manpower that set the tone for assimilation, and the place of any one group on the economic ladder depended more on the degree to which the culture of the former homeland coincided with the values most highly prized in the culture of the new host society. Jews, Scandinavians, and Greeks, for example, were already practiced in the arts of self-employment, individual ambition, and the Puritan ethic with its corollary Gospel of Wealth. For the Catholic peoples, the Irish and Italians, *padrone* and party-boss authority seemed to go hand in hand with their being classified as dull, unambitious, and generally of low intelligence by urban teachers from the earliest days of heavy immigration. Bootstraps were not classroom resources.

The school failure problem was generally tucked away in xenophobic concern for expressions of loyalty and the management problems of running an "efficient" system. And efficiency was measured by the success schools enjoyed in getting more youngsters into the classroom, almost never by academic success or lack of it. "The ratio of the number of children in school to the number in the community who ought legally to be in attendance" was the measure, and academic success was by no means a necessary concomitant.

But if students were to stay in school longer, then the public school structure had to be stretched "by facilitating the progress" of those who were locked hitherto into repeating their grades. As surveyists in

Chicago remarked, "vanishing opportunities of employment" meant that the time had come for "curricular offerings based on ability and purpose."

Once intelligence tests were considered "a measure of potential"— and this was precisely how surveyists, school supervisory personnel, and professors of education viewed IQ tests—it was a short step to the realization that the broadened base of high school admissions meant that academic work in the nations's high schools had to be reorganized. Very soon it was observed, too, that the amount of academic work had been considerably reduced because there were so many more students who previously had not gone beyond the fifth grade. One survey team described them as "the boys and girls of secondary age who show little promise of being able to engage profitably in the activities commonly carried out by pupils of normal or superior ability."

Commitment to more and more schooling, beginning at kindergarten now (although only one in four of the eligible could go as yet) and continuing as long as possible, did nothing to modify the record of poor school performance. Compulsory attendance at higher levels only pushed failure rates into the upper grades throughout the 1920s and 1930s in such cities as Chicago, Boston, New York, Philadelphia, Detroit, and Washington, D. C.

Chicago noted a 65 per cent increase among the "underprivileged" between 1924 and 1931. Elementary school backwardness stood at 61.4 per cent, but 41 per cent of all those entering ninth grade were seriously behind, too; in tenth grade the figure was 32 per cent. Apart from such factors as pupil "feeble-mindedness" as an explanation, there were school difficulties to blame, too. Overcrowding in Detroit, where 13,000 were in half-day sessions and 60 per cent in school were "inadequately housed" in 1925; in Philadelphia, Cleveland, and New York the same overcrowding, unsanitary conditions, and serious financial problems prevailed.

On a scale of nine semesters, Philadelphia high schools lost 65 per cent of incoming students at the end of the first semester, lost another 32 per cent at the end of the fourth and were down to 19 per cent of the total in the final semester. In one instance of a 339-pupil sample established for survey purposes, only ninety-one survived two years. Federal data on schools published in 1937 showed clearly the nationwide "cumulative elimination of pupils in school." While 1,750,000 American youngsters entered grade nine, 86.7 per cent were still in school one year later; by grade eleven, only 72 per cent were left, and finally 56 per cent were graduated. Separate data for New York City showed just over 40 per cent of ninth-grade classes graduating. In the late 1940s, George Strayer recorded the same old story in Washington, D.C., New York City, and Boston. Fifty per cent of Boston's ninth graders failed to graduate; in New York the figure was up to more than 55 per cent. In James Coleman's assessment of *Equal Educational Opportunity* in the nation (1966), in the Havighurst study in Chicago (1964), and in the Passow report in Washington, D.C. (1967), the narrative remains staggeringly unchanged.

The Negro, the individual farthest down, has epitomized the inexorable relationship of success and failure, inside and outside the school. The link between permanent unemployment or chronic underemployment and educational failure is black now, but blacks have inherited a whirlwind no less familiar to them than to lower-class whites. Employment conditions were most severe when it came to the Negro, and school failure rates were at once more glaring and more poignant. But, in effect, the public schools served Negro children as they served the vast majority of others; in Chicago, Philadelphia, Detroit, and New York, that has been the problem since 1890.

But if white lower classes have been vulnerable to the economic market place, the Negro, who worked sporadically and as a reserve force, was constantly a victim. If school success or failure had little meaning in the economic market place for whites, it bore no relevance whatever for blacks. As a result, Negro school failure was quickly isolated as a separate problem early in the twentieth century. When, in the 1940s, Negroes finally entered the lower levels of industrial employment from which they had been excluded, those levels had already become a shrinking sector of the economy, and the massive numbers of school dropouts had no place to go. And so it remained appropriate—even inevitable—to consider Negro school performance as a separate question. But the truth is that academic effort has never been relevant to the place of the poor in society.

In 1931, George Strayer, with a lifetime of school evaluations behind him, looked back on progress in public education over the twenty-five preceding years. Most clear in his assessment of that progress was that not only were the top 10 per cent (in terms of IQ scores) in high school, but that 50 per cent of all eligible students from nursery school through college were involved in formal education. That more of the nation's youngsters were in school was the point of his argument, but still more needed to be put there. He acknowledged that very high failure rates were "still characteristic" of the majority of school systems. That was not a high priority problem, however, but a job "we may certainly hope to accomplish within the next twenty-five years."

The fact is that we haven't, and we haven't precisely because the objectives and priorities of the first twenty-five years of the twentieth century have gone unexamined. Paul Mort, a school surveyist sensitive to the growing alienation of urban community groups from public schools in the 1940s, blamed both the alienation and school failure rates on the historic rigidity of the system, its patent failure to consider or to plan for modification for future needs, and the fire-fighting assumptions that offered more and more of the same, making progress in education no more than the "expansion and extension of the commonplace." The capacity for future innovation and modification has been assumed, because the contradiction between public school pretensions and the measure of its achievement has been entirely disregarded. Consequently, we have no valid education philosophy on which to build differently. And things are unlikely to be much different until we have first exposed our illusions, and finally addressed the problems whose symptoms we fervently wish would go away.

If the assumptions on which public education was founded have gone unexamined, the problem is now compounded by rising aspirations. We could afford failure in the schools as long as the economy had room for unskilled workers and as long as the lower classes accepted without protest what appeared to be their inevitable place. Now, however, there are practically no jobs left for the unskilled, and even if there were, the black lower class no longer is willing to accept only that kind of opportunity—not in a society in which real wealth is increasing so fast.

What this means, in effect, is that in a variety of different ways we have increased our demands on the schools. Thirty years ago the purpose of public education was culturally defined as little more than baby-sitting for all the children. Now, neither corporations, government, suburban parents, nor the black community are willing to accept the school as a mere custodian. Its purpose has been redefined by society: Not only must it serve all children, but it must graduate them all with salable skills.

We criticize the schools and look for change in the present distribution of costs and benefits; we are aware that other social institutions educate, and we have been aware for a long time of the selective nature of public education, but we nevertheless accept the notion that public schools are an assumed asset in the regeneration of society. We have adopted a history based on men and events chosen from the history of democratic ideas in education, while we ignore other men, whom we have labeled anti-intellectual. David Crockett and Horace Greeley, for example, leveled scornful tirades against the creation of elite institutions that served an emerging meritocracy. The land and money, they said, might instead have contributed to a real experiment in universal public education, to make public education truly public in its services, not merely in its uses. Schools have been public only in the sense that what happens in them is typical of what happens outside.

Having assumed the salutary past of the school, we have engaged in discussion and debate over the present efficacy of schools with no question but that schools must be; they are generic to the American landscape. These assumptions preclude debate and scholarly inquiry as to why we maintain schools and what we can reasonably expect of them. Until we can question the validity of these assumptions, we cannot begin to achieve the social restoration of which we speak so eloquently, but for which there is little precedent. We can only continue to generate rationalizations across a variety of disciplines for a national commitment to an ideology that claims simply, but erroneously, that the public schools have always done what they are now expected to do.

ANARCHISM AND EDUCATION: THE DISSENTING TRADITION

Joel H. Spring

The implications of the rise of state supported public schools is often obscured by the lack of a critical tradition. There have certainly existed enough internal criticisms centering around the form, methods, and goals of public schooling which have been treated with great detail by historians. What has been lacking in historical literature is the exploration of a critical tradition which questions the very existence of state supported schools and offers an alternative direction for education. Anarchism as a social and political philosophy concerned with the role and nature of authority in a society has since the eighteenth century raised serious and important questions about the very existence of state systems of schooling and the possibility of nonauthoritarian forms of education. From William Godwin in the eighteenth century to Paul Goodman in the twentieth century, anarchist literature abounds with educational discussions and represents what one might call the dissenting tradition in education.

The central concern of traditional anarchists has been the development of social and economic systems which enhance individual autonomy. Simply defined, autonomy means assuming the responsibility for determining one's own actions. At first glance this goal would not appear radical, but when one begins to work out its implications, it brings into question many of the established and accepted institutions in the modern world. In the first place, anarchists oppose the existence of the state in any form because it destroys individual autonomy by

Source. Joel H. Spring, *Libertarian Analysis (1),* 4, December 1971, 30–42. This article was first published by the Center for Intercultural Documentation (CIDOC), Cuernavaca, Mexico, March, 1971. It has been shortened slightly.

legislating laws which determine individual action. Anarchists in the nineteenth and twentieth century have argued that the state and its laws exist for the protection of the political and economic elite. This rejection of the state includes democratic societies where the individual is required to sacrifice his autonomy either to the majority or a representative. The state has also been viewed as a mechanism which protects economic systems which allow for the exploitation of one man by another man. Working from this perspective, anarchists have found themselves in the interesting position in the twentieth century of being equally opposed to the political and economic system of both the United States and the Union of Soviet Socialist Republics. Secondly, anarchists have believed that individual autonomy means an individual who is able to make a choice free from all imposed dogma. This means that to freely determine one's actions one has to establish his own values and goals. This has meant the rejection of all institutions which attempt to make the individual into something. Of particular importance in this respect has been the objection to the school and the church as institutions which limit autonomy by molding character.

GODWIN: STATE EDUCATION AND FEAR OF SUBSERVIENCE

One of the most important objections made by anarchists to the existence of national systems of schooling was that education in the hands of the state would become subservient to the political interests of those in control. Within this context schooling was viewed as a formidable weapon used by the state to mold and direct the will and character of its citizens so that they would support and maintain existing institutions. Education linked to the national state was viewed as the ultimate form of authority because it limited individual autonomy by directly controlling desires, aspirations, and goals.

William Godwin was one of the first writers in the anarchist tradition to voice these criticisms of national education. Godwin's most important work was *An Enquiry Concerning Political Justice and Its Influence on Morals and Happiness* published in England in 1793 in which he warned that before government is allowed to assume the role of educator "it behooves us to consider well what it is that we do." Godwin argued that education in the hands of government agents would be used to strengthen their positions of power. He stated, "Their views as institutors of a system of education will not fail to be analogous to their views in their political capacity: the data upon which their conduct as statesmen is vindicated will be the data upon which their instructions are founded." Godwin rejected the assumption made by many in the eighteenth and nineteenth century that public schooling would result in individual freedom. That national schooling could be used for totalitarian purposes was not made clear to the Western world until the twentieth century. "Had the scheme of a national education," Godwin warned in the eighteenth century, "been adopted when despotism was most triumphant, it is not to be believed that it could have forever stifled the voice of truth. But it would have been the most formidable and profound contrivance for that purpose that imagination can suggest." Even in countries where liberty prevailed, Godwin argued, one could assume the existence of serious social errors which a national education would tend to perpetuate.

FERRER: OPPRESSIVE INSTITUTIONS AND SOCIAL INERTIA

Godwin's criticisms came at a time when public schools were still in their infancy. His concerns were with what might happen with national education rather than being a critique of actual results. By the end of the nineteenth century some form of national education had triumphed in most industrialized Western countries and anarchists could turn to these institutions for more direct evaluation of the relationship between schooling and the national state. One of the foremost anarchist critics was Spanish educator Francisco Ferrer who founded the Modern School in 1901 in Barcelona. Ferrer's work gained international recognition when in 1909 he was accused by the Spanish government of leading an insurrection in Barcelona and was executed. His execution elicited a cry of injustice from many groups in Europe and the United States and sparked interest in his career and educational ideas. In the United States a Ferrer Society was organized and a Modern School established in Stelton, New Jersey. In Europe the International League for the Rational Education of Children, which had been founded by Ferrer, was re-organized after his death and claimed as its Honorary President, Anatole France.

During Ferrer's career as educator he argued that governments had come to monopolize education. "They know, better than anyone else, that their power is based almost entirely on the school." In the past, Ferrer maintained, governments had kept the masses in a state of ignorance as a means of controlling them. With the rise of industrialism in the nineteenth century, governments found themselves involved in a international economic competition which required a trained industrial worker. Schools triumphed in the nineteenth century not because of a general desire to reform society but because of economic need. . . .

In Ferrer's mind the schools had accomplished exactly the things Godwin had warned of in the previous century. The schools in becoming the focal points for maintaining existing institutions depended on a system which conditioned the student for obedience and docility.

This, of course, was a charge leveled at the schools by a variety of critics. From Ferrer's point of view it was an inevitable result of a school controlled by the state. "Children must be accustomed," Ferrer wrote, "to obey, to believe, to think, according to the social dogmas which govern us. Hence, education cannot be other than such as it is today." For Ferrer one of the central problems for reform was breaking government's power over education. . . .

For Ferrer it was inconceivable for a government to create a system of education which would lead to any radical changes in the society which supported that government. It was therefore unrealistic to believe that national schooling would be a means of significantly changing the conditions of the lower classes. Since it was the existing social structure which produced the poor, education could only eliminate poverty by freeing men to radically change the social structure. An education of this nature would not result from a national education because the government would not teach something which threatened its own stability. . . . What the poor were taught, according to Ferrer, was the acceptance of the existing social structure and the belief that economic improvement depended on individual effort within the existing structure. Developing this attitude in the poor reduced the threat to the controlling economic powers of any major social changes.

STIRNER: FREEMAN OR LEARNER

The critical factor that anarchists were to perceive in a state controlled educational system was that the political dogmas expounded and the attempt to shape the individual into a useful citizen undermined the autonomy of the individual by fixing the boundaries and limits of the will. While state and religious schools were recognized as the greatest threat to individual freedom this did not mean that freedom from these strictures was the sole condition for an anarchist school.

The central issue for anarchists was the meaning of freedom and its relationship to education. Most anarchists have agreed with Max Stirner's statement in the 1840's that the major problem with the stress upon freedom in the nineteenth century was that it "appeared . . . as independence from authorities; however, it lacked self-determination and still produced none of the acts of a man who is free-in-himself. . . ." From an anarchist standpoint this meant that a state might free the individual from direct authority structures but still enslave the individual by determining how he would act through a system of schooling. To be "free-in-himself" required that an individual choose his own goals, ideals, and character rather than having them imposed through a planned system of schooling.

What this meant was that knowledge could be both freeing and enslaving. Whether it was one or the other depended on how one gained knowledge. Probably the most cogent statement of this position was made by Stirner in *The False Principle of Our Education*. Max Stirner, whose real name was Johann Casper Schmidt, was a poor German school teacher who in the 1840's attended meetings of the Young Hegelians in Berlin with Marx and Engels. Stirner's one and only major book, *The Ego and his Own*, was written during this period and so upset Marx that he devoted a large section of the *German Ideology* to an attack upon Stirner's ideas. . . .

Stirner believed that one had to make a distinction between the freeman and the educated man. For the educated man, knowledge was used to shape his character. For the freeman, knowledge was used to facilitate choice. "If one awakens in men the idea of freedom," Stirner wrote, "then the free men will incessantly go on to free themselves; if, on the contrary, one only educates them, then they will at all times accommodate themselves to circumstances in the most highly educated and elegant manner and degenerate into subservient cringing souls." It was Stirner's belief that knowledge should not be taught because this turned the individual into a learner rather that a creative person. The learner was a subservient person because he was taught to depend on authoritarian sources for his beliefs and goals rather than on himself. A learning person was without free will because he depended on learning how to act rather than determining how to act. . . .

To avoid the mere learner, the goal of pedagogy, according to Stirner, should be self-development in the sense that an individual gains self-awareness and the ability to act. For him, the existing schools worked against the freedom of the will. In discussing the development of education up to this time, he argued, that following the reformation education in the humanistic tradition was a means to power. Referring to the humanistic tradition, he wrote, ". . .education, as a power, raised him who possessed it over the weak, who lacked it, and the educated man counted in his circle, however large or small it was, as the mighty, the powerful, the imposing one: for he was an authority." The rise of the idea of universal schooling undermined the authority of the humanist scholar with a system designed to produce useful citizens trained for a practical life. Authority under the system of popular education was not that of one man over another but rather dogmas of what was practical and useful over the minds of men. . . .

For Stirner and future anarchists, the heart of education should be the development of a mind which is able to choose free of dogma and prejudice and whose goals and purposes are self-determined.

Knowledge pursued in this fashion would become a result of self-direction designed to strengthen the will. The individual would not be taught but would teach himself. This did not mean that the individual might not seek a teacher. The acquisition of knowledge would be the result of an individual desire and, consequently, directly related to the will of an individual. . . .

TOLSTOY: CULTURE OR EDUCATION

This approach to education required a careful distinction between what was normally defined as schooling and what anarchists hoped to accomplish. Leo Tolstoy, the Russian novelist and Christian anarchist, who established his own school in Russia in the 1860's, carefully defined these distinctions in an article entitled "Education and Culture" published in 1862. Tolstoy argued that culture, education, instruction and teaching had distinct and important meanings. He defined culture as the total of all the social forces which shaped the character of the individual. Education was the conscious attempt to give men a particular type of character and habits. As Tolstoy stated, "Education is the tendency of one man to make another just like himself." The difference between education and culture was on the issue of compulsion. "Education is culture under restraint. Culture is free." He argued that instruction and teaching were related to both education and culture. Instruction was the transmission of one man's information to another and teaching, which overlapped into the area of instruction, taught physical skills. Teaching and instruction were a means of culture, Tolstoy claimed, when they were free, and a means of education, "when the teaching is forced upon the pupil, and when the instruction is exclusive, that is when only those subjects are taught which the educator regards as necessary."

For anarchists, using Tolstoy's definitions, schooling was to be a process of culture and not education. This meant a school of non-interference and noncompulsion, where the student learned what he wanted to learn. Tolstoy defined a school as "the conscious activity of him who gives culture upon those who receive it . . ." Non-interference in the school meant "granting the person under culture the full freedom to avail himself of the teaching which answers his need, which he wants . . . and to avoid teaching which he does not need and which he does not want." Museums and public lectures were examples of schools of non-interference. They were consciously planned by the institution or lecturer to achieve a certain goal, but the user was free to attend or not to attend. Established schools and universities on the other hand used a system of rewards and punishments and limited the area of studies to achieve their particular ends. Tolstoy's example of the noncompulsory school was one without a planned program where teachers could teach what they wanted and their offerings would be regulated by the demands of the students. The school would not be interested in how its teaching was used or what the effect would be on the students. The school would be a place of culture and not education.

In varying degrees Stirner and Tolstoy reflected general anarchist thought about learning. In the United States, Elisabeth Burns Ferm, writing in the anarchist journal *Mother Earth* in 1907, emphasized the distinction between making the child into something and allowing the child to become something. Using different terms than Tolstoy had, Ferm defined the pedagogue as one who endeavors "to make and leave an impression on the child." Rejecting the pedagogue, Ferm believed the teacher should aid the individual in gaining an awareness of self and, consequently, autonomy. The role of the teacher would be to act as a mirror for students' actions, so that the "individual may see how his act reflects his thought and his thought reflects his act. That thought and action are indivisibly, inseparably one-helping the individual to realize this, consciously, by holding him responsible for every word and act." A teacher serving in this capacity would help the individual, in Stirner's sense, become free-in-himself. Acquisition of knowledge would then become a function of the free choice of the individual.

BEYOND EDUCATION

Most anarchists believed that any form of education would have little meaning unless the family were changed. Emma Goldman, the leading spokesperson for anarchist thought in the United States in the early twentieth century, declared in 1906,

"The terrible struggle of the thinking man and woman against political, social and moral conventions owes its origin to the family, where the child is ever compelled to battle against the internal and external use of force."

From Emma Goldman's point for view, the central problem in overcoming the modern authoritarian family structure was the end of the subservient role of the woman in modern society. Goldman's career was characterized by a life-long fight for women's liberation.

Francisco Ferrer also recognized the importance of the social role of the woman as a factor in anarchist education. Since women had the major responsibility in the care of the child, free humans could never develop until women were free.... Co-education at Ferrer's Modern School in Barcelona was unique not only because it was not generally practiced in Spain, but also because it emphasized the teaching of girls as a means of freeing humanity. He argued this was crucial because so many of one's ideas were wrapped in the emotions of childhood association with the mother. Ferrer did label the male and female with terms that would later be rejected by ardent feminists. For Ferrer the male was the individual and woman the conserver. While this identification was not to be accepted by later groups of women liberationists, his recognition of the necessity of changing the status of women as a precondition for any important social change was to become an important argument in that movement.

TO TEACH ANARCHISM OR FACTS FOR USE

Freeing the child in the family and the school of all authoritarian dogma created an important dilemma in anarchist educational thought. If the teaching of children was to be free of dogma, what exactly would be taught? For instance, Ferrer searched in vain before the opening of his school for books that would meet this criterion. Interestingly, the Modern School was opened without one book in its library because Ferrer could not find one that would meet his approval. There was also a concern about an anarchist education forcing the child to become an anarchist since this would be a product of dogmatic imposition. . . .

Anarchist discussions of this dilemma were often resolved in conviction rather than logic. For instance, the statement of purposes of the International League for the Rational Education of Children founded by Ferrer admitted that there was no neutral instruction and agrued, "We should not, in the school, hide the fact that we would awaken in the children the desire for a society of men. . .equal economically. . .without violence, without hierarchies, and without privilege of any sort." In the next paragraph the League warned, ". . .we have no right to impose this ideal on the child." The League claimed that if the child's conscience, sense of justice, and reason were aroused, this would lead him to work for human emancipation. The conviction underlying this feeling and other anarchist statements regarding education was that reason, which was cultivated free of dogma, would create naturally within the individual a desire for the preservation of his own autonomy and that of others.

It was from this standpoint that Ferrer emphasized the presentation of facts from which the child would draw his own conclusions. Ferrer exhibited a great faith in the ability of the natural and social sciences to yield objective data with which the human mind could reason. It was, of course, open to judgment what constituted objective data. For example, Ferrer argued that arithmetic should be presented without reference to wages, economy, and profit. The substance of arithmetic would be problems dealing with the just distribution of production, communication, transportation, the benefits of machinery, and public works. "In a word," Ferrer wrote, "the Modern School wants a number of problems showing what arithmetic really ought to be-the science of the social economy (taking the word 'economy' in its etymological sense of 'good distribution')." . . .History which emphasized the actions of rulers, governments, and great men conditioned the individual to accept a society where things were done to men rather than men acting. From Emma Goldman's perspective, history had to emphasize the ability of all men to act and shape the direction of history. History presented in the traditional manner enslaved man to authoritarian institutions. History presented as all men acting convinced the individual of his own power to shape history.

ELITE VIEWS
ON AMERICAN EDUCATION
Clarence J. Karier

One of the recurrent themes in American educational literature is that the American system of education is permeated with egalitarian aims and practices. Although, at times, the realities of the very harsh inequities of American educational practices have broken through the myth of equality, the apologists for American education have as a rule been quick to assert that the reason for this lies in America's failure to live up to her ideals. Just how and when these ideals were established remains obscure. Wishful social liberals, writing for sympathetic liberal audiences, usually assume that the American public has embraced egalitarian educational ideals. Such, however, may not be the case. One of the great deficiencies of American writing has been the marked absence of any serious dialogue on basic educational policy. Liberals have had the tendency to talk to liberals, and conservatives to conservatives, thus avoiding any basic confrontation of divergent points of view. Thus conservative elite views of education have coexisted with liberal egalitarian views in American educational thought. Here we shall examine the part played by conservative views in shaping American educational practice.

Source. "Elite Views on American Education," by Clarence Karier from *Education And Social Structure In The Twentieth Century,* edited by George Mosse and Walter Laqueur. Copyright © 1967 by The Institute of Contemporary History (The Weiner Library). Reprinted by permission of Harper & Row, Inc.

Just as the liberal tradition in American education has nurtured the egalitarian point of view, so the conservative tradition has nurtured elite concepts. Since it is impossible to treat the conservative tradition as a whole within a short essay, three figures are here selected for analysis, representing three critical points across the broad spectrum of American conservative thought in the twentieth century, from a mild middle-class position to extreme right-wing conservatism. Edward L. Thorndike aptly reflects the first position; Irving Babbit represents the solid reactionary-conservative point of view, and Lawrence Dennis typifies the extreme conservative or fascist point of view. Taken together, these men do not adequately represent conservatism in America, but they do mark three significant positions within the conservative wing of American political, educational, and social life. While each defined the elite and its function differently, all looked to the elite and not to the masses for the solution to the pressing social problems of their own day. Of the three, Thorndike was undoubtedly most influential in shaping the course of American education in the twentieth century.

Some might argue that John Dewey deserves that distinction. For many, his name was synonymous with the term "progressive education." Yet when one asks pragmatically, "Just how much difference did he make in actual educational practice?" the question becomes embarrassing. Except for his Chicago Laboratory School years (1894-1904), Dewey failed to translate his philosophy into concrete educational practices, although his name was used to justify practically everything in educational practice from nihilism to scholasticism. Educational historians debated, without answering, the question: "Who represents the real John Dewey in American educational practice?" Ironically, it can reasonably be asserted that *the* philosopher of practice had very little influence on practice. Indeed, Dewey's influence on educational practice was in no small degree dissipated by the ability of the educational and social establishment to withstand threats by substituting verbalization for action. As Dewey's philosophy became increasingly bogged down in the morass of the educationalist's jargon, his social philosophy could threaten no one. If, however, one takes the John Dewey of *The Public and Its Problems*, and *Freedom and Culture*, seriously, one realizes that he was no middle of the road "good mixer", but rather a liberal whose ideas about the good society were indeed radical. Some radicals are neutralized by ostracism; others can be more effectively handled by smothering them in praise. Dewey suffered the latter fate.

The remarkable thing is that while Dewey was being feted by young and old alike, American culture was rapidly building an educational system which in many respects was the very antithesis of what he was talking about. While he was writing *Democracy and Education,* forces in American society were at work creating an educational system which was to fall far short of the needs of democracy in the second half of the twentieth century. . . .

Although many educators talked about Dewey's ideas, when it came to practice they seemed to follow Thorndike. Indeed, while Dewey wrote and taught philosophy, Thorndike wrote the dictionaries, textbooks, and teacher manuals used in the elementary school and secondary schools of America. He published some fifty books and four hundred and fifty monographs, and taught thousands of teachers and administrators. From his tireless pen flowed a prodigious number of prescriptions: educational maxims and scales of achievement in arithmetic, reading, English, drawing, composition, and handwriting. In short, Thorndike not only influenced what was taught and how it was taught; he also supplied the criteria for evaluating and standardizing the process. . . .

At various times Thorndike rode the crest of a number of different movements in twentieth-century education. When the classical language came under attack, it was Thorndike and R. S. Woodworth who provided "scientific" justification for the exclusion of the Latin classics from American education. When it came to organizing the public schools on the model of a business establishment, again it was Thorndike who provided the "scientific" test used to classify the students. As George P. Strayer, a leader in the efficiency movement said: "All our investigations with respect to the classification and progress of children in the elementary schools, in high schools and in higher education, are based upon Professor Thorndike's contribution to the psychology of individual differences." Under the banner of scientific efficiency, Thorndike led the Test and Measurement Movement which had a profound influence on both business and education in the United States.

As Chairman of the Committee on Classification of Personnel of the Army, 1917–18, Thorndike demonstrated the use of group intelligence tests on a massive scale. Both businessmen and educators were quick to see the implications. After the war, Thorndike served on the National Research Council and helped to develop the popular National Intelligence Tests. The more he used this and other tests, the more convinced he became that intelligence changed very little, and that its chief determinant was not environment but heredity. He believed furthermore that character, good will, and cleanliness objectively correlated with intelligence. Progress would result, not from extension of culture to the masses, but rather from giving special education to the gifted child. He therefore opposed the upward extension of compulsory education laws, arguing that to raise the aspiration level of the poor would increase not their ability, but only their frustration and resentment.

The social class system which emerged from his statistical charts reflected, he thought, a natural hierachy of native intelligence. Thorndike and others fashioned the intelligence test into a powerful standardizing instrument with which to limit and control mobility on the educational frontier. Under the guise of concern for individual differences, a science of education, and the objective classification of students, American educators proceeded to segregate those said to have superior intellects from their less fortunate fellows within the common school. . . .

Sure that "To him that hath a superior intellect is given also on the average a superior character," he went on to find a positive correlation between intellect, character, and money-making. Thorndike was well within that long tradition of the spirit of American capitalism which repeatedly, from Benjamin Franklin to the present, has mistaken wealth for virtue. . . .

Convinced that it was heredity and not environment which was the chief determinant of ability, Thorndike suggested "that racial differences in original nature are not mere myths". He had reached this conclusion after testing Negro and white children in a New York City high school, and finding that in spite of considerable overlapping between the two races, the white children were "superior in scholarship"; he attributed the difference to original nature, since "The differences in the environment do not seem at all adequate to account for the superiority of the whites". Consequently he saw scientific eugenics as ultimately the only real road to progress. By 1940, in his last major work, he concluded that, "By selective breeding supported by a suitable environment we can have a world in which all men will equal the top ten per cent of present men. One sure service of the able and good is to beget the rear offspring. One sure service (about the only one) which the inferior and vicious can perform is to prevent their genes from survival."

Through the efforts of Thorndike and others, American school administrators, teachers, and curriculum experts learned to objectify and type students so as to standardize the school process. Few seemed troubled by the fact that the standards used were based on white Protestant middle-class values. This was probably the secret of Thorndike's success. His influence on American education may in part be accounted for by the fact that he, more than most, built into his studies his own middle-class values and then dared to call them "scientific". More important, he was saying exactly what a growing middle class wanted to hear about itself and its schools. His positive correlations of morality, wealth, intelligence, and social power could only endear him to the established power structure, just as his empirical finding that "the abler persons in the world in the long run are more clean, decent, just, and kind" would make him a patron saint of the well-washed middle-class American educators. Thorndike embodied the attitudes and values which came to underlie the American public school. Such a school system placed a premium on middle-class virtues, repeatedly confusing morality, wealth, social power, and cultural advantage with native intelligence, racial superiority, and real achievement. . . .

While Professor Thorndike was publishing works so congenial to the rising middle class, another professor was attempting to resuscitate the values and ideals of a declining nineteenth-century educational tradition. With his back to the twentieth century, Irving Babbit (1865-1933) fought a bitter, but losing battle in the name of belles-lettres and the genteel tradition.

From the serenity of Harvard Yard, Babbitt, Professor of French Literature, was drawing the intellectual guidelines of a new humanism in *Literature and the American College* (1908); *The New Laocoön* (1910); *The Masters of French Criticism* (1912); *Rousseau and Romanticism* (1919); and *Democracy and Leadership* (1924). As Greek disappeared from American education, and Latin declined, Babbit mobilized the classical ideas about the nature of man and the good society and sent them into battle against the humanitarians who, he felt, had been undermining the very foundations of American culture. The crisis he saw in America was part of a broader cultural sickness affecting the entire West. It had begun with Bacon and the utilitarian worship of science on the one hand, and with Rousseau and the romantic worship of the primitive on the other; both traditions if left unchecked, would end in the complete destruction of western civilization. Science and romanticism fed the Frankenstein of mass culture, the myth of progress, and the idea of the perfectibility of man.

For Babbitt, God had died, and with him vanished the credibility of the Christian myths which held the passions of the masses in check. As naturalism and romanticism demolished the last remaining sanctions of the moral order, the idea of progress and the perfectibility of man began to be substituted for the idea of God. Although men continued to live off the moral capital of a past age of faith, the time was rapidly approaching when they would have to create their own moral capital or perish. To Babbitt the latter was a very real possibility.

Babitt believed that the human condition was a tragic one: man, he said, "is intellectually incompetent and morally responsible". Collectively, men produce the fruits which sustain life, but morally each man stands alone. Men had achieved considerable material, but not moral, progress through collective action. Morality, for the humanist, is always an individual concern. Those who believe that science can and must be employed in the service of humanity, and that humanity can progress both morally and materially, were, for Babbitt, humanitarians. Humanitarianism was fed by faith in science and faith in a romanticized humanity. "A person who has sympathy for mankind in the lump, faith in its future progress, and desire to serve the great cause of this progress," and is committed to either the utilitarian ideal of knowledge for power or the romantic goal of service to humanity, should be called a humanitarian, not a humanist. . . .

Humanitarianism had corrupted the house of intellect, destroyed age-old standards of taste, and ushered in an age of nihilism. All, however, was not lost. Babbitt argued that perhaps it was still not too late for the humanist to reorient the liberal arts college towards its true classical centre. What was needed was an aesthetic elite trained in the classics, who would embody and exemplify for the modern world the great ideas of the "noble dead . . ."

A truly educated man was one who had so disciplined his ethical will that he could refrain from action. The liberal arts colleges, therefore, must educate a classical elite of sound taste and moderation. This elite would learn how to channel the passions of the masses, and realize that the main purpose of government is not to raise the material welfare of the masses, but to create advantages for the upward striving of the exceptional. In this aristocratic view of the good society, the masses were trainable in the humanitarian sense but fundamentally uneducable in the humanist sense.

"Some persons will remain spiritually anarchical in spite of educational opportunity, others will acquire at least the rudiments of ethical discipline, whereas still others, a small minority, if we are to judge by past experience, will show themselves capable of more difficult stages of self-conquest that will fit them for leadership."

The masses cannot lift themselves by their bootstraps; they need and are receptive to leadership. The critical need is for humanistically educated leaders.

In practice, Babbitt's views had relatively little effect on the direction the American college took in the liberal thirties, but his ideas remained very much a part of the conservative criticism of progressive education. By the more conservative decades of the fifties and sixties, others such as Peter Viereck, Russell Kirk, Gordon Keith Chalmers, under the banner of the new conservatism, and James D. Koerner of the Council for Basic Education, carried out the neo-humanist assault on the humanitarian educational establishment.

By 1933 it was clear to most observers that Babbitt's kind of reactionary conservatism did not measure up to the demands of the future. A new and more radical conservatism was in the making—a conservatism which would satisfy the need for security and "belonging," and overcome the feeling of alienation so prevalent in a mass society by the use of myths designed to make a non-rational appeal. Paradoxically, the more rationally ordered society became, the more non-rational became the needs of the individual in that society. The radical conservatism of fascism offered all the advantages that the reactionary conservative offered, such as order and security, and the extra emotional satisfaction of being part of a cause far larger than the limited loneliness of the existential self in crisis. Western man and western society indeed were in crisis. Perhaps a philosophy which assumed that men were rational enough to live without myths or illusions was a false philosophy. Falling back in fear and dread on his own resources, modern man constructed a new feudalism in the form of a fascist state. Its leading advocate in America was Lawrence Dennis.

After giving up a successful career in international banking, Lawrence Dennis wrote *Is Capitalism Doomed?* (1932), *The Coming American Fascism* (1936), and *Dynamics of War and Revolution* (1940). Dennis believed the remedy for the chaos and confusion of the depression was to be found in the charismatic elite asserting its control over the means of production, communication, education, and government, and directing those activities towards a single national purpose. The function of any humane education, he maintained, was to integrate the individual into the society. Modern man suffers not so much from poverty as from alienation.

"To be successfully adjusted, an individual does not have to have two cars or even a full stomach. He merely needs to have a place, or, to belong ... People don't mind suffering. On the contrary, some of them love to suffer all of the time, and all of them love to suffer some of the time. What people cannot endure is not belonging. The tragedy of capitalism—unemployment—does not inhere in the phenomena of want and privation, but in the spiritual disintegration of large numbers of people from the group culture. Hitler can feed millions of his people acorns, and yet, if he integrates them in a spiritual union with their community, they will be happier than they were while receiving generous doles from a regime which gave them no such spiritual integration with the herd."

To be spiritually integrated with the herd is to be fed the myths which satisfy the irrational need to belong. In this respect Hitler was most rational in realizing that what people wanted was not more reason but emotion. . . .

Dennis maintained that American democracy had declined long ago and had left in its place a chaotic liberalism which bordered on anarchy. A charismatic power elite was needed to weld the disparate elements of American society into a single cause behind a single party and a single leader. . . .

A charismatic elite which shed its outworn values of social democracy must step forward to manipulate the herd in its own best interests. It would use education as one of its instruments. . . .

The school was, however, only one of the lesser agencies of education through which the elite would indoctrinate the masses. The mass media were more important. . . .

The function of education is not to produce free men, nor is it to educate men so that they can, as Jefferson maintained, "recognize tyranny and revolt against it." The function of the school as a tool of the dominant elite was to indoctrinate the young with the right values. Right values, Dennis argued, are always determined by those who have the power to enforce them. Those who look to the school to impart ideas neutrally, as if they "can be dispensed like cigarettes wrapped in cellophane", are as naive as those who believe the schools can reconstruct the social order. The schools can do neither. They can only follow the will of the dominant elite who either "buy or shoot their way to power". Those who claim that the function of the school is to educate the young to criticize and rebel against the injustices of the power elite make two gross errors. First the kind of person who freely chooses to become a teacher is seldom a revolutionary; second, no real power elite would permit an effective revolutionary to exist in its schools. . . .

The function of the school was to inculcate the right values. The teacher was one of the propagandizing agents through which the elite in power effectively organized and secured their control of the social system.

In *The Coming American Facism* (1936), Dennis warned his countrymen against American involvement in any war against Germany on the side of the Soviet Union. The only result of such a war would be a fascist America left alone to halt the expansion of communist Russia. To most observers in the thirties, Dennis's ideas about a fascist America seemed far-fetched. After twenty years of cold war, with the concomitant expansion of massive military establishment, of racial conflict, of the rapid growth of right-wing influence in American culture, the idea of a coming American fascism seemed more plausible than before. In 1958 Robert Welch organized the John Birch Society, which rapidly became the leading rightist organization in American politics, exemplifying better than any other organization the American fascism envisaged by Lawrence Dennis. By 1965 its membership approached 100,000, equalling the membership of the Communist Party of America at its peak in 1944. It had 5,000 cells and a budget of more than a million dollars a month. By 1966 it was the leading organization on the fascist right attempting to influence American education.

The phenomenal rise of the fascist right in America during the sixties can best be understood in the light of the fears of the American people. Just as the Communist Party gained influence in the liberal thirties, so the fascist right has grown in influence in the conservative sixties. Neither group has seriously threatened to gain control of the vital centres of American politics or American education. However, the ideas of Lawrence Dennis represent what American education would become if the fascist right ever gained effective control.

Although all three representatives of the conservative tradition examined here looked to an elite of leadership to solve the major social issues of the century, each saw the role of the school in relation to the elite quite differently. Thorndike sought an elite of achievement, shaped and standardized by middle-class values. Babbitt, on the other hand, represented a more conservataive position, calling for an elite of "culture" based on the presumed excellence of classical values. For Babbitt the Golden Age had passed. The best that could be hoped for was that the schools might train the masses to support themselves and that the natural elite might be educated in the liberal arts and become exemplars of culture. Babbitt assumed that some men were rational enough to know the truth and act accordingly. Dennis represents a more radical conservative position. Denying rationality to any man or group of men, Dennis found security in an elite of power which existed not because of the school but in spite of it. The school, like all other social instruments, such as the churches and the mass media, was viewed as an instrument to be used by the power elite to manipulate the masses and satisfy their irrational needs. Dennis called his radical conservatism what it was—fascism.

Babbitt, the reactionary conservative, represents what American education would become if Russell Kirk of the neo-conservatives and James D. Koerner of the Council for Basic Education were free to shape American education. Lawrence Dennis, on the extreme right, represents what American education could be expected to become if the John Birch Society continues to increase in influence in American politics and education. Thorndike, on the other hand, as a middle-class conservative, represents what American education largely became: a system of schooling which specially rewards children of white, Protestant, middle-class backgrounds. Although the American school historically has had its exponents of the liberal tradition, it seems more realistic to describe it as basically serving a conservative function. Perhaps the confusion about the goals of American education arises, in large part, from the fact that at various times the American public has taken the rhetoric of liberalism seriously and therefore expected more than a conservative, elite function from its schools. At such times, the confusion was compounded by the many educators who skilfully verbalized a liberal view of education, but carried the educational views of Thorndike into practice.

THREE

The Social and Cultural Dimension: Family Background and Educational Opportunity

Peter Schrag and S. M. Miller show persuasively, in the selections that follow, how the limitations of family background and social class are built into the structure of public education. They argue further that the promise of American education has made little sense for large segments of the population. Generally, sociologists of education, quite contrary to historical myths, make a strong case that schools serve the socioeconomic structure in which they exist. Unfortunately, this has led many educators to assume that schools are hopelessly subservient institutions and to neglect the exploration of how and what schools might do to redefine their relationship with other institutions and with society as a whole.

END OF THE IMPOSSIBLE DREAM

Peter Schrag

It is ten years later, and the great dream has come to an end. We thought we had solutions to everything—poverty, racism, injustice, ignorance; it was supposed to be only a matter of time, of money, of proper programs, of massive assaults. Perhaps nothing was ever tried without restraint or dilution, perhaps we were never willing to exert

Source. Copyright © 1970 by Saturday Review Co. First appeared in *Saturday Review,* September, 1970. Used with permission.

enough effort or spend enough money, but it is now clear that the confidence is gone, that many of the things we *knew* no longer seem sure or even probable. What we believed about schools and society and the possibilities of socially manageable perfection has been reduced to belying statistics and to open conflict in the street and the classroom.

Twenty years ago we took as fact the idea that American public schools—that *the school system*—could be reformed, first to make the education enterprise more intellectually rigorous and selective, and then to make it more democratic. Thus we had our decade with the Rickovers, the Bestors, the Conants, and the Zachariases; men who believed that students did not know enough physics or French or English, and that through new programs, or a return to "the fundamentals," or through adjustments in teacher training, students could become superior academic operators and, above all, better qualified candidates for the university. And then, beginning in about 1960, we had our decade with the democrats, the integrationists, and the apostles of universal opportunity: Kenneth B. Clark, Thomas Pettigrew, Francis Keppel, and John Gardner, who believed that by changing teacher attitudes, or through busing, or through fiscal and geographical rezoning, all children could have equal educational opportunities.

In the first instance the reformers represented the aspirations of the enfranchised, the suburban parents of affluence who once sent their children to Harvard by right of birth and now had to do it by right of achievement. In the second, the reformers demanded for the deprived what they thought the advantaged were getting, believing in the magic of the good school and accepting the rhetoric of individual accomplishment. Now, suddenly, the optimism is gone, and the declining faith in educational institutions is threatening the idea of education itself.

If we want to understand why the schools have "failed," we have only to state the criteria of success. The schools achieved their reputation when they did not have to succeed, when there were educational alternatives—the farm, the shop, the apprenticeship—and when there were other routes to economic and social advancement. Every poor little boy who became a doctor represented a victory. Poor little boys who became ditch diggers disappeared from the record. As soon as we demanded success for everyone—once there were no alternatives—failure was inevitable, not only because the demands were too great, but because they were repressive and contradictory. No other nation, wrote Henry Steele Commager in a representative flight of self-congratulation, "ever demanded so much of schools and of education ... none other was ever so well served by its schools and its educators." We expected the schools to teach order, discipline, and democracy, the virtures of thrift, cleanliness, and hard work, the evils of alcohol, tobacco, and later of sex and communism; we wanted them to acculturate the immigrants, to provide vocational skills, to foster patriotism and tolerance, and, above all, to produce a high standard of literacy throughout the population. All this they sometimes did and still do.

The impossible demand was enshrined in the mythology of the American dream itself; that the schools constitute the ultimate promise of equality and opportunity; that they enable American society to remain somehow immune from the economic inequities and social afflictions that plague the rest of mankind; that they, in short, guarantee an open society. . . . Thus, if the school system fails, so does the promise of equality, so does the dream of the classless society, so does our security against the inequalities of society. The school system has failed.

Evidence? Is it necessary again to cite statistics, dropout rates, figures on black and white children who go to college (or finish high school), comparisons of academic success between rich and poor kids, college attendance figures for slums or suburbs? The most comprehensive data on hand indicate that, in the final analysis, nothing in school makes as much difference as the economic background of the student and the social and economic backgrounds of his peers. There is no evidence that increasing educational expenditures in a particular district will produce greater achievement, and a fair amount of evidence that it will not. But this sort of argument is still misleading and, in the final analysis, rather useless, because it presumes that we agree on what constitutes success. Failure to complete high school is regarded as some sort of cosmic failure, a form of personal and social death. Dropout becomes synonymous with delinquent. Yet the evidence indicates that in some school systems the smart ones drop out and the dumb ones continue. Self-educated men used to be heroes; now they are prejudged unfit, or, more likely, they just don't appear in the social telescope at all.

Then why have the schools failed? Why boycotts and strikes, why the high school SDS, why the battles over long hair, underground newspapers, and expressions of independent student opinion? Why are there cops in the corridors and marijuana in the gym lockers? Why is it that most students panic when they're invited to work on their own, to study independently? Why is it that most students are more interested in what the teacher wants or what's going to be on the test than they are in understanding the subject that's ostensibly under study? Why bells, monitors, grades, credits, and requirements? Why do most students learn to cheat long before they learn how to learn? Yes, there are exceptions—there are teachers who ask real questions and schools that honor real intellectual distinction and practice real democracy. But a system that requires all children (except the very rich who can buy their way out) to attend a particular school for a specified period— that, in other words, sentences everyone to twelve years of schooling— such a system can and must be judged by its failures.

Everything that we could not, or would not, do somewhere else we expected to be done in the schools. And in the process we thought we saw what in fact does not exist. The greatest failure of American educational journalism in the last decade is that its practitioners refused to believe what they saw, and reported instead what they were supposed to see. Thus we have been inundated with millions of words about the new math, the new physics, the compensatory this and advanced that, about BSCS and PSSC, about IPI and SMSG, about individual progress and head start, upward bound, and forward march. And thus also we have read, with increasing incomprehension, about student uprisings, protests and boycotts and strikes. But few of us ever described the boredom, the emptiness, the brutality, the stupidity, the sheer waste of the average classroom.

What choices does a fifteen-year-old have in the average high school? Choices as to courses, teachers, or physical presence? What does he do most of the day? He sits—and maybe listens. Follow him, not for a few minutes, but for six hours a day, 180 days a year. What goes on in the class? What is it about, what questions are asked? Is it about the real world? Is it about an intellectually honest discipline? Is it about the feelings, passions, interests, hopes, and fears of those who are present? No. It is a world all of its own. It is mostly about nothing.

It worked as long as the promise of schooling itself appeared credible, that is, as long as the proffered reward looked more like a rainbow and less like a mirage, before the end of the road was crowded with people reporting back that the trip wasn't worth it. . . .

Earlier, I spoke about contradictory objectives. One is the objective of "equality of educational opportunity;" the other is to reinforce and legitimize distinctions. For many years, these objectives were, in fact, consistent. They share certain behavioral values that are honored and enforced in the average classroom: discipline, order, certain kinds of manners, styles of speech and dress, punctuality, cleanliness, and so on. Kids who do not meet these standards are ridiculed, punished, and demeaned. The two sets of values also share a declared commitment to certain skills: reading, writing, the skills of the average intelligence test—and a disdain for other attributes: originality, curiosity, diversity. They share, in other words, a linear standard of success and failure.

Slow and bright, average and retarded, all fall on one scale, one straight line that runs from zero to one hundred, from A to F. Any teacher in any school can tell any other teacher in any other school about his good, average, and slow students, about his difficult students, and about his cooperative ones, and both will know precisely who and what is being described. (Occasionally, of course, some school or teacher honors a "difficult" child, or a genuinely curious one, or one who has skills—in music or dance, for example—which are outside the normal scale of classroom success. But those are rare instances.)

About a decade ago, something began to change. Until then "equality of educational opportunity" was understood in simple (and misleading) terms. It was the equality inherited from social Darwinism: Everyone in the jungle (or in society, or in school) was to be treated equally: one standard, one set of books, one fiscal formula for children everywhere, regardless of race, creed, or color. Success went to the resourceful, the ambitious, the bright, the strong. Those who failed were stupid or shiftless, but whatever the reason, failure was the responsibility of the individual (or perhaps of his parents, poor fellow), but certainly not that of the school or the society. It was this premise that fired the drive for school integration. Negro schools, we believed, were older, more poorly equipped, badly financed. By equalizing resources, and perhaps throwing in a little compensation to offset differences deriving from "cultural disadvantage," everybody would be competing in the same race. Thus Head Start and "counterpoise" and "early enrichment." Every program launched in the past decade assumed a linear standard of success; each took for granted that schooling was a competitive enterprise and that life was a jungle where only the fit survive. Integration was, more than anything else, a political attempt to win white hostages to black education: Where white kids went to school with black there would be better resources and teachers. Apparently it never occurred to anyone that as long as we operated by a linear standard (bright, average, slow, or whatever) the system would, by definition, have to fail at least some kids. Every race has a loser. Failure is structured into the American system of public education. Losers are essential to the success of the winners.

In the process of compensating and adjusting, of head starting and upward bounding, the burden of responsibility shifted subtly from the individual to the school and the society. Failure used to be the kid's fault; now, increasingly, it seems, at least in part, to be the fault of the system. And thus all was thrown into confusion. Do we measure equality by what goes in or what comes out? That is, do we measure it in terms of resources provided, efforts made, or by achievement? Assuming some form of cultural pluralism (not yet proven or even argued)—assuming, for example that certain groups in the society are not merely "disadvantaged" but culturally distinct, and that those distinctions are valuable—assuming these things, what does equality mean when it comes to education? Equality before the law, yes; equality in medical treatment, yes; equality in the hiring of plumbers and mechanics, yes. But equality in education? James Coleman, who directed the huge federal study called "Equality of Educational Opportunity," subsequently wrestled with the question (in an article in *Public Interest*) and concluded that "equality of educational opportunity implies not merely 'equal' schools but equally effective schools, whose influences will overcome the differences in starting point of children from different social groups." This is the statement of a homogenizer, hardly different from that of the DAR lady who, sixty years ago, gave the schools a similar mission. "What kind of American consciousness can grow," she asked, "in the atmosphere of sauerkraut and limburger cheese?" The differences, in these views, should be equalized away: All comers should be transformed into mainstream, middle-class competitors (or consumers?) who are equally able to run the race.

There was nothing insidious or sinister about these things; they are as American as the flag. Our dream, as a society, was in the possibilities of transformation: frogs into princes, immigrants into Americans, poor children into affluent adults. And now, with other options closed, the schools, which always have received a major share of the credit for such accomplishments, are expected to do it all. But the schools never did what they were praised for doing; many immigrant groups, for example, did not achieve economic and social success through the public school, but through an open market for unskilled and semi-skilled labor, through sweatshops and factories, through political organizations and civil service jobs. There are more poor whites in America than poor blacks, and if the schools can be credited with the success of those who made it, they also have to be blamed for the failure of those who did not. But to say all this is not to say very much, because in the definition of making it, in a competitive race with one set of criteria, one man's success is defined by another's failure.

Then what do the schools actually do? More than anything else they certify and legitimize success and failure. "Equality of educational opportunity," even if it has no meaning, is necessary because it says to the loser, "You had your chance." Therefore equality remains a significant political and moral imperative, a tune that has to be sung by politicians, guidance counselors, and other apologists of the status quo. . . .

The common school, quite simply, no longer exists, except as public rhetoric. With the large-scale movement to the suburbs after World War II, much of the American middle class seceded from the common school by physically removing its children to what it regarded as a more salubrious educational environment. For the successful in the suburbs the schools became contractual partners in a bargain that trades economic support (higher taxes, teacher salaries, bond issues) for academic credentials and some guarantee of advancement in the form of college admission. They went there seeking not equality but advantage, a head start for the rich. And who can blame them? We all "want the best for our children." Education, and especially higher education, is regarded as the *sine qua non* of position and power in this society. The "new class" of managers and technicians, as David Bazelon has said, is not based on birth or social standing but on educational skills (or at least on credentials). Cash and power, in other words, can be converted into degrees, then reconverted into more cash and power. The suburban school, the current demands for community control, and the concomitant failure of integration are all massive testimonials to the end of the common school.

What is being ignored is that the suburban schools don't actually do anything for most kids, other than bore them. Their prime function (aside from baby sitting) is to certify skills and reinforce characteristics and attitudes that are produced somewhere else. The money, in other words, did not buy much learning. But it did buy exclusiveness. They come in at this end, bright and shiny, and come out at that one, ready for Harvard or Cornell. The schools are, in brief, selective mechanisms, and through their selections they appear to justify (and are, in turn, justified by) the distinctions the society wants to make.

This is why we are fighting about schools and why we are in such serious trouble. Part of the fight—in the cities at least—is over a share of political power, over jobs and patronage and control. But the ideology that gives that battle energy, the ideas that help rally the troops, is the belief in the schools and in what remains of the dream of opportunity. But if *the* school system is the only mode of access to social and economic salvation, and if there is only one officially honored definition of such salvation (house in the suburbs, job at IBM, life insurance, and a certain set of manners), and if the school excludes any sizable minority from such salvation, then we have obviously defined ourselves into a choice between revolution and repression. The great dream of universal opportunity originated in an era of social alternatives, when schooling was one of several options for advancement; the school therefore could demand certain kinds of conformity. Individuality and pluralism could take refuge and sustenance elsewhere. But for the moment all advancement (we are told, are indeed required, to believe) begins in school, and we are, for this reason if for no other, no longer an open society. . . .

Inevitably, there are questions about the demands of a technological society and the necessity for universal literacy. Haven't many schools succeeded; don't we have one of the highest standards of literacy in the world? Don't schools make selections according to the demands that the technology and the culture impose? The answer is complicated, but there is nothing in it that makes the existing system of schooling imperative or even desirable, except—as always—the maintenance of the status quo. Which is to say that the system is necessary if the system is to be preserved. . .

Even if the school system were proficient in training people to deal with a world defined as technological (which it is not), it would still be guilty of the worst sort of parochialism and idolatry. Part of the significance of technology, we are told, is to free man from all those boring, menial tasks, maybe even to free him from the necessity of working at all. To prepare for this, the school system imposes boring, menial tasks. The very propaganda of technology would suggest other worlds, other options, time for other concerns. It suggests more, not less, pluralism, more leisure time, more lonely moments, and the necessity for more personal resources for recreation, satisfaction, and human encounter. But what actually happens is that by deifying technology, or by joining the rest of us in so doing, the schools are reinforcing the existing linear standards of judgment and selection—are, in other words, employing the rhetoric of the brave new world to coerce kids and parents rather than to free them. . .

Mathematics and history and literature thus become tokens of acquiescence rather than instruments of liberation. They are used by teachers to maintain order, reinforce distinctions, and intimidate or embarrass students. Complexity becomes a club and technology a prison. We are training a generation of people who regard the disciplines of the intellect as instruments of oppression.

One of the things we learned in the past decade is that we don't know very much. We don't know much about kids, about learning, or about motivation. One of the more fundamental assumptions of ten years ago was that curriculum planners sitting in some university, a foundation, or a central school office could invent programs (for teachers and students) and thereby engineer pedagogical success. What we discovered is that most of the time it couldn't be done, which may well be a good thing. If our pedagogical instruments were really powerful, we would have in hand one of the most totalitarian instruments imaginable. . . .

What we do know is that children are different, and that different people learn different ways, that some people think better in numbers than in words, that certain groups perceive and understand mathematical relationships more easily than verbal relationships, and that still others are particularly skillful in manipulating spatial problems but relatively incompetent with literature. Most of all, we know that personalities, backgrounds, and interests differ. It may well be that certain levels of literacy and ability in arithmetic constitute "fundamentals" for survival in America or anywhere in the Western world. But it does not follow that learning these things can be achieved by a single set of techniques, or that any teacher can be trained to them. More defensible is the assumption that, while drill, order, and tight discipline may be suitable for some students and teachers, they may be destructive for others; that "permissive" classes or Deweyan practices may work well with certain personalities but not with everyone. It is even possible to assume that the "fundamentals" should not always precede music or auto mechanics, but may, in many cases, grow naturally from other activities and from curiosity stimulated in other ways. We know that illiterate adults, properly motivated, have learned to read and write in a few months, and that recruits who almost failed Selective Service intelligence tests can be trained to operate computers and maintain radar equipment.

More important, we should have learned in the last decade that there is no magic in the single school system or in any set of curricular prescriptions, and that the most successful motivating device may simply be the sense that one has chosen what one wants to learn and under what conditions. In urban areas there is no reason why children in one neighborhood should be forced to attend one particular school for a specified period of time; why there should not be choice as to place, subject, style of teaching, and hours; why, for all children, French and history and algebra should have absolutely equal value; why, for some, art or dance or music should not be given more time than history; why reading a book is more of a humanistic activity than making a film or playing an instrument; why children should not be allowed to choose between permissive and highly structured situations (and many would choose the latter); why parents and children should not have the economic power to punish unsuccessful schools (by leaving them) and reward effective ones; or why single, self-serving bureaucracies should continue to hold monopoly power in what is probably the most crucial, and certainly the most universal, public enterprise in America. Wealthy children and middle-class parents have some options about schools; lower-class children have none.

What I am arguing for, obviously, is a restoration of multiple options and, as much as possible, multiple values. Christopher Jencks and others have proposed a system whereby parents are given educational vouchers that they can spend in any school or educational activity of their choice. The voucher would be roughly equal in cash value to the amount that the local school system spends each year on the education of one child, and it could be spent in any school that does not charge more in tuition than the voucher is worth. With support from the Office of Economic Opportunity, Jencks will try the system over a period of eight years in a place yet to be chosen. No one claims that this is the only way of restoring choice, options, and multiple values. It is conceivable that single public school systems might, on their own initiative, introduce the kind of pluralism that the voucher system is designed to achieve. Clearly, many have become more "flexible" and more cognizant of individual choice. And yet the pressure within a single system is likely to be the other way; it is likely, always, to demand a certain caution. Separate schools, accountable not to public vote and citizen support but only to their clients, may be immune to such pressure; they will have to make their way on the basis of performance. Ideally, moreover, vouchers would be usable in apprenticeships, in community-operated schools, in projects of independent study, travel (for older kids), or simply for learning resources to be used at home.

There is, obviously, no certainty that changes in the structure or financing of public education will generate a situation in which individuality is honored and where the system does not impose the fearful price it now extracts from the young in the name of "growing up." But such changes may, at least, remove some obstacles. They may, if nothing else, represent a social declaration by the system—by the state and the citizen—that education is not simply the acceptance of impersonality and conformity, and that schooling is not merely the training and selection of candidates for corporate life. The practice of encouraging, through a new structure, the idea that personal fulfillment is the first responsibility of an educational system, and that human dignity is not founded on a single standard, may do more than anything else to mitigate the alienation and hostility of the angry young. What the ideal system would do—not in rhetoric nor with slogans from the principal, but in practice—would be to declare itself unequivocally to be the ally of difference, of individuals, and of the tolerant against the invidious; it would recognize its own limitations in choosing for people and recognize their ability to choose for themselves, and it would, in all cases, stand at their side against the imperious collective demands of crowds, machines, and bureaucrats. All of that may be a vain hope, but given the impossible and possibly destructive hopes of social engineering that we entertained in the Sixties, it is, at least, a hope worth hoping.

EDUCATION AND SOCIAL MOBILITY

S. M. Miller and Pamela Roby

The poverty programs of the Economic Opportunity Act of 1964 were largely youth programs; the intent was to break the connection between the situation of low-income parents and the prospects of their children. These programs aimed at increasing the rate of intergenerational social mobility of low-income youth. More generally, questions of equality and social justice involve issues of social mobility. Life chances are defined largely as questions of opportunity for an individual to rise occupationally in his lifetime or for his children to move into better situations in society, thus surpassing the economic level of their parents. Americans generally point to the educational system to support their ideology that equal opportunity exists for all; the equitable distribution of this education is frequently unquestioned.... The importance of education is illustrated by the findings of Wilensky and Duncan that it is the only variable which consistently ranks all the white-collar strata above each of the manual and farm strata. In addition to its economic role, educational experience affects the way individuals are treated by other people and by various kinds of organizations and bureaucracies. An individual with low education is an outsider, less able to take advantage of the opportunities that exist, and is treated less well than those with the same income but a higher education. . . .

Why treat education and social mobility independently? Does not improvement in family income *automatically* result in improvement in chances for social mobility? The data in Fig. 1 do not support this conclusion: the education of a family, in most situations, is more important than the income of the family in affecting how far the youth goes in school. Furthermore, two families of the same income obviously fare quite differently in other respects if the offspring of one have a much better chance of higher education and resulting better job prospects than the other. To some extent, then, social mobility is a dimension of well-being deserving of separate attention. It is one of the most crucial indicators of a socially democratic society. In this chapter, therefore, we will deal first with education and then with social mobility.

Source. From *The Future of Inequality* by S. M. Miller and Pamela Roby. Copyright © 1970 by Basic Books, Inc., Publishers, New York.

Figure 1. Percentage of Youth, Age Sixteen to Twenty, Who Were Enrolled in or Attended College in 1960 (by father's education and family income)[1].

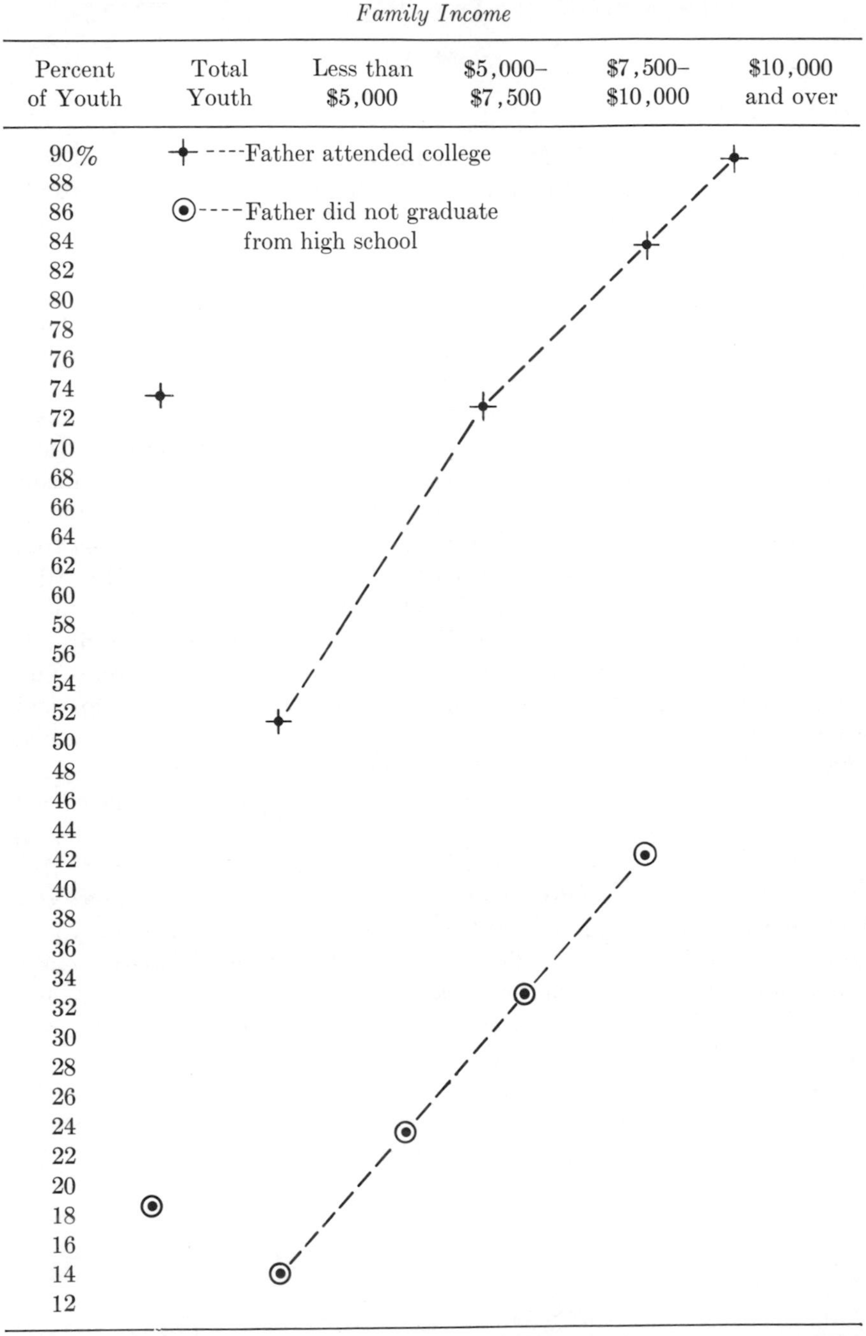

Family Income

Percent of Youth	Total Youth	Less than $5,000	$5,000– $7,500	$7,500– $10,000	$10,000 and over

90% ──┼──── Father attended college
88
86 ◉──── Father did not graduate
84   from high school
82
80
78
76
74
72
70
68
66
64
62
60
58
56
54
52
50
48
46
44
42
40
38
36
34
32
30
28
26
24
22
20
18
16
14
12

[1] From Pamela Roby, "The Economic Prospects of High School Dropouts, Graduates, and College Graduates," Syracuse University Youth Development Center (1965, mimeo). Adapted from U.S. Bureau of the Census, *Current Population Reports*, Series P-20, No. 110 (July 24, 1961), p. 15, Table 10.

EDUCATION

In education, we may examine various types of indicators of input and output. One input indicator is expenditure data—how much is spent on children of different income levels? The importance of school expenditures is indicated by the finding that the proportion of National Merit finalists is related to a locality's support for education. Data for the city of Chicago in 1963 show that for children in the ten lowest socioeconomic schools, only 63 per cent of the teachers were fully certified; in the ten highest socioeconomic schools the figure was 90 per cent. The significance of this difference is highlighted by Project Talent findings, which show that teacher experience is highly correlated with student achievement. In turn, teacher experience is related to salary.

EXPENDITURES

Despite the growing attention to class differences in education, educational resources are probably not being redistributed in favor of the low-income and the black. The Syracuse University study of school expenditures by Alan Campbell, Jesse Burkhead, Seymour Sachs, and associates shows that in 1962 in thirty-five of the largest metropolitan areas, expenditures in central cities—where there are many low-income children—were $145 per pupil less than in their contiguous suburbs— where there are few low-income children. One of the most disturbing findings in this investigation is that state educational funds give relatively more to the suburbs than to the cities; schools in the suburbs receive $40 more in state aid per pupil than schools in the cities. Even more disconcerting, the gap between cities and suburbs is growing; the difference in 1962 did not exist in 1958, when the two areas were spending the same amount. More recent data are not available but many believe the gaps to be at least as great as in 1962.

Vast regional differences also exist in the distribution of educational resources. Average per pupil expenditures were $413 in Mississippi and $1,125 in New York State during the 1967-1968 school year. . . .

When differences in the quality of the product—the return per dollar of expenditures—are considered, the gap is probably even greater than the gross education figures indicate. It is likely that fewer and poorer services are rendered per dollar in low-income than in higher-income schools. Thus, the gross inequities revealed by the expenditure figures are accentuated by the quality differences.

Table 1. Percentage of Male High School Graduates Who Entered College within One Year after Completing High School by Aptitude Level and Family Income

Family Income	Aptitude Level (Percentile)				
	0–49.9	50–74.9	75–89.9	90–97.9	98–100
Less than $3,000	19.6	48.2	75.4	87.9	100.0
$3,000–$5,999	27.3	52.5	73.3	86.7	96.1
$6,000–$8,999	31.9	59.7	80.6	88.6	95.2
$9,000–$11,999	40.2	66.8	83.9	92.5	95.9
$12,000 plus	49.7	79.7	90.1	96.7	98.5

Source. U.S. Congress, House, Committee on Education and Labor, Subcommittee on Education, *Hearings*, 88th Cong., 1st and 2nd Sess., 1963–1964.

Table 1 indicates that adequate financial aid is probably available to the top 2 per cent of the nation's high school graduates. Even for those who fall within 2 to 10 percentage points from the top in ability, family income is an important determinant of who shall go to college.

After questioning the level and distribution of educational resources, we must also ask, "If we had adequate monetary resources, would we have the capacity to implement our educational goals in the way we know they should be implemented?" The answer is probably, "No." Not only money, modern school buildings, and technological equipment, such as teaching machines, but *people*—teachers and administrators—are required for effective education. Like so many other things, the capacities of teachers and principals are distributed roughly along a "normal curve." Only a few are very effective; a few are very ineffective; and most are "average." Money that is devoted to new methods of training and guiding teachers and administrators may improve the effectiveness of the poor and average teachers, but it is doubtful whether any technique can make all teachers as effective as those few talented and concerned individuals who stand out as great. These outstanding individuals are the most important educational need of low-income youth in Appalachia, Harlem, or Watts. The need is not easy to fill.

BLACK EDUCATION

Since 1960, young blacks have radically narrowed the education gap that traditionally existed between nonwhites and whites. But the current situation is uneven. Between 1960 and 1968 the difference in median educational attainment of whites and nonwhites twenty-five to twenty-nine years old shrank from 1.9 years to 0.4 years. The difference between the percentage of nonwhites and whites possessing high school diplomas also declined. On the other hand, the gap separating the percentage of whites and nonwhites twenty-five to twenty-nine years old graduating from college increased: the percentage of nonwhites completing college increased from 5.4 per cent in 1960 to 7.7 per cent in 1968, while the numbers of whites doing so increased more rapidly from 11.8 to 15.6 per cent. This gap is significant since the college diploma increasingly separates the "haves" from those who "just get by" in society.

Compounding the educational gap is the disturbing fact that blacks have not reaped the monetary or occupational rewards which education delivers to whites. At every educational level, nonwhites earn less than whites. In 1966, nonwhite college alumni still earned less than white high school dropouts. Between 1958 and 1966, the income gap separating nonwhite and white males with one or more years of college grew from $2,131 to $3,095. A portion of the discrepancy between black and white earnings may be accounted for by differences in the quality of black and white education. Another fraction may be attributed to the higher concentration of blacks working in the South, where wages are low. But discrimination is the only factor which accounts for a major portion of the difference.

Sharp differences exist not only between the earnings but also between the occupational distributions of blacks and whites. Even college graduation does not completely protect blacks from being treated differently than whites in the occupational arena. Differential treatment is experienced at all age levels. In 1964 only 8 per cent of nonwhite high school graduates, as opposed to 30 per cent of white high school graduates, sixteen to twenty-one years old who had not enrolled in college, were able to obtain clerical and other white-collar jobs.

At every educational level not only are nonwhites employed in lower-paying, less prestigious occupations than whites, but their chances of obtaining work are also considerably lower than that of whites. . . .

Discrimination continues to intervene between education and income, between education and occupation, and between education and chances for employment. Education is important for the advancement of blacks—we do not wish to be interpreted as arguing otherwise. With education, blacks and other minority groups do gain higher incomes, more prestigious occupations, and a smaller risk of unemployment. The gain is, however, incomplete. The roots of black poverty lie in the discriminatory practices of the larger society as well as their own lack of education. As long as discrimination exists, education alone will not solve the problems of redistributing incomes and occupations between whites and minority members.

LIMITED POSSIBILITIES

Although education is very important, it cannot solve all the problems that produce poverty in American society. "Education" can become a slogan to escape from the wider responsibility of aiding the poor. If educational strategies are not viewed in perspective, an overemphasis on education can be self-defeating, for it may lead to neglect of economic assistance programs. . . .

By forcing all persons to enter the occupational world through the school gate, we have drastically underestimated and underutilized the potential of many low-income youth. Today nearly one-fourth of white youth and nearly one-half of black youth are dropping or being pushed out of school before they complete high school. In ghetto communities, the proportion is higher. . . .

Today dropouts who have gained valuable experience in the work world find that this experience is ignored by employers because the label *dropout*, assigned at age fifteen or sixteen, persists throughout a lifetime. Consequently, individuals who may have outgrown the issues which propelled them out of school continue to be economically disenfranchised. With our increasing emphasis on academic credentials, our Chinese walls of exclusion grow ever higher for persons who are ignored because they lack the magical diploma, although their occupational experience and performance prove them qualified. The loss resulting from an overemphasis on credentials is society's as well as the individuals'.

For education to enrich rather than constrict, men must be free to choose to use or not to use it. It is one of the paradoxes of our time that education, considered to be a liberating force, has become a prison for many. . . .

SOCIAL MOBILITY

As societies become increasingly future-oriented, a crucial dimension of stratification is what happens to the children of different strata. Current positions of families only partially denote future positions.

Many governmental policies are aimed at reducing the correlation between the economic position of the child and that of his parent. The aim is toward intergenerational social mobility rather than improvement of the conditions of the poor today. In the War on Poverty the emphases on job training programs (for example, Job Corps, Manpower Development) and education (for example, Head Start, Elementary and Secondary Education Act) are essentially programs in social mobility. The programs aimed at the young, such as Head Start, obviously aim toward intergenerational mobility, while those designed for older persons, such as many of the Manpower Development and Training Acts programs, seek intragenerational mobility.

What is the value of casting these poverty and manpower programs in the language of intergenerational social mobility? In some cases, the mobility perspective points out that program goals are too low. In some job training programs, for example, success is recorded if the individual secures a job, even if the job pays no more or is no less of a dead end than his previous job. Similarly, low-wage, full-time employment may not be a substantial mobility step over unemployment or irregular employment.

The mobility approach may also indicate the possible importance of stratum or group mobility. Important gains may be achieved not only by moving individuals out of particular low-wage occupations, but by securing a substantial improvement in the relative position in terms of wages, status, and conditions of currently low-level occupations. The large percentage of families living in poverty that are headed by males who are working full time suggests the need for that change. Increasing returns for certain kinds of work may be crucial if poverty is to be rapidly reduced. The stratificational approach also encourages study in the factors which impede or promote mobility. Lack of education may be a less important barrier than current common sense suggests, while discrimination may continue to bar many from jobs or career mobility.

Surprisingly, the United States has lagged behind many other nations in conducting a national study which is mainly addressed to issues of social mobility. In 1962, this lack was remedied by the very useful investigation of the Bureau of the Census, which was stimulated by and conducted in close cooperation with the sociologists Otis Dudley Duncan and Peter Blau. We will use this study. It would be very useful to conduct such a study every five years to record the changes in rates and patterns of social mobility in the United States.

The results of this study show that children of families at the bottom of the occupational hierachy have much less chance of moving into upper-level jobs than children who are born in families at these levels. The son of a black manual worker has less than one-fifth the chance of the son of a white-collar non-black to obtain a white-collar job. The white manual worker's son has nearly twice the chance of the black manual worker's son. . . .

The data on blacks are disturbing. The educational attainments of blacks are consistently lower than those of whites with the fathers' education constant. In addition, the black mobility rate from lower manual occupations is 51 per cent that of whites from these same occupations. More disturbing is the finding that among black sons of higher white-collar fathers, 72.4 per cent fall into manual-occupations, as compared with 23.4 per cent of non-black sons. This rate of downward mobility is spectacular even when we allow for the likelihood that for some the movement may be into manual occupations that pay as well or better than marginal middle-class occupations.

What is the target in social mobility? Obviously, income, occupational and social contacts of families, know-how, and educational support all combine to make it difficult to reduce sharply competitive advantages. But substantial curtailing is possible, and specific targets over a ten-and twenty-year period are probably desirable to reduce social mobility differentials in that time period. The improvement of the education of those at the bottom of society, reduction of the emphasis on educational credentials as intrinsic to occupational entrance, and more effective reliance on up-grading and training on the job are among the ways that social mobility patterns can become political questions. But it is doubtful if high social mobility rates can be produced without a relative improvement in the income of those at the bottom. For the conditions of the family affect the possibilities of the children.

Cutting the link between the parent's position and that of the child is one of the core goals of a fluid society. (One can argue that the goal is to break the link only for those at the bottom, not those in more advantaged positions.) Careful collection and analysis of data of this kind are essential to keeping the issue under public scrutiny.

Obviously, there are important questions concerning the significant economic-political-social boundaries of high and low position. Social stratification analysts have been slow to refine the manual-nonmanual divide. Our conclusion is that the increasingly important social division is not between the manual and nonmanual groups but between those with and without a college diploma—between those in professional and managerial occupations and the rest of society. . . Important differences obviously exist below the professional-managerial level, but the expanding "diploma elite" is becoming distinctly advantaged in society. Their advantage is not only economic but social and political as well. The diploma elite manages to achieve deference and decent treatment from governmental organizations and at the same time—perhaps because of this—is able to organize effectively as a political voice. As the complexity of life in the United States increases, we may expect the importance of education to grow.

The increased concern with intergenerational social mobility means that it cannot rest as a residual of other acts in society. What the rate of mobility will be is a political concern today. . . .

The hope has been in the United States that the doors to (educational) opportunity could be flung open without raising the (income) floors of the families of the youth. In the late 1960's, income, rather than opportunity alone, became an issue. In the 1970's, the balance between the two—between directly increasing the income of the disadvantaged and improving the schools—will be of central importance.

FOUR

How Schools Are Financed: The Economic Foundations of Education

The economics of education is generally viewed one-dimensionally in terms of the costs of a very narrowly defined range of benefits. In its most sophisticated form, this view is accompanied with serious questions about the way taxes are raised and used to support public education and about alternatives for the redistribution of costs and benefits. John E. Coons, William H. Clune, and Stephen Sugarman help to provide a much needed, larger view. They argue that the economics of public education should be more than a reflection of existing economic values; instead, it should incorporate new values that are more humanistic and more relevant to emergent societal priorities.

SCHOOL FINANCING: ITS USES AS AN APPARATUS OF PRIVILEGE

John E. Coons, William H. Clune, and Stephen Sugarman

The pioneer effort to translate the philosophy of equal educational opportunity into a viable state finance program adjusting for district wealth variation was made by George D. Strayer and Robert M. Haig in 1923 and later refined and developed by Paul R. Mort. The program came to be known as the foundation plan. Modified, scrutinized,

Source. Reprinted by permission of the publishers from *Private Wealth and Public Education* by John E. Coons, William H. Clune, and Stephen D. Sugarman, Cambridge, The Belknap Press of Harvard University Press. Copyright © 1970 by the President and Fellows of Harvard College.

criticized as it was, the program remained the paradigm of state aid to education until after 1960. The philosophy of the movement that produced it is described in its extreme version by the authors of the plan: "The state should insure equal educational facilities to everyone within its borders at a uniform rate throughout the state in terms of the burden of taxation. The tax burden of education should throughout the state be uniform in relation to taxpaying ability, and the provision of the schools should be uniform in relation to the educable population desiring education." The goals expressed are similar to Cubberley's; the practical program—like Cubberley's—deliberately falls far short of the rhetoric. The gap between description and deed exercised a pernicious influence for two generations. The failure to articulate the fact that the "solution" in reality permits wealthy districts to perpetuate their advantage left the erroneous impression among education amateurs that the problem had been solved. The allure of an ornamental equalizing grant formula that still permitted local incentive for better schools captured the loyalty of the average reformer with little time for technicalities and provided the basis for what can only be described as the equalization myth.

Shortly we will examine the mechanics of the foundation plan and observe it in operation in several states. Its operation can be complex, and we will proceed with accelerating sophistication. Starting at the beginning, simply put, under the Strayer-Haig scheme the state establishes a dollar level (foundation) of spending per pupil which it guarantees to every district; this can be set hypothetically at $500 per pupil. To qualify for the guarantee a district must tax at a certain minimum property tax rate, hypothetically 1 percent. The amount raised by a district at that tax rate will be supplemented by state aid to the extent necessary to insure the district the foundation level offering. Thus if a 1-percent tax in a given district raises $400 per pupil, state aid will come to $100. To preserve incentive, the district is allowed to tax more than the minimum rate whenever it wants additional local revenues.

It was Charles S. Benson, in his book, *The Economics of Public Education*, published in 1961, who finally rallied the arguments against the foundation program and began to dismantle the myth that it provided equal educational opportunity. Benson saw that the crux of the problem lies within that part of the formula which guarantees local incentive. The foundation plan has never provided that all districts can have the same offering if they make the same effort; the state will not equalize local ability to tax above the foundation level. Rich districts can turn out a better offering at every level of local effort above the minimum rate. The effect, of course, is to radically exacerbate disparities between rich and poor with every tax increment above the foundation level. Local incentive—subsidiarity—is useful only to the rich. Furthermore, what is empirically demonstrable is that in most states nearly all districts, rich and poor, do tax at a level above the minimum, so that the foundation program is indeed but a foundation upon which the districts with richer tax bases continue to build much finer houses than do poor districts. Under this plan, equal opportunity in terms of balancing offering, wealth, and effort is a hoax.

Unfortunately, rather than concentrating on its structural inadequacy, for many years reformers worked merely within the parameters of the foundation plan. Their attention focused upon (1) refining the measures employed in the Strayer-Haig scheme and (2) detailing the shortcomings which beset the plan, even within its own modest goals, when put into practice by the states. These two efforts provide concepts which are useful to an understanding of any sophisticated school financing plan, and they illustrate how for many years the reforming zeal was dissipated in confrontation with minutiae.

Implementing the Myth

Mort was principally responsible for clarifying the three basic steps in the formulation of the foundation plan; the analysis which follows is based upon his work.

Determine the Unit Cost of the Minimum Program. The first step in the foundation plan is the legislature's determination of the minimum level of education that all districts will be guaranteed if they tax at some minimum rate. This minimum education must be phrased in terms of number of dollars per task unit. Mort, however, felt that describing the program in dollars per pupils in average daily attendance (ADA) was too crude an approach; there had to be additional refinements of control to assure that the districts would be judged by the same standards. Thus, one very important criterion for state aid was the universality of a program. If almost every school has a kindergarten, kindergarten should be part of the minimum program. Secondly, there should be adjustments for those additional undertakings, such as transportation in rural districts, which are necessary to make the basic program possible. This approach sought to standardize the dimensions of the program.

Then Mort focused on refining the task unit. For the foundation scheme his approach was to divide school costs into two groups, classroom costs and all other costs. He noted that classroom costs tend to vary greatly from place to place depending on the kind of factors identified by Cubberley, whereas other costs remain fairly constantly related to number of pupils. Mort's solution was the "weighted pupil," a system for multiplying the number of students in a school by a certain factor depending upon the size of the school. He also devised a technique for including the cost of transportation in the weighted pupil measure; this, too, was computed by multiplying the number of students in average daily attendance by some factor. The result of this first step in constructing the minimum foundation program then, is a *unit cost per weighted pupil* which purports to cover the real costs of a certain level of education throughout the state. Granting that these adjustments are difficult to make with precision, their attractiveness is clear. Many states have nevertheless continued to base their plans on a simple per-pupil formula; on the other hand, some of the same states have adopted special grants to help defray costs arising from diversity of districts, for example, a special transportation fund.

Determine the Nature of the State-Local Financing Partnership. Establishment of the level of fiscal obligation which must be undertaken by a district in order to participate is next in order. As noted earlier, insofar as the minimum foundation program achieves equalizations, it does so by supplementing what is raised locally by a minimum tax rate. Of course some districts may be so rich that, at the minimum tax rate, they raise as many or more dollars than the foundation plan guarantees and are therefore entirely out of the aid plan. The original planners did not seem to intend this to happen often; they typically set the minimum rate so that none or only a few districts would exceed the foundation level.

One peculiarity of Mort's proposal was that existing state flat grants were to be subtracted from the basic program in order to determine the state share under the equalizing grant. Thus, if the state were already supplying $2 per pupil for textbooks, that amount would be subtracted from whatever the state aid otherwise happened to be. If a district, under the formula, were to receive $50 per pupil under the foundation program, it would not, in effect, receive the flat grant as well. This made some sense from the standpoint of the pure philosophy of the program. State aid purported to assure payment of the full costs of a "basic" education, so why should it support a greater level? Nonetheless, even within the foundation philosophy, from the point of view of equalization the flat grants should have been eliminated and textbook aid supported through the equalizing fund. Otherwise this combination of state forms of aid has an undesirable impact, as appears later. In any case, Mort's refinement was made meaningless; the states typically did not support the unit cost of even a basic education, let alone a substantial one.

Determine Ability to Pay. As the third step, the equalizing of sacrifice at the foundation level requires a rational measurement of local ability. Assessed valuation of property (often realty only) is nearly everywhere the measure of ability, and, in turn, the tax rate on that ability is the measure of sacrifice. Refinement in this case meant the acquisition of standardized ability data and was difficult because of the varying local assessment practices.

These then are the three chief elements of the foundation plan; but their adoption has not been uniform. Too often the admonitions of Mort and others regarding meaningful implementation of the plan are ignored, rendering individual programs almost complete shams. It is possible to particularize the kinds of inadequacies which contributed to the failure of the foundation to reduce inequalities even to a respectable minimum level. They include:

1. Political compromise —task unit distribution. An important weakness of the Strayer-Haig system is the political sensitivity of the foundation level. The theoretical goal of the foundation program is to determine and support the real cost of some basic and substantial educational offering. The structure of the guarantee—usually simply a certain number of dollars per pupil—lends itself from the outset to political compromise. The support level always remained below the real costs of any substantial level of education and became an index merely of the available resources and the educational politics of the particular state legislature, not of any job to be done.

2. Static nature of the support level. The needs of education have steadily outgained support levels. There are two reasons for this, one the fast-growing cost of education. Mort admitted in one of his last publications: "The level of support used in the State Aid formula did not rise automatically with the cost increases. Only population increase was in any degree reflected in the formula." Second, school expenditures have shown great "expansibility" (a tendency to branch into new areas), far beyond what Mort had anticipated. Hindsight makes it obvious that the political process has been ill-suited to produce the continually strengthened support required.

3. Lack of flexibility in meeting local needs. A foundation program tends to produce uniformities of two kinds among poor districts: one is uniformity of expenditures because of the great burden of raising additional funds, the other is the related uniformity of educational style. At the "basic" level of spending the districts are far less free to experiment and diversify. Their meager resource is largely consumed merely in the struggle to meet state standards, including the traditional starting point of any system, teachers' salaries. Experimental or light

house programs become such by virture of the dollars available above the educational subsistence level: light house districts are invariably rich districts.

4. Continued presence of flat grants. Most states use the Strayer-Haig distribution and employ flat grants of the specific or general purpose type as well. These grants often reduce the equalizing nature of the foundation program, usually obscure the realities of district needs, and always contribute to the vulnerability of the program to political compromise.

5. The minimum rate—reducing state support from below. The technical machinery of the plan, by which it achieves whatever equalization occurs, has also been an obstacle to the achievement of equalization. This point requires some elaboration.

The minimum foundation rate is usually chosen with reference to some district in the state in which the minimum rate will produce enough local money to meet the foundation program. That district would represent the level of wealth at which state aid would cease. Thus, assume that the foundation level is $1,000 and that the richest district in the state is assessed at $100,000 per pupil. A 1-percent tax would then produce the minimum program in the richest district; and if 1 percent were chosen for the participation tax, every district in the state would have to work equally hard to produce the $1,000. In fact, it was never seriously urged that the richest district be used as the standard for the participation rate, for often it was freakishly wealthy; rather, it was recommended that a "key" rich district be chosen. In practice, however, the average district more often became the "key." If the average district were assessed at $50,000, a 2-percent tax would have to be chosen as the participation rate (the rate necessary to raise $1,000 in that district), and equalizing grants would be distributed only to districts below the state average valuation. Superficially, one might think it is more equalizing *not* to give any state aid to districts richer than average. Unfortunately this result is achieved by giving the poorer districts less, because the minimum rate must be set higher (2 percent instead of 1 percent) in order to produce the guaranteed amount in the average district.

This means that, even within the foundation plan itself (that is, at the participation tax level), districts richer than the "key" district can exploit wealth. If all districts sacrifice at the participation level, there will not be equal offerings. Only the poorer ones will have the same dollars, because the richer half even at that tax rate will exceed the guaranteed minimum. Of course, beyond the foundation tax level there is *no equalization* for any district. What is produced by a given tax effort is precisely relative to wealth at all levels above the average. Thus we may say that choice of the average district as key does not even ameliorate the problem of wealth variations—except as to the lower half of the districts, and then only up to the minimum participation rate.

The problem with characterizing inadequacies of the foundation plan this way—from within the framework of the theory—is that it fails to focus upon the behavioral response of the districts. Let us therefore assume a state without these inadequacies, in which the foundation level is continually adjusted upward, in which only foundation aid and no flat grants are employed, in which the plan is keyed to a rich district, and, most importantly, in which the support level is sufficient to provide a substantial educational offering. Consider the probable behavior of districts in response; if the foundation is still inadequate to satisfy the objectives of local educators, school board authorities, and local citizens in a number of districts, some will tax locally above the participation rate to supplement the state guarantee. The wealthier districts, of course, will have a far easier time raising the additional money, and it is inevitable that they in fact will raise more. This is the typical result in even the most progressive states. On the other hand, if few districts had aspirations to exceed the foundation level, there would be less tendency for individual districts to raise significant amounts of additional funds locally. That is, local variation in wealth diminishes in importance to the extent that local incentive disappears. Still, so long as any two districts desire to exercise local incentive, the richer will have an advantage over the poorer. To avoid this, revisions would have to be built into the Strayer-Haig approach which would change its very nature. Districts would have to be prohibited from spending more than the foundation amount. To effect this, either that amount must be high enough so that no district will want to exceed it with local collections, or any excess collections must be rebated to the state.

With a fixed effort level and fixed expenditure level the foundation plan would be transformed to a centralized system, and statewide incentive would become the sole source of educational betterment. This is not what the foundation program contemplates: it would then no longer be a foundation, but a ceiling. Nor is it the solution we urge. It is not necessary to eliminate local decision-making concerning the level of the child's offering in order to terminate variation by wealth among districts.

TYPICAL FOUNDATION PLAN IN ACTION: THE OHIO PLAN

... The Ohio support program represents a very traditional application of a Mort-adjusted Strayer-Haig system. The state support level is not fixed in terms of so many dollars per pupil in ADA, but rather is cast in terms of "classroom units." This concept is a modern example of a basic process we have already seen—a way of adjusting the task unit so that instructional, administrative, and other burdens, which fall on districts differently because of size, location, and other characteristics, might be fairly taken into consideration in the aid formula. The program remains based on an equalized guaranteed dollar minimum of support for each student in average daily membership (ADM). Of course, if the district wants to spend more on its schools, it simply taxes at more than the minimum. (Or in cases of the very rich, more dollars are raised even at the foundation rate).

The Ohio aid program has been altered in amount a number of times in recent years, although the approach has remained fundamentally the same. Details of the plan adopted in 1967 to govern future school terms are worth explaining. Classroom units for each district are awarded (a) one for every sixty kindergarten pupils, (b) one for every thirty elementary and high school pupils, (c) some for vocational and special education burdens, then (d) one additional unit for each eight units in order to compensate for administrative and operational demands, plus (e) some other minor adjustments.

The foundation level under the plan is variable but tends to be upwards of $8,000 per classroom unit; fundamentally it is calculated as the sum of (1) a sliding salary schedule amount for certified teaching employees and (2) $2,425 per classroom unit. On the basis of these two factors, for example, a district would be supported up to the level of $7,625 for a classroom unit if it had a certified employee with a B.A. and one year's experience ($5,200 plus $2,425). The amount of state aid is determined by the difference between the foundation amount and the amount raised locally by a levy of 17.5 mills. The Ohio program also includes a guarantee that no district will receive aid from the state of less than $3,050 per classroom unit.

Note that the sliding salary part of the Ohio aid program is anti-equalizing. It is an allowance based on a revenue task unit which stimulates districts to hire teachers with advanced educational training. Thus, for example, the state will support a higher foundation for a unit in which the teacher has an M.A. Richer districts, of course, can more easily take advantage of this aid.

The 1967 version of the Ohio aid plan is a marked dollar improvement over the previous plan: that is, the foundation level has been substantially raised (along with the participation rate). Impetus for this change seems to have come in part from the proposals made by a committee of education experts for the Ohio Foundation in 1966. The program represents a change in degree, if not in kind; the committee proposed more sweeping changes than were adopted, including a shifting of the entire Ohio focus away from the foundation system, but the general structure remained intact. The data to be generated for the 1969-70 school year should manifest fewer and less dramatic differentials than those we are about to examine from the 1965-66 year, but the differences will be there and they will be substantial. The system makes them inevitable.

SPENDING AND WEALTH IN OHIO

Analysis was made of the 162 city school districts in the state in terms of their expenditures per pupil in average daily membership for 1965-66 (including state aid). The range of current expenditures was a high of $806.93 to a low of $329.40. The weighted mean was $457.41 and the mean $448.80. . . .

A look at the state's big cities demonstrates significant discrepancy in terms of the average amount of money spent on each child depending upon where he lives:

Table 1.

City	Expenditure per Pupil in ADM
Cincinnati	$501.84
Cleveland	481.90
Dayton	479.44
Akron	441.19
Toledo	412.30
Columbus	410.68

Accounting for the variation in expenditure per pupil in the 162 Ohio city districts requires analysis of the ability of the local district to do its own financing. The Ohio plan in effect until recently is a good test of the tendencies of the Strayer-Haig approach to tie educational opportunity to wealth: it presents a relatively simple Strayer-Haig state aid pattern plus state participation at a relatively low level (that is, the foundation support level is clearly not adequate by itself to operate the school system).

The results of wealth-expenditure analysis clearly link what is produced with ability to pay. The wealth measurement used was the district's assessed property valuation per pupil. The 162 cities, ranked in terms of expenditure per pupil, were divided into quartiles and

Table 2.   Ohio City Districts: Wealth and Spending Comparison by Number of Districts in Each Spending Quartile

Wealth Status	Spending Quartiles[a]			
	$Q_1(40)$	$Q_2(41)$	$Q_3(40)$	$Q_4(41)$
Above average wealth	38	24	17	2
Among 20 wealthiest	16	3	1	0
Among 10 wealthiest	9	0	1	0
Among 20 poorest	0	1	3	16
Among 10 poorest	0	0	0	10

[a] Includes state and federal aid; Q_1 is highest.

analyzed, and the assessed valuation per pupil for the median district was found to be $13,300. Table 2 portrays the relation of expenditure to wealth; 38 of the 40 best offerings are by districts with above-average wealth and of the ten wealthiest all but one have offerings in the top quarter. When we consider the extremities of the wealth spectrum in Table 3 we see an even more dramatic contrast.

The dominating impact of the wealth factor could hardly be made clearer; but another perspective can be gained by looking at the wealth and spending figures for the 5 largest city school systems in the state (Table 4), which account for more than 20 percent of the total number of Ohio school pupils. The wealthier the community, the better education for the children, consistently. Of course the correlation in not perfect, and other factors may exert some influence, including cost of living differences (likely not to be large among these big cities), economies of scale (also probably not a differentiating factor among large systems) and willingness to support schools through tax effort. Thus, for example, Toledo, the sixth largest district, while third in terms of wealth is fifth in expenditure among the top six.

The range of assessed valuation among Ohio city districts is from $5,358.27 to $85,174.20 per pupil. Some extremes are naturally to be expected. More important is the range of $8,500 to $25,000—approximately a 3-1 ratio—which separates the richest and poorest of the middle 80 percent of the districts (cutting off, that is, the extreme 10 percent at each end so as to eliminate "freaks"). Given such polarization of wealth, no matter how hard a poor district tries it is not likely to catch up with the rich one without more state help.

The Ohio legislature, by delegating the financial responsibility to local districts and by engaging only in tokenism from the state

Table 3. Ohio City Districts: Numbers of Districts Ranked by Spending and Wealth

	Districts in Terms of Spending per Pupil (State and Federal Aid Included)		
Wealth Status	Top 10% (90–100 centile) (total 16)	Middle 20% (40–60 centile) (total 32)	Low 10% (0–10 centile) (total 16)
Districts with wealth above median	16	17	0
Districts with wealth below median	0	15	16
Districts ranking among 20 wealthiest	12	0	0
Districts ranking among 20 poorest	0	0	8

Table 4. Spending and Wealth of Five Largest Ohio Cities

City	Expenditure (dollars) per Pupil in ADM[a]	Assessed Valuation per Pupil (dollars)	ADM
Cincinnati	501.84	20,514.56	87,681.28
Cleveland	481.90	18,555.34	151,986.24
Dayton	479.44	16,126.50	59,658.17
Akron	441.19	14,801.14	58,297.95
Columbus	410.68	13,087.93	103,550.09

[a] State and federal aid included.

treasury, transmuted the proper private advantage of the rich into a public institution having the essential economic characteristics of a private system. The new plan will do little to change this. In Ohio, a child's public education is dependent for its quality upon the private wealth of his district. It is as simple as that. . .

A Preview of the Solution

There are a number of ways to satisfy the basic principle that wealth should not determine the quality of public education. One, of course, is the abolition of public education. Another is. . .the creation of a completely centralized state system with expenditures either equalized on a per-pupil basis or rationalized according to need and/or other criteria. . . .

Our approach depends for its practical effect upon manipulation of tax systems. Equal district power is the key. The concrete financing proposal may be stated thus: equal tax rates should provide equal spendable dollars. That is, the local unit would be empowered to fix the tax rate (effort) to be imposed upon a specific class of local wealth. For every level of local tax effort permitted by statute, the state would have fixed the number of dollars per task unit (probably per pupil) that the district would be empowered to spend. The state also guarantees that this number of dollars will be available to the district. Assume, for example, that by statute a fifteen-mill district tax rate makes $600 per pupil available to the district. If the local levy raises less than $600, the state makes up the difference from a fund generated by taxation of general state wealth. If the local tax produces an excess (it can be set so that it never does), that excess is redistributed to poorer districts within the system.

The local share would come probably from a levy on real property, though income would be superior as a fair measure of the district's ability. Whatever the source, it must be a reasonably accurate measure of wealth, and it must be reasonably local in its incidence, for the aim is to provide a measure of the district's sacrifice.

The state tax that supplements insufficient district collections in theory should be progressive to the degree that the decisions of individual taxing units about their appropriate sacrifice for school expenditures are all made on an economic parity. Such a fine adjustment may be too much to expect, but in any event it should not be a regressive tax.

A highly oversimplified example may help. Imagine a state divided into two school districts, A and B, each with 100 pupils. District A has a total wealth of $10,000 ($100 per pupil). District B has a total of $90,000, or $900 per pupil. Each decides to tax its wealth at the rate of 10 percent for schools, yielding respectively $10 and $90 per pupil. Under our basic value judgment, district A is $80 short—it tried just as hard, so it should be able to buy just as good a school. The $80 must come from a state tax. Since the total wealth of the state is $100,000, in order to raise the $80 per pupil for district A the state chooses to levy a flat 8-percent tax, producing $72 per pupil from district B and $8 from district A. Now look at the example from the other side. In *gross taxes* per pupil district A has paid $10 (local) plus $8 (state), or $18. District B has paid $90 (local) plus $72 (state), or $162. As a *percentage of local wealth, each total tax is exactly the same,* while the redistribution of wealth has produced equal expenditures. Each is taxed at 10 percent locally and 18 percent totally, each has $90 to spend—from each according to his ability, to each according to his effort.

We call the scheme "power equalizing." It may be used to equalize either governmental units such as school districts or it may be applied to families. It is imperfect; it is probably feasible; it is vastly superior to any existing system; it preserves most of the present systems. It takes advantage of an interesting phenomenon: poor districts show a tendency to tax themselves as hard as or harder than rich. Under existing systems this sacrifice by the poor is unrewarded, for it is imposed on an inferior tax base and produces inferior education. The solution suggested would sacrifice nothing but the right of the rich to have superior public schools with less effort. It would insist that if you want to be number one, rich or poor, you must try hardest.

FIVE

Who Controls Education: The Politics of Education

The increasing fury over the issue of community control gives the impression that primary control over education is exercised on the local level. This impression is deepened even further by the important and active role that local school boards play in the administration of public education, especially in matters related to finance. However, the visibility of school boards in local educational affairs should not be equated with power. Primary legal power over public education resides on the state level. Finally, all decisions regarding public schools are subject to state authority.

The formal structure of educational control provides only partial insight into the politics of education, however. When the focus is switched to the actual participants in critical educational decisions, the clean lines of governmental organization charts fall away and are replaced by zigzag lines that enlarge the control picture beyond local and state levels. From this latter perspective, public-school policy turns out to be heavily influenced by a highly complex national network of graduate school professors, university administrators and trustees, corporation directors, and government bureaucrats who weave business values and needs into the fabric of schooling. So that even the reforms that first appear to be sweeping in their scope inevitably prove to be small changes geared to narrow-gauged problems and designed to make what exists more effective rather than change it.

Real reform, that is, reform that is concerned with basic causes as well as techniques, necessarily requires a serious change in the pattern of control over public education. Obviously, those in power will not initiate reform that threatens their positions. How, then, is significant reform to be achieved? How can those without power achieve it? At best, answers to these questions are elusive. Yet, until a new politics that is both rational and sensitive is found, educational failure will not only continue but will grow.

Political questions are largely ignored in educational studies. In many ways, the Jencks selection can be read as a plea to restore politics to an important place in the study and practice of education. A radical analysis of American education, Jencks tells us, must begin by answering this question: Who controls our schools?

Ridgeway's argument that universities are deeply involved with big business suggests that the professors—who, Jencks tells us, shape curricula, school structure, and staff patterns from kindergarten to graduate school—are unavoidably influenced by their positions in business-oriented universities with massive corporate interests.

The role of big business in education is most directly represented by the work of major philanthropic foundations. As Wolfe points out, although many of the reforms the foundations sponsor appear radical, in reality, they amount to little more than the strengthening of the sectors of the existing system that serve big business.

WHO SHOULD CONTROL EDUCATION?

Christopher Jencks

American liberals have traditionally believed that many of the country's problems were susceptible to gradual and comparatively painless solution by combining education and technological innovation. In part, this assumption is correct. But most of America's problems are rooted not in technological or intellectual ineptitude but in genuine conflicts of interest. These problems cannot be solved merely by learning more; they can be solved only by taking the right to make certain decisions away from some people and giving power to others. Whether the problem is the arms race or America's enthusiasm for minding other nation's business, racism or poverty, illness or crime, the solution is not to be found in the classroom. If it were, there would be no need for radicalism in modern America.

The inability of schools to cure America's social disorders comes as a continuing disappointment to almost everyone (with the possible exception of teachers). Americans have always tended to assume that good schools could offset all the numerous defects of American homes, churches, and employers. Our dependence on schools and colleges to socialize the young has increased steadily during recent years. The

Source. "Who Controls Education," by Christopher Jencks. From *Dissent*, March/April 1966, pages 145–156. Copyright © 1966 by Dissent Magazine.

reason for this is not the megalomania of educators. Nor is it the instinctive faith of laymen in educators; on the contrary, such faith has been conspiciously lacking. The reason is that parents, clergymen, and employers have found it harder and harder to meet their traditional responsibilities.

The inability of the typical American home to prepare its young for adult life needs little documentation. The world is changing too fast for parents to feel confident about imposing the values of their own youth on their children. They look outside the home for guidance; to their neighbors, to the mass media, to Dr. Spock and Margaret Mead, and to the schools. If elementary schools suggest that it is more important for children to get along with one another than to acquire adult virtues, most parents will acquiesce. If high schools sanction cars and cigarettes as normal to adolescent life, most parents will do the same. If colleges take sex and liquor for granted among undergraduates, most parents will protest only feebly.

The parent who would resist this pattern, soon discovers that his powers are extremely limited. The days are long gone when parents could or would spend most of their time with the young, either in household or farm work. By the time most students reach adolescence they have become expert in outwardly seeming to conform to parental demands while actually adapting to the less easily evaded expectations of their classmates. They have found, too, that their schools are in fact ersatz families, competing with parents for control over the young. The modern "schoolchild" is in many respects just that: the child of an institution. For him the school provides the mirror in which to discover himself. In large part, moreover, this mirror is the creation of his classmates, not his teachers. If the child is successful by his classmates' standards he becomes confident in a way that he never does if he succeeds only in pleasing his elders. Yet he can seldom be healthy or satisfied unless he also has the skill to make some kind of peace, however fragile or fraudulent, with adult expectations.

The decline of the family as a shaper of the young has been matched by the decline of the churches, and for similar reasons. The geographic mobility which has made it easier for children to anticipate that they will sooner or later be freed from the parental shadow has also made it possible for everyone to change churches more easily, creating a buyer's market in religion. The growing complexity of the economy has created a variety of occupations which rival or surpass the clergy in erudition and breadth of experience, thereby reducing the authority of the pulpit as the arbiter of community morals. As a result, education has become a kind of secular religion, and teachers a sort of lay clergy.

Industry is also eager to transfer responsibility for the socialization and training of prospective employees to the schools. Employers have wanted to put vocational and professional training under public auspices to save themselves money and effort. Labor unions, professional associations and the like wanted their training programs in schools and colleges to give their callings status. Both have agreed that such a transfer of responsibility would provide more equality of opportunity and more assurance that the young would get high quality training. The roots of this change go back to the nineteenth century, when schools of medicine, law, and theology were established in the better American universities. In this same era, land-grant colleges were set up to provide scientific training for farmers and engineers. Later, with the help of federal grants-in-aid, vocational training won a place in the secondary schools. In recent decades even business and public administration, the last prestigious holdouts against professionalization and academic preparation, have begun to fall into line. Today there is little real debate about the necessity of providing occupational training in school as well as (and in some measure instead of) on the job. The only serious debate is whether particular kinds of training need be extensive or brief, and at which educational level they should be provided.

It is clear, then, that schools and colleges are being asked to assume a large measure of responsibility for the personalities, attitudes and competence of the next generation. It is also clear that they are not set up to meet this responsibility. In the first place, America has assigned a comparatively small share of her resources to the task. Expenditures on education are usually reckoned at between five and six per cent of the Gross National Product. Less than three per cent of the adult population is employed in teaching, and except at the graduate level and in a few colleges this three per cent includes only a few of America's most talented men and women. Even our commitment of time may well be inadequate for the tasks we expect to accomplish in the classroom. The average American goes to school only 12 years out of almost 70, and during those years he is in school only about 180 days out of 365, and usually only about 6 hours each day. He devotes only about two per cent of his lifetime to formal education. Academically talented or socially fortunate children are, of course, likely to give more of their lives to educational institutions: often as much as four, and sometimes even six per cent. In some of these cases the impact of what happens in school is so strong that it helps shape the rest of the student's life. But this is the exception. Often enough, life outside the school is so much more compelling than life inside that a student is psychologically absent even during the hours he spends in class.

The basic reason why schools and colleges cannot cure our major social disorders is not, however, their lack of resources; it is that they are part of the system which produces the disorders. The resulting limitations are illustrated by looking closely at one of the many problems education is normally expected to solve: poverty.

American society is organized on the assumption that if you want to live comfortably you have to perform some kind of work which society values. Those who cannot perform such work are, with certain exceptions, condemned to live at or below the subsistence level. It is therefore usually assumed that the cure for poverty is an educational system which gives everyone the skills for doing some kind of valuable work. In other words, if everyone were literate, ambitious, and socially poised, everyone could earn a comfortable middle-class living.

Unfortunately, however, skills are not absolute but relative—and hence competitive. If the least adept students are given slightly better instruction, while instruction of the most adept gets substantially better, the competitive position of the least adept will deteriorate rather than improve. If that happens, poverty will grow more widespread. If the schools want to end poverty, they must not only improve the position of the poor pupils; *they must improve it faster than they improve the position of the rest of the pupils.* Parents of the better pupils (middle-class parents by and large) inevitably resist such efforts. They do not, of course, defend giving the inept students an inept teacher or poorly equipped classroom. But they do not want talented teachers diverted from work with gifted children to "remedial" or "vocational" work, nor do they want improvement of slum schools given higher priority than the improvement of their own schools. The middle classes realize quite well that American life is competitive, and that if their children are to prosper they must get "the best" education. Both "the best" and "the worst" are defined by comparison with the rest. If "the worst" gets better, then middle-class parents will want "the best" improved even more. Given today's political realities, educators can seldom resist such middle-class demands. Nor do most educators have an impulse to resist, even if they could. They typically argue that "the best way to improve the education system is to start at the top." This is probably true. But improving the system in this way will do nothing to eliminate poverty, and may even intensify it. If we want to end poverty we must concentrate not on increasing the absolute educational level of the population but on narrowing the gap between the best educated and the worst educated.

As this example suggests, the social role of education is at bottom a political rather than a technical question. Schools and colleges can only play a major role in solving America's social problems if control over them passes to new individuals and interests which expect to benefit from solving these problems. If the poor, for example, want to narrow the gap between what their children learn in school and what the children of the middle classes learn, they will have to fight for a larger voice in the allocation of personnel and money among competing schools and competing programs within schools.

A radical analysis of American education must, then, begin by focusing on the question of who controls our schools and colleges. At first glance this appears to be a fairly simple question, which can be answered by studying the legislators, philanthropists, and parents who put up most of the money for education, and the boards of education and trustees which nominally control most schools and colleges. This kind of analysis shows quite clearly that education is a virtual monopoly of the middle classes, and that the great conflicts are in large part intraclass conflicts. The battle over church-state relations, for example, is largely a struggle between middle-class Catholics who want "the best" education for their child and don't want to pay for it twice, and the middle-class non-Catholics who think religious separatism a national menace. The battle over racial segregation, too, is largely a struggle between lower-middle-class Negroes who want to escape the ghetto mentality and lower-middle-class whites whose status and self-assurance are too fragile to accept Negroes as equals. (This is not to say that poor Negroes accept segregation willingly. But for the most part they are not ready to organize and they are more interested in new buildings and good teachers than in integregation *per se*.)

Most conflicts over education are not, however, conflicts among lay interests but between one or another lay group and the professionals. Formally, of course, these battles are fought in the lay arena. Typically there is a "liberal" group which takes its cues from the professionals and supports their demands, and a "conservative" group which opposes the dominant professional opinion on the subject. The classic example of this pattern is, of course, the perennial struggle over educational finances, in which the educators ask for more money, the "liberals" support the demand, and the "conservatives" oppose it. Another recurrent example is the struggle for "academic freedom," a term which can mean almost anything but is generally used in debates about the political, theological or moral content of a teacher's classes or reading lists. Again, the pattern is one in which the "liberals" support professional autonomy while the "conservatives" argue for the layman's right to decide what goes on in a school or college. With the major exceptions of racial and religious questions, this pattern characterizes almost the full range of educational politics. Sooner or later (mostly later) victory in such struggles usually goes to the liberals.

The result is that the educators have more and more control both over their own affairs and over their students'. The reasons for this trend deserve careful attention, for until they are understood it is impossible to map a realistic program of educational reform, radical or otherwise.

Ours is an academic age. All of the major professions have come to depend on universities, not just to train their recruits but to provide old-timers with new techniques and ideas. Business and government are in many respects as dependent on the universities as the professions are. The universities generate many of the ideas which give politicians and civil servants a sense of purpose; they invent many of the scientific and managerial techniques which make it possible for both governmental and corporate bureaucracies to achieve their purposes; and they train men to do the more complicated jobs in business and government. Even such a symbolically pre-academic man as the yeoman farmer has come to depend on the university extension service.

The vital link between formal education and workaday world is usually the graduate professional school. These schools, concentrated in a few dozen universities, train almost all the important educators, doctors, lawyers, engineers, economists, and literary critics, as well as many of the leading businessmen, government officials, and even military officers. They put an imprimatur on the young which tells outsiders that a particular man is an insider. They also shape the state of mind which this imprimatur symbolizes: acceptance of the needs of your employer-client, be he the Pentagon or a neurotic four year old, as legitimate and inevitable; keeping personal feelings and emotional impulses to yourself; knowing more about the problems you tackle than anyone else; not getting hung up on questions that are too big or too fundamental to be "manageable". Over any considerable period of time the men who teach in America's leading graduate schools determine for the rest of us not only what is true and what is false but in large measure what is "done" and "not done." Since the graduate schools are usually a generation ahead of whatever segment of the society they lead, their influence at any particular moment always looks modest. Over the years, however, they are perhaps the single most important source of innovation in society.

There are, of course, differences among graduate schools. The world of medicine is not the same as the world of physics, economic advice is not offered in quite the same way as legal advice, literary criticism requires a different temperament from library management. And all these differences are mirrored in the graduate schools. Nevertheless, the similarities between graduate programs are generally more striking than the differences. I shall therefore lump all of these programs under the general rubric "graduate schools," and will assume that all graduate schools are professional schools, even when the "profession" for which they prepare is archaeology or musicology.

Standing as they do at the crossroads between education and employment, the graduate schools have enormous potential influence on the rest of education. Nor have they been slow to exercise this influence. The customs and concerns of the graduate schools increasingly mold undergraduate education. This applies not only to undergraduate education in the universities but to the supposedly independent liberal arts colleges, and even colleges nominally dedicated to saving souls, training teachers and preparing young ladies to become Southern matrons.

The reasons for this hegemony are several. First, the graduate schools are the principal source of college teachers. These teachers tend to regard their years in graduate school as a model of what all education should be like. They seek to re-create this model in the college, both by adding graduate programs and by reorganizing undergraduate programs in the image of graduate ones. A second reason for the hegemony of the graduate schools is that the proportion of undergraduates who plan to go on to graduate school appears to be steadily increasing. As a result, the faculty has more leverage in its struggle to impose graduate school standards on undergraduates. The student who a generation ago would not have cared whether he got an "A" or a "C" in European History now does care. This means that his professors can make him act like an apprentice historian while he is enrolled in the course. And now that he sees himself as a prospective graduate student he is often *eager* to play the amateur Ranke. There are, of course, still plenty of colleges where the majority of students reject all this and intend to go to work in what they see as an anti-intellectual business community. But such colleges and such students have less status than their more academically rigorous competitors and are increasingly on the defensive. Everyone concerned agrees that the graduate schools are the wave of the future.

If outside laymen still controlled colleges as tightly as they once did, the recruitment and expectations of faculty and students might make little difference. But the fact is that college trustees and administrators are more and more responsive to the collective views of the academic profession, less and less to other pressures. As a result, college faculties have increasing power to shape their institutions. One reason for this is the rising importance of federal and foundation support, compared to such traditional sources as state legislatures and alumni. Both the foundations and the federal government are inclined to consult professional rather than lay opinion in deciding how to spend their money. They also often deal with faculty members rather than going through administrators and trustees. Thus the faculty have more independent initiative, and the trustees and administrators are more dependent on the faculty to bring in money. With so much money available for research, even institutions which have done little to push back the intellectual frontiers are anxious to do more—or at least to *seem* to do more. This anxiety has produced an unprecedented concern about that elusive attribute "quality" as well as about its more measurable (if largely meaningless) counterpart, "credentials." Faced with a shortage of distinguished or even competent scholars, boards of trustees and administrators have nevertheless shown unprecedented eagerness to maintain standards, and in many cases have even struggled to raise them. As a result, colleges compete to improve salaries and working conditions. More and more faculty can "write their own ticket."

The rising bargaining power of the academic profession and its rising prestige in the eyes of laymen have reduced the control of the special interest groups which founded most colleges: The Catholics and Baptists, the Negroes and Irish, the teachers and farmers, the feminists and aristocrats, the home town boosters and regional patriots. Academicans are subject to less direct pressure from these groups, either with regard to their own affairs or in their dealings with the young. Indeed, academicians are more and more looked to by these interests to mediate between their traditional claims and the newer, more cosmopolitan and "national" vision of society which many members of the groups see emerging. This does not, of course, mean that academic and professional freedom is universal or irreversible; but any look at the past suggests that the trend is toward more and more autonomy for the professors, less and less authority for the laymen.

Nor is this trend confined to the colleges. It is also apparent, if to a lesser extent, in the elementary and secondary schools. Indeed, the relationship between graduate and undergraduate instruction is in many respects paralleled by that between undergraduate and secondary education. Most of the secondary school teachers have been trained in the colleges (some have also had some graduate work), and their definitions of what is worth knowing and how it should be taught are at least partially acquired in college. These colleges, moreover, are increasingly cosmopolitan. The old teachers college in which the student never met a creative scholar or scientist is slowly on the way out.

At the same time, the proportion of high school students who graduate and go on to college is rising steadily, and this means that more and more high school students care about good grades and can be forced to do whatever academic tasks their teachers set for them.

These changes have many by-products. The "curriculum reform" movement, for example, is primarily an effort to remake the secondary (and to a lesser extent, the elementary) curriculum in the image of the college and the graduate school curricula—only better. Professors from the leading universities have been involved in preparing curriculum materials and in training teachers to us them. "Advanced placement" courses are another sign of the times. High school teachers of these courses give instruction which is avowedly and deliberately similar to what has traditionally been given to college freshmen, and many colleges now give credit for such work if students do sufficiently well on a national exam devised for the purpose. The growing emphasis on academic preparation for secondary teachers, and the feeling that the skills and training required for a college teacher are essentially the same as those required for a high school teacher, are a natural consequence of such trends.

In the elementary and secondary schools as in the colleges, the power of lay boards of control appears to be diminishing. Partly this is a financial change. The local school board depends more and more upon state and federal assistance to balance its budget and is therefore subject to the decisions of state and federal legislators about how money should be spent. For a variety of reasons best known to politicians, the professional educators seem to have substantially more influence over decisions made at the state and federal level than over decisions made locally. One reason may be that state and federal legislators are typically better educated than the local school board members, and may therefore be more deferential toward the claims of educators. Then too, neither state nor federal legislators can easily punish educators who mobilize public opinion against them or try to push them in directions they don't want to go. The teacher who criticizes a local school board, on the other hand, may find himself unemployed. Yet even at the local level teachers have in recent years shown unprecedented readiness to organize, lobby for better schools, and withdraw their services if they don't get what they want. While much of the controversy over teachers' unions, strikes, and "professional sanctions" has focused on salaries, the teachers' right to a direct voice in shaping school policy has also been a vital issue.

What do these developments portend for the future? So far as educators are concerned, the picture seems clear. They are building a unified educational system, running from pre-school to graduate school, all of whose parts will be increasingly articulated with one another. The wellsprings of authority in this system will be the graduate schools, which have direct contact with the dominant institutions in the larger society and which therefore embody and symbolize the demands of the "real" world. The leading universities will have far more influence on the rest of the educational system than the system has on them. This will be clear to teachers at all levels, and the result will be an increasingly widespread desire to work in a major university where most research will be done, where most graduate students will be trained, and where the rest of the educational system will be increasingly shaped. The teachers will, moreover, find it easier than in the past to satisfy their perennial impulse to work in or near the centers of power and influence. Graduate programs will undergo enormous expansion, creating more jobs for men with good scholarly credentials. This will not only decimate undergraduate classrooms but lure many talented teachers away from the elementary and secondary schools.

The hegemony of the universities will almost certainly accelerate the nationalization of the whole educational system. Already the academic profession has an essentially national outlook, and tends to be impatient with the parochial interests of local boards who assume that the educational system under their control should have a special mission or standards. Academicians use whatever leverage they have to enforce their more universalistic viewpoint, and they find that the federal civil service and to a lesser extent the President and the Congress are their natural allies in such struggles. Thus there will be more and more pressure for federal "leadership" and federal "standards" at all levels, and the result will be more federal "control."

For the students, a system dominated by the academic profession and the top universities will mean several changes. First, and perhaps most important, such a system will be increasingly organized and run on the assumption that students at each level are going on to the next level. The high schools will be run for the benefit of those who plan to attend college, the colleges will be run for those who plan to attend graduate school. At any particular level, this assumption will be correct for more and more students, even though in the forseeable future the great majority will continue to drop out *somewhere* along the path to a graduate degree. The dropouts, however, will be more and more on the defensive in the nonacademic world. Adults will assume that a "normal" youngster should go on to get a graduate degree, and that those who fail to follow this course are stupid, rebellious, inflexible, or in some other way socially tainted. As a result, there will be a growing consensus among educators and laymen that "improving" education at each level consists not of preparing students better for the nonacademic world, but preparing them better for the next higher level.

These trends will affect students in several ways. For one thing, the present emphasis on admission to the "right" college will probably be

more and more overshadowed and supplanted by emphasis on admission to the "right" graduate school. Students will tend to view
college as they now view secondary school: mainly as a way-station
from which one progresses to the next level. Many such students will, I
think, be willing to attend "comprehensive" public commuter colleges
during their undergraduate years, just as they now attend
comprehensive public high schools. In that event the undergraduate
colleges attached to major universities may go the same way as the
academic high schools of an earlier era: surviving and even prospering,
but still appealing only to a small, cosmopolitan and highly motivated
minority. Similarly, the private residential liberal arts college may, like
the boarding school of an earlier era, price itself out of reach of most
families. (Costs have in recent years risen much faster than personal
incomes.) Some such colleges may fold, while the rest will come to
serve the same mixture of education-conscious upper-middle class
families and carefully selected scholarship students now found in the
better private schools.

The present influence of the elite undergraduate college may be
further eroded if, as seems likely, it becomes increasingly difficult for
any undergraduate program to attract big-name teachers. Without distinguished faculties, the difference between an elite residential college
and a "comprehensive" commuter college will be more and more a
matter of "tradition," and "atmosphere." How many parents will be
willing to spend a large fraction of their income on such "intangibles"
if there is a cheap and respectable public college just around the
corner, and if this college seems to ensure its more gifted BA's entry
into the nation's top graduate schools? Parental reluctance to invest
large sums in undergraduate education may be particularly marked if
federal support for graduate students lags behind costs, so that the
parents expect to be asked for substantial contributions to their
children's graduate education. Only the most prosperous parents, who
can afford to support their children at *both* levels, seem likely to opt
for expensive undergraduate education. In this respect, as in others, the
undergraduate pattern of tomorrow is likely to mirror the secondary
school pattern of today.

Students in this system will find themselves under pressure to grow
up faster than they have in the past. Educators generally, and
university scholars particularly, tend to gear the educational program
to precocious and talented youngsters such as they themselves usually
were. Today this tendency is somewhat restrained by the power of
laymen. Parents, speaking through the board of education, complain if
their children are worked too hard or "can't keep up." Students both in
school and college conspire tacitly or explicitly to restrict output. For

reasons already suggested, however, these limitations on academic power and pressure are diminishing, and the pace of learning is accelerating. Today's students study languages in elementary school which were once saved for secondary school, they read books in high school that were once read only in college, and they write papers and perform experiments in college which would once have been reserved to graduate students. Conversely, students whose failure to learn was once accepted as normal and predictable are now defined as "problems," and are segregated into "remedial" programs of one kind or another. . .

UNIVERSITIES AS BIG BUSINESS

James Ridgeway

America's 2,200 colleges and universities are the largest body of secret organizations in the nation. The trustees of the private institutions are self-perpetuating groups who meet *in camera* and do not publish reports of their operations. Although the regents or trustees who rule public universities periodically hold open meetings, their real business is transacted at confidential executive sessions. The universities have been so successful in safeguarding their privacy—particularly with respect to their finances—that few people are aware of the extent to which the worlds of higher education, big business, and banking are linked through interlocking relationships among professors, college presidents, and trustees, industry, and government—relationships whose chief victims are the more than six million students the universities are supposed to teach.

In fact the American university today resembles a conglomerate corporation. Its sprawling enterprises include graduate institutes, computation centers, and propaganda headquarters where sociologists test the citizenry's political attitudes. There may be campuses in Madrid, Florence, or Lima, and teams of researchers carrying out inquiries for AID or CIA in Ethiopia or Thailand. The university may own a press, a ball park, a couple of hotels, some ships, and—for complete diversification—an amusement park. Some holdings are more exotic: Purdue, for instance, ran an airline for a time; Dartmouth has a timber-producing forest; Connecticut's Wesleyan put out a children's magazine,

Source. Excerpts from "Universities as Big Business" as it appeared in *Harper's.* Copyright © 1968 by James Ridgeway. Reprinted from THE CLOSED CORPORATION, by James Ridgeway, by permission of Random House, Inc.

the *Weekly Reader*, before selling it to Xerox for several million. The University of Wisconsin is responsible for the world's leading rat poison, and New York University gets the profit from a spaghetti factory.

Very likely there will be a defense-systems laboratory or an AEC installation near the campus and a sprawl of companies created by some of the professors. These academic entrepreneurs who dash back and forth between campus, government, and business see themselves as Renaissance men.

The defense electronics business started this trend. But nowadays the "spin-offs," as the professors' companies are called, may sell educational games, run Job Corps camps, schools for small children, community-development centers in the slums, or prepare a "menu" of options to better motivate laggard black businessmen.

Deans and presidents take a benign view of such activities, often encouraging the professor to start a new company, and then sitting on its board of directors or that of a local bank, where they can lend a hand in financing and coordinating the whole works. The older graduate students provide cheap labor pools, useful for keeping the undergraduates in tow and for assisting the senior professors in carrying forward their inquiries within the university or in some private company. Teaching undergraduate students is not especially interesting compared to working on the outside in one of the new companies, and some professors tell you it is now obsolete as well: the students learn more by working in the "real world laboratory," which is to say on a professor's experiment outside the university. They refer to the profit motive as the "reward structure."

An archetype of the new arrangement is at Stanford University in Palo Alto, California. On part of the 9,000 acres left to the university by Leland Stanford, there is now an industrial park which houses fifty companies, also involved in research and development. They keep in close touch with the university's electronics laboratory, whose scientists pioneered in the development of vacuum tubes and microwave equipment. One, for example, is George Barry, a radio engineer and physicist. When two of his colleagues figured out a way to measure the area covered by Voice of America broadcasts, Barry quit his job as professor and, with his colleagues helping out in their spare time, started the Barry Research Corporation, which submitted the winning bid for the new equipment. Another Stanford scientist helped the government to evaluate the proposal. . . .

An even more impressive model is in the environs of Cambridge, Massachusetts. Studies by Edward B. Roberts and Herbert A. Wainer of MIT indicate that more than a hundred different companies were begun by professors departing from MIT labs and academic depart-ments. While the bulk of their business at first comes from government contracts, after four or five years 40 per cent is in commercial markets. The new companies needed very little to begin with, usually starting on personal savings of a few thousand dollars. Once operating, they were able to tap ample sources of risk capital around Boston. . .

Sixteen spin-off companies have been established since 1950 around the Ann Arbor campus of the University of Michigan. Probably the best known is Conductron, which makes radar and optical equipment. It was begun in 1960 by Keeve M. Siegel, then a professor of electrical engineering at the university. Siegel recruited twenty-five university people, fifteen of them professors. Then Conductron shunted $250,000 of research funds into the university's engineering department, where several members of the company's staff were still professors. At the same time the university handed out a $39,000 subcontract to Conductron. When the university's laboratories performed advanced research in detection of underground explosions, Conductron applied these techniques to machinery for evaluating data from underground explosions in oil drilling. In 1966 Siegel sold control of the company to McDonnell-Douglas, the aircraft company, and started another firm. He is estimated to have made $5 million on Conductron.

Another successful spin-off is Tracor, Inc. Begun by University of Texas professors, the company now makes $50 million a year, much of it for work on defense systems. One of the most enterprising members of the Texas faculty is Dr. George Kozmetsky, Dean of the College of Business Administration. A graduate of Harvard Business School, he has taught at Carnegie Tech, and is one of the founders of Teledyne, a highly successful electronics company. . . .

The computer business is perhaps the prime example of the new business-university partnership. International Business Machines, which sells more than 80 per cent of the nation's computers, dominates the industry. Computers in operation around the country are judged to be worth $7.2 billion, and the market increases by 25 per cent every year. IBM achieved its supremacy by shrewd and farsighted marketing techniques. Nearly 200,000 college graduates annually use computers; if they all learned on IBM equipment, their future employers would avoid a training problem by buying IBM hardware rather than another company's. To this end, during the past twenty years IBM has made discounts of more than two-thirds on equipment to universities, which are themselves a rapidly expanding market, using computers now worth about $160 million for planning, administration, and teaching as well as for research. IBM now says its educational allowance ranges from 10 to 30 per cent for colleges and universities.

By making research grants and offering the machinery itself at large discounts, the company gets "free science" as professors develop projects on IBM machines which may result in new products or new uses for the machinery. . . .

Currently in vogue is the theory that the techniques of systems analysis employed in making complicated missile and defense systems can be used to solve political and social problems. In other words, the engineers and scientists who could send a rocket to the moon, could also learn how to build a fine school system or end poverty.

The technique involves collecting data, which can be built into a model that will simulate, or imitate, human activity. If one could quantify human activity—so goes the theory—one might also be able to predict and control it. These possibilities have given rise to companies engaged in "social problem solving."

Simulmatics Corporation . . . was organized in 1959 by Edward L. Greenfield, a public-relations man, and three professors—Ithiel de Sola Pool of MIT, William N. McPhee of Columbia, and Robert P. Abelson of Yale. In the 1960 Presidential campaign the Simulmatics predictions turned out to be remarkably accurate, and trading on this success, the company went on to other work. The company has made models of the Venezuelan economy for AID and drawn up a computer program called Dynamark, which can "assess brand loyalty" by evaluating results of the test-marketing of different products.

It also produces educational games, including a very popular one for youngsters called the Life Career Game. Students are divided up into teams of two or three people. Each team is assigned a fictitious student, and the idea is to plan a worthwhile life for this hypothetical person. In another, the Legislative Game, sometimes called the Direct Democracy Game, players pretend to be Congressmen. They are provided with cards that tell how the people back home vote. Then they simulate Congressmen at work. This game calls for sessions in a cloakroom where the players can swindle one another, and they have a chance to act out the less meaningful forms of parliamentary procedure on the floor of Congress.

The educational games were designed by a group of professors at Johns Hopkins headed by James Coleman, then marketed through Simulmatics, where Coleman is a vice-president and director. Simulmatics has purchased polling data from the Furst Survey Research Center, Incorporated, which is owned by Sidney Furst, who at the time was also a vice-president and director of Simulmatics. (Furst is no longer associated with the company.) Simulmatics hired its own vice-president, Professor McPhee, as a consultant, through Columbia University's Bureau of Applied Social Research, where he was employed. Fifty thousand shares of Simulmatics stock are owned by Pool, who is a professor and chairman of the political science department at MIT, and director of the research program for international communication at the Center for International Studies. (The center was originally financed by the CIA, and Pool sometimes consults for the agency. Pool is mainly concerned with propaganda. At MIT one of his major interests is in studying mass-media propaganda techniques in communist countries; on the side, through Simulmatics, he conducts secret research in South Vietnam for the Pentagon's Advanced Research Projects Agency. . . .)

The endowment funds of American universities now total around $12 billion. Harvard is one of the wealthiest private institutions, with an endowment of $1 billion. Decisions as to where and how to invest these funds are made on advice of the treasurer by the six members of the self-perpetuating corporation which runs the university. The treasurer is George F. Bennett, who is also president of State Street Investment Corporation, which manages three mutual funds with assets of $600 million. It also handles investments for Harvard. (Francis H. Burr, a partner in the law firm of Ropes & Gray, also sits on the boards of both the Harvard Corporation and the State Street Investment Corporation.) Bennett, in addition to his earnings as president of the investment company, draws a fee, said to be $25,000 a year, from Harvard for investment advice. While Bennett's mutual funds in themselves are not very large, when he combines them with Harvard's funds he enters the market with imposing leverage. The arrangement between State Street and Harvard was initially set up by State Street's founder, Paul C. Cabot, who preceded Bennett as university treasurer. Initially it was specified that when securities held by both Harvard and the State Street mutual funds were involved the latter would lead in buying or selling; so at least in theory, Bennett can purchase a stock for State Street Investment and then drive it up by using Harvard's money. Or, in selling, he can dump a large holding belonging to State Street and then sell Harvard on a lower market. However, Bennett claims it never works out like this, and that oddly, Harvard often does much better than the mutual funds.

State Street owns 485,000 common stock shares in Middle South Utilities, Inc., a holding company which controls electric companies in several Southern states, including Mississippi and Louisiana. Harvard has 543,719 shares; Harvard-Yenching Institute, an organization devoted to promoting higher education in Asia, of which Bennett is deputy treasurer, has 18,668 shares; Bennett himself holds 2,000 shares and is a director of the company. In recent years Harvard undergraduates unsuccessfully challenged the university's Middle South holdings on the grounds that the Southern companies were managed by racists, members of the Klan, and White Citizens Councils. Bennett says he regards these utilities as public-service companies, regulated under state laws: "I made a personal investigation and satisfied myself that the officers were law-abiding citizens," he said. When asked about the investment at a public meeting, Harvard's President Nathan Pusey said, "Our purpose is just to invest in places that are selfishly good for Harvard. We do not use our money for social purposes...."

Dealings between business and universities have on occasion led to murky complications. One such episode occurred in 1965 at the University of Michigan and resulted in the resignation of Eugene Power, who had been a much-respected regent for nearly a decade. He was also president of University Microfilms, which sells microfilm copies of out-of-date and rare books and is now a subsidiary of Xerox. In October 1965 the campus newspaper, the *Michigan Daily* reported that University Microfilms in effect enjoyed a monopoly in copying graduate students' theses. University Microfilms was also making profitable use of a valuable book list prepared by the university library. The company had set up its equipment in the library basement where it could photograph fragile or rare books which could not be taken out of the building. The State Attorney General Frank Kelley began looking into the matter and Power left the board. Kelley later said, "There is no question of Mr. Power's motives, his integrity, or his devotion to the interest of the university...." He added, however, "For Mr. Power to maintain his position as a regent while his company has its present relationship with the university is inconsistent with the requirements of the Michigan constitution relating to 'substantial conflict of interest.'..."

Unpleasant incidents of this sort have rarely come to light. Indeed the cozy relationships between universities and industry are widely considered not only respectable but desirable. For example, Franklin D. Murphy, who until 1968 was chancellor of the University of California's Los Angeles campus, also sat on the boards of Ford Motor Company, Hallmark Cards, McCall Corp., and the Times Mirror Company, which publishes the *Los Angeles Times*. The last two companies were also represented on the university's board of regents. When I talked with him, Murphy conceded that the relationship between universities and industry created some problems. "If you have your professors running around consulting all over the place, they are not around to talk to students," he said. "If you can keep it under control, and I think that there are ways that you can manage this at the university level, this is enormously valuable from my point of view. Number one, it does provide this necessary expertise (something that the French and Germans want to talk to us about—how to strengthen university relationships with industry when both need it). Secondly, it does provide for the university professor the technique of guaranteeing to some degree that he will not be in an ivory tower and that he will be dealing in the teaching process with things that are germane and contemporary, not entirely theoretical. . . .

REFORM WITHOUT REFORM

Alan Wolfe

When Clark Kerr was fired as president of the University of California in early January 1967, two things were immediately apparent. One was that it would be difficult for him to find another job that matched in stature being the head of one of the largest and most prestigious universities in the United States. The other, which could do nothing but add to his prestige, was that he was an ideal martyr. Victim of verbal abuse from the left, yet unceremoniously and contemptuously dumped by the right, he appeared as the tragic political figure of our times, just trying to be competent in a world of political extremism. Clearly here was a man, many felt, who could continue in some way to have an impact on higher education, if only the right job could be found for him.

It was. Shortly after Governor Reagan announced Kerr's dismissal from the University, then-acting president of the Carnegie Corporation Alan Pifer called a press conference in New York. Clark Kerr, he announced, would head a major study of higher education in the United States, one that would have a profound impact on the shape and destiny of education beyond the high school in this country. According to Pifer, Kerr had agreed to head this study, on a part-time basis, before the regents had taken their action. Now, with no other entanglements, Kerr would be free to give the project more time. Other members of the study commission were announced, and some deadlines were established.

That was four years ago. Now Ronald Reagan has been reelected for another term; Alan Pifer is the permanent head of the Carnegie Corporation; and Clark Kerr and his associates have published a series of

Source. "Reform Without Reform: The Carnegie Commission on Higher Education," by Alan Wolfe. From *Social Policy,* May/June 1971, pages 18–22, 27. Copyright © 1971 Social Policy Corporation. Reprinted by permission of the Social Policy Corporation, New York, New York 10010.

reports advancing their notions of how higher education must be reformed in order to meet the challenges of the years between now and the year 2000.

Perhaps it is because we live in what some behavioral scientists call a "temporary society," but somehow we never expect that things will be delivered as promised. When the Kerr Commission was announced, there was a good deal of publicity. Now that it is in the process of making its reports, few seem to have taken the time to analyze very closely what it is saying. To be sure, professional journals and newsletters connected with higher education have duly noted and summarized the reports; and an occasional newspaper, usually *The New York Times*, has devoted front-page space to the commission's recommendations. But Pifer had said that the work of the commission would be enormously influential, and he was probably right. If that is the case, some attempt to evaluate what has been published so far in a critical and over-all way is needed, especially if the commission's influence has a chance of being pernicious rather than beneficial.

Such an analysis must begin with the Carnegie Corporation itself. What is it, and why is it interested in the future of higher education? It is named, of course, for that most introspective and visionary of all the so-called "robber barons," Andrew Carnegie. The schoolbook version is that Carnegie, never formally educated himself and feeling guilty about the money he had accumulated, decided to become a philanthropist in his old age and began giving money to libraries and other educational institutions throughout the country. Guilty he may have felt, but his motives were hardly completely philanthropic. Foundations were created as a device through which industrialists could pass on to their descendants both their wealth and their political power with the tacit blessing of the state, expressed through tax exemptions. The result was so beneficial to them that all the leading capitalists of the nineteenth century bequeathed to our generation extraordinarily powerful institutions bearing their names, institutions which operate as if they were governments, but over which citizens have no control, since they are still considered "private."

At the present time the three major foundations—Rockefeller, Ford, and Carnegie—are committed, above all, to the maintenance of the existing political and economic arrangements in this country. Indeed, they make few secrets about their political preferences. Ford and Rockefeller projects and studies, for example, are designed to preserve the "free world" and to administer defeats to those who question that priority. As then-president of the Rockefeller Foundation Dean Rusk once told the 83rd Congress, foundations support only "those patriotic institutions which recognize their obligations to serve the public interest." But at the same time, the foundations, because they are not corporations pursuing immediate profits, can focus on the long-range strategies needed by the corporate order. This, combined with the flexibility provided by no public control, means that they can support some controversial projects that few others in power can do. Thus the Ford Foundation, realizing that American schools were a disaster and were helping nobody, could sponsor an experiment in community control in New York City. Although temporarily allied with radical groups, Ford's motives were not radical. Foundation directors knew that as far as public education was concerned, some changes had to be made to keep the whole society functioning.

The Carnegie Corporation traditionally has been less powerful and wealthy than the Ford or Rockefeller Foundations. In order to compensate for this, its directors have concentrated its activities in two areas, international relations (through the Carnegie Endowment for International Peace) and education. From its very beginning, the Carnegie Corporation has given large financial support to a subfoundation, the Carnegie Foundation for the Advancement of Teaching (CFAT); and periodically the CFAT has provided money in places where reforms were needed.

In 1910, for example, the CFAT sponsored the Flexner Study of American medical schools, designed to upgrade and regulate the quality of medical education being offered in the United States. Other important projects have included the creation of a pension plan for college teachers, the Teacher's Insurance and Annuity Association (TIAA), whose own financing has turned it from a relatively insignificant plan to a powerful institution in its own right. (The TIAA now insures college teachers all over the country, and its proceeds have financed such things as the construction of the new Gulf and Western skyscraper at New York's Columbus Circle.) The so-called "Pennsylvania study" of the CFAT, in the words of Alan Pifer's report for the year 1966, "gave impetus and respectability to objective testing as a means of educational measurement." Finally, the most recent major study of the Foundation before the Kerr appointment was a comprehensive review of the American high school, under the leadership of the ubiquitous James Bryant Conant. (Indeed, Pifer compared Kerr's mission with that of Conant and said that he expected the Kerr Commission's eventual reports to have the impact that Conant's *The American High School Today* had when it was published).

The interesting thing about all these reforms is that they were actually attempts to rationalize important sectors of the educational system in order to make them more effective. Medical education was a disaster area before the Flexner reforms; and so long as quacks could call themselves doctors, public confidence in medicine would be minimal. Reform here would have little impact on providing mass medicine, but it would benefit the legitimate doctors, and that is why they supported reform. Similarly, educational testing was a necessary reform if more and more people were to go to college. Given mass education, mass measurement was needed. Far from changing education in any significant way, educational testing simply made it easier to continue along a direction already started. The Conant study of the high schools grew out of the Soviet advances in science, and the reforms proposed were not so much designed to make high schools humane places within which to work and study as they were intended to turn out more scientists as rapidly as possible.

It follows that a main consequence of the Carnegie Foundation for the Advancement of Teaching has been what can be called "reform without reform," changes geared to certain narrow-gauged problems and designed to make what existed more effective rather than to change it. Radical alternatives to the present might be considered, but only to be undercut.

It is worth keeping this in mind when we turn to the Kerr Commission, which shortly after its creation decided to call itself the Carnegie Commission on Higher Education. It was obvious from the very composition of the commission that far-reaching reform was beyond its purview. Generally it is considered good politics to give a commission as much breadth as possible by appointing people from all walks of life. So a "safe" labor leader, a Black quasi-militant, a woman, a student, or other such person is often appointed to give the impression of balance. Yet the Carnegie Corporation chose not even to take this minimal step in appointing the Kerr Commission. Its members were, with one exception, either industrialists or highly placed college administrators. All were white, there was only one woman, and nary a person was younger than 45. When they looked at each other across the table, each commission member saw a reflection of himself.

Yet lack of balance in and of itself was not the major problem in the commission's composition. More startling was the total identification of its members with those institutions of power that have demonstrable stakes in the maintenance of the *status quo*: the 14 members of the commission, excluding Kerr, were directors of at least 14 major corporations, including such giants as American Airlines, New York Life Insurance Company, First National City Bank, Kennecott Copper, Scott Paper, McCall Corporation, Northern Pacific Railroad, and Crucible Steel Company. Four commissioners were full-time board chairman—of the Cleveland Electric Illuminating Company, the Marine Midland Bank, Time, Inc., and Hunt Foods. Among these 14 people were trustees of 8 schools and colleges, including Harvard, Yale, Pennsylvania, and Reed. Many of them were directors or trustees of the Ford and Rockefeller Foundations, and nearly all of them had served the Carnegie Corporation in one capacity or another before their appointment to the Kerr Commission. The college presidents among them had served in official capacities with established educational organizations such as the American Council on Education and the Association of American Universities. Finally, two of them were trustees or consultants of the Rand Corporation; and among the 14 could be found directors of such institutions as the Council on Foreign Relations, the Institute for Defense Analysis, the Educational Testing Service, and the Teacher's Insurance and Annuity Association. By any standards, it was clear from the beginning that all of the commissioners were associated with political and economic power in the most direct of ways.

Such imbalance seems to have embarrassed even the commission itself after a while. As it progressed, the commission added to its members an Englishman, a Black woman (two categories for the price of one) associated with a law firm close to Hubert Humphrey, a Yale psychiatrist noted for his sympathetic (yet critical) studies of young people (thus filling the "youth" category somewhat indirectly), and two college administrators from the West and the Southwest, correcting a geographic imbalance. But the changes were not very meaningful; and they hardly covered up what the initial appointments had revealed: that this was one commission that would play things pretty close to the chest. One does not have to be a strict economic determinist to conclude that a commission with this composition would shy away from reforms that would affect the existing distribution of power and wealth in the society. . . .

Quality and Equality: New Levels of Federal Responsibility for Higher Education was the first publication of the commission, dated December 1968. At a time when federal aid to education, a new policy first instituted by the Johnson Administration, was just three years old, the commission strongly recommended massive federal aid to colleges and universities. Under its various proposals, aid would be nearly doubled in a six-year period from an estimated $7.03 billion in 1971-1972 to a projected $12.97 billion by 1976-1977.

The money was urged for very specific kinds of programs. Student aid programs, for example, would be intensified through equal opportunity grants (". . . all college students with demonstrated need will be assured of some financial aid to meet expenses at institutions which they select"), federal scholarship grants directly to institutions of higher learning, work-study programs, graduate "talent search" programs, and increased counseling and information programs. All student aid, however, even when totaled, adds up to only a fourth of the commission's proposed budget.

Cost-of-education supplements are to be provided directly to the colleges to meet the expenses caused by the influx of students, and they can be used as the colleges see fit. Projected expenses for construction are also taken into account, although here the commission sees a decline over time as enrollments taper off in the 1980s. Commenting on, and approving of, the trend toward government aid for research, the commission makes a strong plea for more than doubling federal aid to research. In addition, the commission makes recommendations in various other areas: medical education programs, library support, new colleges, and international studies programs (shades of the Ford Foundation).

Tying all these recommendations together is a proposal to create a National Foundation for the Development of Higher Education, on the model of the National Science Foundation, "to provide encouragement, advice, review, and financial support for institutional programs, designed to provide new directions in curricula, strengthening of essential areas that have fallen behind or that have never adequately developed because of inadequate funding, and development of programs to improve educational processes and techniques."

Doubling federal aid to education within a six-year period is quite a large order, especially in a time of unemployment, inflation, and recession; and it took some courage to recommend such a push, given the general resistance to increased taxes in such a period. The commission seems to want to go far and to upset some cherished notions in order to improve education beyond the high school. Yet ten years ago these recommendations would have seemed more controversial than they do now. Federal aid to education was once a major issue (I remember being assigned a book, to read in college, that contained arguments on both sides of the issue, and that was exactly ten years ago). But by now, when the federal government provides aid to so many things, the issue would seem to be not whether federal aid should be increased, but for what purposes it should be used. This the commission does not imaginatively deal with. The vision of college education behind its proposals is substantially the same as the present reality of higher education. What exists now is taken as given; the only policy is to spend more money to expand it. Perhaps, it could be argued, our problems are not financial, but political and moral, in which case doubling the money simply doubles the problems.

If the commission is not particularly visionary, why does it urge such increased federal support? It is not the first to ask the state to intervene on behalf of institutional aid. The major corporations in the

United States realized by the time of Woodrow Wilson that the government would not harm them if it was already helping them, and so they turned to the state and demanded regulation in order to stabilize the economy and create an atmosphere in which profits would be steady and would accrue most to the biggest companies.

Behind the Carnegie Commission's report lies a similar appeal. "The economy," it notes, "is dependent upon basic research and advancing technology, and upon the higher skills needed to make that technology effective, to assure national economic growth and well being." What has occurred is that technology has made demands for skills, from scientific research to lower-level tasks like computer programming. Corporations could teach those skills themselves, but since all are pursuing a profit, they see no reason to do so as long as other institutions will do it for them. Traditionally, one of the functions of the American university has been to train future corporate workers at public expense (and at the expense of the student himself). Now this program is no longer efficient; the demands of technology are such that the colleges cannot keep pace—hence the need for increased federal aid to education. As it has done in the past, the government will step in and provide to the private sector what that sector does not want to provide for itself. Thus federal aid to education is essential to the maintenance of a corporate-dominated economy oriented toward private profit.

There are other advantages to increased federal aid to education, and I do not mean to demean their importance. It is important to the schools themselves to have more money; their financial situation is desperate and is becoming worse. Increasing student aid will naturally benefit the student and, if intelligently applied, will also benefit those who would like to be students but cannot afford to be. These are all vital needs, and the commission did well to recognize them.

My point is only that the commission's vision is one that, however noble, never took it beyond the kind of society that now exists and that is largely responsible for many deficiencies in the educational system. Thus, when it was announced that this report had caused some disagreements and would be substantially revised as of June 1970, one waited to see some fundamental changes, only to discover that the point at issue was the amount of money involved. In the second report, the "liberals" within the commission managed to increase the projected budgets and even win a parenthetical aside in the introduction saying that some members felt that expenditures should be even higher. But the revised version never touched the way in which the questions were phrased, and thus accepted the previous definition of reality.

The remaining three commission reports published to date deal with more specific aspects of higher education.

My criticism of the commission is not intended to suggest a conspiratorial and nefarious plot against the public good by a small group of people hidden away in key places. Rather, I am suggesting that there is a style of educational reform concerned only with technique, not with basic causes. Growing out of a fondness for the existing economic and social system, such a style of reform accepts as a given the very cause of the problem—the fact that a few still benefit from welfare-state capitalism at the expense of many more. When those who obtain the benefits turn their attention to a problem like education, their main interest must inevitably be in preserving the system.

In effect, then, the Carnegie Commission on Higher Education is telling us how *not* to go about reform if we really want to see some meaningful changes in our educational system and the wider social system of which it is a major part. My feeling is that it represents a false path, one which assumes that the expansionist economic system and education's service to it will leave the colleges in the same position they are in now, except with more money and more students.

Education in International and Comparative Perspective

There is much to be gained from the study of education in other countries. Many of our most basic and far-reaching reforms have been patterned on educational practices originally developed in other parts of the world. A most recent example is the popular open-classroom movement that owes much to English education. Equally important, the study of other educational systems provides fresh insights and new perspectives on our own system.

Jackson and Marsden, authors of *Education and the Working Class,* from which their selection is extracted, have written a most original and penetrating research study on the difficulties English working-class children encounter in school. Their study was published over 10 years ago, and certainly much has changed in English education since then. And there are so many differences between English and U. S. education, it is difficult to imagine how a study of English education could have any meaning for the U.S. educator. Yet, with all the changes and with all the differences, the basic problems related to social class and public education dealt with in the study are as serious in England today as they were when the study was done, and the basic problems are as pervasive in the United States as they are in England. This study is still timely and important, and it merits the fullest possible reading by all educators who are concerned with the pain and alienation that results from the way in which social class and schooling are entwined.

EIGHTY-EIGHT WORKING CLASS CHILDREN WHO SUCCEEDED IN SCHOOL

Brian Jackson and Denis Marsden

Before we begin the illustration of school and college days, it is useful to indicate the crucial difference between the middle and the working-class home. Such pointers as could be gleaned from the slender middle-class sample drew attention to the father as the dominant parent in matters of education. But behind the schooldays of working-class children, it is clear that the centres of power usually lay with the mother. . . This could not altogether be accounted for by the mother's education or her superior station before marriage, though both these mattered. Its roots seemed to push much deeper into the basic rhythms and expectations of working-class life, belonging to that whole pattern of social living in which the mother rather than the father was the organic centre.

But this does not mean that husbands were not prominent: often they were—but usually supported by their wife. Many of the working men were resentful of their lot, and eager for hard bread-and-butter reasons that education should come to their children. "To put it bluntly," said Mr. Beresford, "I didn't want him to finish up in the same street as I'm in—whistled up at half-past six in the morning, working on short time. I had seven solid months off work just before we got married, and I knew that if he got educated, he wouldn't be in the same position as me. That's the top and bottom of it." Others spoke of strongly "cultural" expectations, of pictures and Shakespeare becoming meaningful to their children; but perhaps the commonest feeling was that education promised a kind of classless adulthood in which you could mix freely and talk with every kind of man and woman. . . .

It was no wonder then that out of this mesh of hopes and anxieties the moment of birth itself should look so especially rich in promise; almost oracular even. "When our Richard was born, he had a funny head," said Mrs. Beckworth, "he had the funniest shaped head that you can imagine. It stuck out here, like that! And I said, 'Oh Dr. Sykes, look at his head. I've never seen one like that.' And Dr. Sykes said, 'I have. It's a long time since I've seen one like that. Don't worry Mrs. Beckworth, those are brains. Those are brains pushing out, and as

Source. Excerpts from *Education and the Working Class* by Brian Jackson and Denis Marsden, 1962, pages 82–153. Reprinted by permission of Routledge & Kegan Paul Ltd., Publishers, London.

long as you take care of him until that head's firm, you mark my words, something will come of this'."

As the child began to talk and play, there was sometimes distinct parental effort for a more than common correctness of speech, for a purer English than the parents themselves had hold of. With this might go rules on play with "rougher" children, a whole series of *extra* precautions, demands, and trainings, in which love has a tang of harshness and restriction for the growing child. "His auntie came over, and she said to him, 'Let's have you talking, give me your pandy,' and I said, 'I'm not having any of that! If they are going to speak, they are going to speak properly, right from the beginning. We're not going to have any of that sort of talk here!' "

PRIMARY SCHOOL

Nevertheless, when the moment came for schooling to begin, many of the parents were less sure of their choice and guidance. This was the point of entry to unfamiliar worlds. Those families with blood relatives in the professional classes, or with middle-class links through church or club, sometimes took advice about the choice of primary school. . . . Like most cities, Marburton is divided into loose zones with a primary school in each. The working-class population tends to accept the zone together with its school. This after all unites with convenience and the many ties of "neighbourhood." When the middle-class population resides close together it too tends to take over a distinct school, and is satisfied. But the whole system, as elsewhere, is reasonable and elastic and a certain degree of free movement to schools out of the native zone is tolerated. Now there are many critical areas in the city where very good and less successful primary schools lie close together, or where several less successful schools command a whole sector. Middle-class parents are much more aware of the relativity of procedures of selection and rejection, much more aware that these things are not decided by acts of God or infallible scientific procedures. They know that all kinds of advantages may flow in from choosing the best school for results, rather than accepting the school which is simply nearest. Consequently they use the system's elasticity, and by doing so reinforce differences in standard, tone and expectation.

Few working-class parents fully realized this. Apart from those with middle-class connections, they accepted the local school in a natural "neighbourhood" spirit. When they seemed equidistant from two schools, their reasons for preferring one rather than the other were warm and child-centred, but extraordinarily short-term. . . .

The children selected for this study were the able ones who had taken easily and quickly to primary school. Not surprisingly, there were no stories of children being pulled through by extra coaching outside school, if their gifts had not immediately begun to develop. Parents were not in touch with this kind of thing, even if they could afford it; nor was as full a knowledge disseminated about the selection examination at that time, as there is today. It is worth suggesting that for the working-class child *early* success in the primary school was a pre-requisite to any further achievement.

Early success meant firstly a quick and eager mastery of reading. A facility with figures counted next: but to begin with, it was from the ones whose literacy came young that the successful children emerged. Many parents reported their child's relative quickness with the printed page, their almost hypnotic concern to unravel written language. "One summer's evening talking to our neighbour," said Mrs. Robinson, "we looked out and there was our Arthur sat on the wall at the bottom of the garden. It was a windy night, and there were bits and scraps of paper being blown along. A bit came rolling on just past our Arthur's feet, and didn't he off and pick it up, and sit on the roadside and start to read it! There you are! Read owt, read any scrap of paper that came his way. 'That lad'll be Prime Minister one of these days,' said my neighbour. . . ."

At school the children discovered themselves sorted out into 'top groups', special classes, and similar bodies marked by the teachers as good prospects for selection. In all but the smallest schools there were systems of pre-selection enabling the teachers to give particular attention to the needs of those likely to go to grammar school. Some, for instance, were moved up into the "scholarship" class two or even three years in advance. For most this meant that hard work, many tests and a thorough grounding in those skills of arithmetic and language to be examined by the "eleven plus," began at seven or eight years of age. A certain "apartness" from less successful children was experienced even before the examination was taken.

As the eleven plus drew nearer, one or two children were hurriedly moved across a vital boundary line, on to the side where there was more substantial grammar school provision. These were cases where the family had middle-class relatives or friends. "I never thought anything about this exam.," said Mrs. Waite, "until Mrs. Beardsell came down to talk to me. She was Peter Beardsell's mam, and he was our boy's age. She came down and she talked and she talked until in the end we took him away from the school and sent him to Broadbank." But few parents were aware of these important discrepancies, and though many were looking forward hopefully to their child's success, many others did not properly understand the significance of the exam. . . .

With the results of the exam. came warm scenes, full of pride, excitement and promise, remembered still with remarkable precision. "I was cooking down in the cellar (I do all my cooking down there for fear of accidents) and he came in and stood at the top of the cellar head, waving an envelope, and I said to him, 'What's that, love? Has the post been or something?' and he shouts, 'I've passed my exam., mam, I've got my exam. I'm going to grammar school.' " Other children responded to their own fears and their parents' anxieties in curious ways. Lillian Ellis said how she "ran home and went into the house, and do you know what I did? I said my name hadn't come on the lists, and I waited until her face fell, until it really dropped. Then—it was a cruel thing to do—then I told her I'd passed. What do you think of that?" And in some homes they were met with a more worldly-wise reception. "When I passed," said Kathleen Holdsworth, "I came home and told them it was a load off my mind. They said I needn't be so cocky—it was a load *on* theirs." But for almost all it was a moment to be eagerly recalled ("When I passed....") and a moment that seemed to bring overnight the most perplexing weight of worries.

To begin with there was the grammar school to be chosen. For the girls this was fairly easy since there was not so much grammar school provision anyway. But for the boys there was in the city both a first grade and a second grade grammar school, and for many it was the choice between these two that was so difficult.

Knowledge as to the best and the second best only circulated freely in those families with some history of grammar school education or with middle-class connections. Many of the other parents had obviously been quite concerned, but both ignorant and embarrassed at their own ignorance. Those with church, union or political connections held a distinct advantage when it came to seeking advice. Others tried the neighbours, workmates, even a friendly bus driver. Some went to the school, but in that atmosphere felt antagonistic or defensive.

The result of this ignorance, embarrassment and bewilderment was that in many cases a vital decision was taken for quite trivial reasons. A school was chosen because it was near enough for the child to come home at dinner time, or because it meant one bus journey instead of two, or because its situation seemed to offer a greater abundance of "fresh air." Faced with a lack of knowledge, there was at this and many future points a strong tendency to choose that which was nearer, less divorced from the world of home. There were, of course, those homes (very few) in which the surface hesitation had nothing to do with lack of information, but mirrored the more reluctant depths. The most extreme case of such hesitation was one in which not only the responsibility for choosing the grammar school was left to the child (for this frequently happened), but the basic decision itself was abrogated.

GRAMMAR SCHOOL

The first weeks at grammar school were strange. For the children who already had contacts, they were exhilarating, the exciting prelude to promised satisfactions. Whole new areas of inviting study presented themselves—Algebra, Physics, Latin, French. "I took to Marburton College like a duck to water," said Ronald Turnbull. For children who had broken most friendships and connections with the old neighbourhood, here were fresh children, fresh clubs and societies, the school scouts and the school corps to join. The invitation was irresistible, and many were glad to accept it in full and become from the earliest days loyal and eager members of the school. Their wholeheartedness was naturally reflected in their first pieces of work, and finding themselves soon well placed in class, they were conscious of latent power thrusting through, of their ability to command new and more testing situations. . . Most of the parents came from the very upper reaches of the working-class, and once their child reached grammar school, these parents were whole-heartedly behind the enterprise. In very small ways they influenced their children to accept, to belong. Both grammar school and home supported the child in orthodox and receptive attitudes. But under particular strains and pressures, this home support could, and did, break down; and this happens more and more often as either the school disturbs the parents. . . or the parents find no way of obtaining vital knowledge, or coming to terms with the middle-class ethos of the grammar school. The parents may have been 'sunken middle-class', but many of these discover how different this can be in knowledge and evaluation from that range of middle-class life endorsed by the grammar school.

For the majority of the (working class) children, unlike Ronald Turnbull, the entry to grammar school was uncertain and confused. They had suddenly lost in some measure that mesh of securities, expectations, recognitions, that we have called "neighbourhood." "I had this feeling of not *belonging* anywhere," said Patricia Joy. They found themselves surrounded by more middle-class children than they had ever met before. These children spoke better, seemed more confident, some already knew bits of French and Latin, their fathers had told them what "Physics" was about, a few even knew the teachers. *They*, evidently, seemed to belong. This insecurity was heightened by confusions over getting the right books, the right sports equipment, the right uniform. "I didn't like it," said Rita Watson, "my uniform seemed too big all around—long sleeves—I suppose my mother had to do it like that so it would last longer, but I felt awful. All the other girls' uniforms seemed all right. *I* was wrong." On top of this came the new subjects, the new vocabulary (not "kept in" but "detention," not "playtime" but "break"—and was it "yard" or "playground" or "cloisters"?) the masters' gowns, the prefects, the whole body of customs, small rights and wrongs, that any well-developed grammar school holds. Some of the schools made a practice of teaching the new children aggressively for the first weeks, to "break them in", and, presumably, to nip behaviour problems in the bud. The effect on children already bewildered was to knock them off balance rather than 'break them in' and to create rather than cure behaviour problems. . . . For some of the working-class children, confused by a genuine loss of part of their social life ("neighbourhood"), perplexed by the strangeness and sheer difference of grammar school, conscious of new *social* barriers thickening the normal barriers between pupil and teacher, and unable to turn to parents for explanation and understanding—for these children the beginnings could seem almost hallucinatory. "I had that feeling like when you were in the forces," said one boy, "after you got your jabs and you got inoculation fever, you felt away from it all. You felt in a bit of a haze, everything was a bit bleared. Well, that's how school felt at first. I felt just as I did later when I'd got inoculation fever. . . ."

For many the "haze" always seemed to hang about grammar school. And not grammar school only, the world outside had suddenly changed. If they forgot to speak to someone in the street, or failed to notice a passing neighbour, there were sharp accusations of "snobbishness." Even neighbors who had never been spoken to much before were illogically insistent that they were now being scorned. Sometimes they had grounds for their charges ("I must have condescended to them. I thought how unlucky they were not to have been to grammar school"), and perhaps small children compensated for their insignificance at school by their surface confidence at home. But many were very scrupulous about these matters, they soon learned what a remarkable tact was required for them. . . .

CLASSROOM

Eighty of the children were in grammar school years in which there was some form of streaming, of dividing into "A", "B" and "C" classes. This division had usually taken place by the end of the first year, and sometimes was complete after eight weeks. It looks as if it decided a lot about the future for these children. Sixty-six were in "A" classes, and only two came from "C" classes. For them there was not much movement between streams after the first decision. We only recorded five such instances. Almost all those children who were graded "B" or "C" at this early stage did not last for the sixth form course. At this stage we must either credit the grading system with very remarkable accuracy, or wonder whether working-class children, lacking a particular kind of parental knowledge and support, and rubbing against the school in all kinds of ways, did not over-accept the gradings given them. Once declared "C" children, did they not begin to learn, play, act, think and feel as "C" children; precisely that?

From now on then we are, to a large extent, talking of children in "A" classes. And to begin with we must report what thorough workers they seemed to be. As they felt it, the atmosphere was sharply competitive...Success here was a peculiarly potent security, and even those children who refused to identify themselves with the school, largely identified themselves with the *work*. Its compulsions could have touches of "guilt" and "obligation" about it. One boy summarized it with "I always had the feelings that I ought to do well in exams because I *owed* it to somebody being at grammar school. . . ."

Meanwhile some of the social difficulties were resolving themselves and some of the "haze" beginning to clear. Speech and accent had been an early difficulty. Some spoke of their sudden self-consciousness over accent, of their discovering that they actually had an accent. Boys were troubled at having to read aloud in class, girls feared to ask questions. "That bothered me quite a lot. I thought that if I mispronounced words or said them wrongly the other girls would pick me up and correct me and tease me. . . . Oh yes, they did. Oh yes, they certainly did. These things did happen." But, as confidence gathered, some of these troubles were deliberately overcome. Parents with middle-class ambitions were as conscious over this particular difficulty as their children, and a small number (especially girls) were soon taking elocution lessons. Others spoke of themselves as good "mimics" who quickly learned to speak as others and the teachers spoke. . . . But accent, even if changed, was still a burden and created other difficulties. That it offended the neighbours and old friends goes almost without saying ("stuck up", "speaks la-di-dah"), but this time it cut into the home and family life. Again the need was above all for "tact", and there were children who became bilingual, speaking B.B.C. English at school but roughening up when they got home. But the situation was not as automatic as this, and the tact was not always forthcoming. Some kept the new accent at home as well as at school, and though this was approved by parents paying for elocution lessons, it thrust a touch of discord into other working-class homes.

Yet, as social difficulties altered and most children began to melt into the school, to become *of* the school, other problems arose. As early as the second year important decisions were being made by teachers or by the children as to the range of subjects they would study. There were decisions about going into a "science" or a "language" class, about dropping or keeping geography, or Latin or chemistry, or physics or German. Many working-class children knew what in the long term they were deciding when a subject was dropped; and no working-class parent ever raised objections at the time on such grounds. So the decisions, if the child's, were taken for childish reasons. "I chose the Latin stream because I couldn't manage the bunsen burner and I'd got told off." Or else they were taken in the familiar "haze." Clifford Tate recalled, "The others seemed ready to take decisions and look after themselves. They'd go and talk to the teachers. They knew what they were doing. Whereas I very seldom knew what I was doing. I daren't ask and I didn't seem to know what was going on. There were a lot of decisions you had to make at 11 or 12. You had to decide between Latin and German, and you had to choose between history and geography, and as it turned out the subjects I dropped would have been a lot more use to me. "The extent or seriousness of this dilemma was hard to measure, for of course it is a common indulgence to blame present weakness on past decisions; but without being able to offer anything near precision, two areas did locate themselves. Firstly children who had ambitions to be doctors discovered very late in the day that they had made things extremely difficult for themselves by wrong specialization from the age of 12, and with most, their ambition was defeated by discovering themselves at 16 or 17 so far along the wrong path. Secondly, some who later wanted to go to university, and some who obtained sufficient marks to get a scholarship there, were startled to find that they lacked basic qualifications for entry.

HOMEWORK

The schools usually had a graded system of homework. In the first year something up to an hour a night might be expected, by the end of the fifth form it would have risen to near two hours. There were children who kept to these times, and there were children who did it in less. But for most, the prescribed time was merely nominal and a considerable under-estimation of the hours they spent. This was not because the schools were demanding an excessive weight of private study, though there were instances where a too-fast timetable spilled heavily over into evening work. It had more to do with the children's own need for success, for marks—a need we did not encounter at this intensity with middle-class children.

Few working-class homes had easy provision for home study. Some children went into the front room, others retired to a bedroom, but many did their homework in the living-room/kitchen at the very centre of family activity. This immediately produced difficulties. Should the wireless be on or off? Could the younger children play noisily? Could the father stretch his legs and tell the day's tales? To ask for silence here was to offend the life of the family, was to go against it in its natural moments of coming together, of relaxation. So many learned the early habit of working with the wireless on and the family talking, of building a cone of silence around themselves. To a certain extent this worked well, but it meant that the boy or girl had to continue at his tasks after the others had gone to bed, or he had to learn to snatch those moments of emptiness in the house immediately before tea or breakfast or during the week-end. And the family was not always untroubled at this, for the private concentration could produce an abstraction, a forgetfulness, an off-handedness that also gave offence. Those who retired to front rooms and bedrooms met with other difficulties, especially in winter, when they could hardly ask—in their peculiarly dependant and "obliged" position—for two rooms to be heated. "Sometimes he used to go up into the bedroom and do it. Aye, he'd have the eiderdown wrapped all around him to keep him warm, wouldn't he? And many's the time he'd be up early on a morning— before breakfast—working away at his problems and things. They gave him such a lot." But it wasn't simply a case of their being given "such a lot." Other children, no more able, managed it within the time.

There were arguments; arguments in which the children tried to explain the urgency to them of their work. Mrs. Lynch recalled, "He'd stopped up till midnight studying, and I said to him, "Surely you know enough to pass by now, Clifford?' And he said, 'I don't just want to *pass,* I want to do *really well.*' " And these arguments flared into the open when one of the parents (often the father) was reluctant about the whole grammar school undertaking. "Our Alfred would be doing his homework in the front room, and his father wasn't a bit understanding. He'd make it in his way to go through that room as many times as he possibly could—to disturb him. First he'd go for his coat, and then for his cap, and then for his collar and tie. Eeh, we'd have some rows in this place on a Saturday evening when Alfred was doing his homework! His father would start off talking about Rugby League and stuff like that, and I'd tell him to shut up," These long homework hours, even more than "accent", cut into the vital centres of family life, dislocated the whole household's living. It could generate hostility, misunderstanding, irritation, jealousy; and many mothers had to make a special effort to take it under their protection, to create a new rhythm around it.

SCHOOL VERSUS NEIGHBOURHOOD

There was some evidence to suggest that the third year had been an important kind of pause, a point after which it was clear whether you were for the school or not. We were not asking for particular statements about this in the interviews, for it was only as the survey developed that the conflict begain to claim more of our attention than we had foreseen. But, without prompting, 48 children spoke clearly of themselves as being identified with the school ("I was very much an establishment man. I was all establishment man!") whereas 15 were just as clear that they had declared *against* the school, and 25 held some intermediate position. As pointed out above, being *against* school did not necessarily mean being against school *work*. For all kinds of children interest here was intense, and success of supreme importance.

We pay a great deal of attention to the children who refused to accept the school. This is because we believe that they often represent the very large numbers of gifted working-class children who abandon grammar school at 16, and do not progress (as well they might) on to university and the professional life. Certainly the children we spoke to remembered large numbers of dissident pupils up to the fifth form, but few of these remained at school after this. . . .

The essential choice which the working-class children faced in the early grammar school years was one between school and neighbourhood. Some children had begun with few neighbourhood links, and for them this was no crisis. But the others who found themselves firmly, or sporadically, against the school, were boys and girls who were still involved in neighbourhood life, and who preserved their other style of living. It was more than a matter of joining a youth club rather than the school scout troop; it had to do with deep differences in response, feeling, judgment—which recoiled against common images of "dominance" of "leadership": school uniform, teachers' gowns, prefects, the Honours Board, the First Eleven, the Scout Troop, the School Corps, Speech Day, Morning Assembly, Expected Public Decorum. The children who drew back from this spent their evenings in youth clubs, or with cycling groups or roaming the parks and streets in large inclusive gangs. . . .

Sport was a critical point of conflict. So much of the grammar school tradition was overt here, so much expected. The boy who clung tenaciously to neighbourhood modes of feeling and doing had first of all a rather different idea of what came under the title of "sport," and further he had a much freer sense of what was meant by "the team". . . There were those whose interest in snooker was more intense then their interest in cricket, and there were still others for whom sport meant the lonely skills of cycling, the more individual emphasis of table tennis. The sports do not of course quite separate out into two camps, it is rather a matter of emphasis. For the team games had their place too. A recurring situation at Marburton College seems to have been the desire of working-class boys to play rugby league football (the northern professional game) instead of soccer. When this reached the state of groups of boys organizing themselves into something like unofficial school or house teams at this unofficial game, then the school might put out feelers for compromise, and suggest the difficulties of catering for *rugby union* as well as soccer—difficulties, say, over fixtures of the better kind. The whole point, of course, of the rugby playing was lost in this, for the school failed to see that whereas rugby league was very close at heart to northern working-class life, and whereas soccer could occupy a kind of neutral and classless position, rugby union was almost as remote as lacrosse, and not what was wanted at all.

But difficulties over the right style of playing football were as nothing to the disagreements over cricket and its rituals. Richard Beckworth tried to reconcile playing for the school at cricket with playing for a local club, and this is how he spoke of "official" school cricket. "Simon Carpenter was captain, and he was dead keen that we all walk on the field in a straight line behind him, like professionals. Well, I'd never do that, nor would my pal Hopkins. And then the master, Rylands, he always insisted that we had whites, white shirt, white shorts, white shoes, white socks, all dressed *properly*. Well, George Hopkins would come along wearing green corduroy pants and one of those tee-shirts with cowboys across the front, and I'd wear my shirt outside my trousers. No. . . .I don't seem to have that certain something that makes cricketers and prefects and officers. I don't know what it is. . . ."

It was odd to hear these consistent incidents in which children—often quite shy children—had taken a painful stand against the school over something which must have looked quite trivial to the teachers. It was not a case of the lack of money, though this might reinforce a stand, and it was not that the children could themselves explain why they were having nothing to do with this or that aspect of the grammar school. All they could say was, "I won't," and stick.

On the other hand, it was by no means clear that the school understood either, and often there was the sense of two strange worlds finding themselves side by side, yet with neither fully aware of the other's sheer difference. Head teachers saw that some boys and girls retained neighbourhood links through youth clubs and similar bodies. Most tried to dissuade their pupils from membership. . . .

Daily from the teachers came a host of warnings, injunctions, suggestions, that spoke of the gulf existing. Working-class children felt themselves being separated from their kind. The choice between school and neighbourhood was faced daily in small concrete incidents. For the teachers these incidents were merely part of the pattern of manners, part of that training in 'tone' which distinguished the grammar school from the general community. They were honourably conceived and held, but for the child something much more central to his living was being locally but continually strained. "She said you weren't allowed to eat ice-cream or sweets in the street. All sorts of silly things like that you'd have done *naturally.* ..."

We recorded a lot of evidence about the school's insensitivity and the child's hypersensitivity; the school's determination to hand on the grammar school modes, to spread its standards as the best and the only standards, and the child's awkward, clumsy and stubborn desire to preserve the other ways, to remain 'natural'. . . And the children who clung to "neighbourhood" seemed to attract to themselves the full weight of the school's punishments. Again it was all part of the "haze." "I got showers of detentions, showers of them, and "Saturday mornings" as well. Canings, tests, detentions, crying at night over my arithmetic homework—that's all I can remember of those years. I don't know why I got so much punishment. I was quite a mild child, and I was interested in my way, too. I just don't know how it was."

So it was not then such a simple case of being anti-school. School had its attractions, and for these, its very deep satisfactions, but it was only a part of life and often an alien part of that. "No," said Alec Shapley, "we weren't anti-school. School didn't enter into it. School was like work, you went to school in the daytime and in the evenings you went out to enjoy yourself." Those who tried to keep their evenings to themselves seldom lasted into the sixth form, though some did. Others were caught in the tensions between the evening life and the need to do well, to establish themselves securely in terms of marks—as a counterpoise to the ambiguities, the discords, the losses of living. By the third year the lines were clear: on the one hand were the working-class children who had thrown their total self into the school; on the other hand were those children (largely in B and C streams now) who clung to neighbourhood, and whose attitude, clumsiness and inarticulate divergencies attracted that rebuke and punishment which merely stiffened the will to resist. Most of these children were moving towards the escape from grammar school at the end of the fifth form. From their ranks only the very small minority survived.

BROTHERS AND SISTERS

We have not the space to fully report on what happened to the brothers and sisters of our 88 working-class children. But a few general details inserted here, and one suggestive instance, may be helpful.

There were only 55 families with more than one child. Out of these only seven families had a boy remaining at a secondary modern school, and only 11 families had a girl there. So most of our children had their brothers or sisters at grammar school with them. The situation of the child who had a brother or sister at a secondary modern school was very much a minority one. Or to put it another way, the selective process in the schools picked out and held not just gifted *individual* children, it selected *families*. Because of this, families were not usually divided through differences in children's schooling. But what happened when this *did* take place? One of the most suggestive instances that we met was the one of Jean Ash and her sister, Margaret.

Jean Ash was the only girl whose sister went to a secondary modern school. In the acuteness of her discomfort and her feelings of loss and abnormality, she became articulate precisely *because* her family situation was so unusual. She experienced in her relationship with her sister a much more intense form of the same discomfort that she felt with many of her day-to-day working-class acquaintances. And her separation from her family and the life of which they were part made it easier for her to talk about them, even though she still complained of feeling disloyal.

Her sister, Margaret, was two years older. During the early years the two sisters were close playmates; and they played together with the many other children nearby, went to parties together, and slept in the same bed at night. Jean felt very keenly the separation when Margaret had to go to school at the age of five, and two years later when her turn came to go to the same school she was disappointed to find herself in a different class. But it was the same school and they still had friends in common. When the scholarship examination came Margaret was away ill: Mrs. Ash said, "I don't think she'd have passed. She's not the type." Jean, when her turn came, passed out top and went to Ash Grange, leaving Margaret behind with only one year further to do at school before she left school.

They no longer had school matters to talk about: Jean was reluctant to talk about Ash Grange at home in case she was thought uppish, and she seldom brought her few Ash Grange friends home. Her sister's friends visited regularly, but Jean did not know them now. Margaret went to work in a shop. "She started going out with boys a lot sooner. She was working, you see," said Mrs. Ash, "and you do when you're working. Jean didn't really start going anywhere until she was 17." To Jean, "She was always two years older, but just then she seemed to shoot away from me. Whilst I, well I was still a schoolgirl. She did seem very old. She was older really at 14 when she left school than I was when I was 18. She was much more adventurous. She'd come home and say, 'I'm *going* to do something,' whereas I'd say, '*Can* I do so and so.'"

SIXTH FORM

. . . Those who had identified themselves with the school, taken pride in its uniform, joined its scout troup or O.T.C., now came into their own. They became the formal leaders of the school community. Forty-eight of our sample were made prefects. Fourteen became either head or deputy head of their school. The proportions are high.

For the orthodox children, school was a smooth process, once they had learned to fit in. They had their difficulties and tensions all right, but these hovered around the life at home. Previously at school they had taken extra care over their accents. In the sixth form this was bearing a certain fruit. Many schools had readings or speeches from their sixth formers at their annual public prize giving. And here again working-class children seemed to do not only as well, but a little *better* than others. On the public platform the orthodox working-class child spoke the idiom better than the native born. It was worked into the very grain of their ambitions. "In the sixth form we were always talking about 'the cultured man.' It was really exciting, we'd listen and we'd want to be 'cultured men.' And when it came to Speech Day I was given the chance of doing the 'English speech' and that was from Eliot's *Notes Towards a Definition of Culture:* that shows you I spoke very well even then."

. . . At school they worked hard, played hard and were rewarded for it. Their dress was smart and correct, their accent was good. Sometimes classmates forgot such a child's working-class origin, and only redis-covered it, to their surprise, in later life. Outside school, links with neighbourhood life or non-grammar school children had largely gone. One girl came across her former elementary school companions at a Sunday school; "But I stood out. I felt different. I know I talk York-shire but they talked, not 'broad,' but shipshod—not grammatical. I only went along to play the piano. You can't blame them, I know, but—I *looked* different."

. . . But if neighbourhood ties were lost or weak, relationships at home were also changing. . . The social life of school and the particular fields of study were both now out of the parents' reach. Together with this had gone changes in tone, manner, accent, friendships, which often troubled home relationships. The boy or girl knew that the important educational decisions must be taken by himself not his parents, and his sense of "life" and "knowledge" was often such that fathers and mothers began to seem very dull and limited indeed. "I thought my parents were terrible, and very badly educated. They were always doing the *wrong* things." With some this was no more than a passing hubris, but there were others perceptive and candid enough to admit that these things could bite down to the very roots. . . .

The imbalance could be established in many ways, but the orthodox child belonged to two worlds—school and home—and sometimes developed two identities to match. "And then I had these two personalities. At school I was extrovert, confident, full of life. I knew what I was doing all the time. I was heroine in the school play, first violin in the school orchestra, captain of netball, captain of the school, captain of the house, top of the class, sometimes. 'Miss Ash Grange,' my husband calls me. But at home I was oh, so quiet, so timid, never said a word out of place. I just shrank inside myself and mother ruled the roost." Behind the assurance of the school personality was frequently this lack of reciprocal flow between parent and child. Their assured and successful school identity was in a kind of suspension, almost disconnected. . . .

As the sixth form course drew to an end thoughts began to concentrate on university or training college. The middle-class children had a fairly clear idea of where they were going, and of how to get there. The situation with working-class children was much more mixed. There was the small number whose parents were intent on thrusting them through to university despite all obstacles. . . But by this stage many of even the most ambitious parents had, in a sense, been left behind. They might originally have hoped for their children to get a good grammar school education and then move in a local bank or office: university was a strange new thought. . . .

University and college were approached in a mood in which elements of sheer ignorance, general perplexity, or mere lack of initiative were hard to disentangle. Lack of initiative there certainly was, and this may have had something to do with the "automatic" nature of education so far. Everything had always run along smooth lines, once you accepted the school's ways, and a few had realised that a stage was now reached where they were expected to fend for themselves. But it would be misleading to leave it at that. Sheer ignorance was also there to a startling extent. Two girls were thinking of Oxford or Cambridge, but "didn't know it was possible to stay three years in the sixth form to do this. I know it's silly to say this, but I just *didn't* know, and I went feverishly looking around for a place, and in the end got into the School of Tropical Medicine and Hygiene—and it turned out to be absolutely the wrong course for me." Neither girl—their qualifications were excellent—knew when she left school that she could have stayed longer and prepared for Oxbridge. Again, neither Mr. and Mrs. Lynch nor their son had realized that there were grants above a nominal sum of £10 or £20 for university courses. The boy left under this misapprehension at 18 though he had a perfectly reasonable chance of going to university. . . .

Another boy also "knew there were State scholarships and things and I knew they paid for your fees and your books, but I didn't know they'd see you through. It seems daft now, but you *don't* know."

. . . Simply, the channels of communication were not open: nor was the need for clear primary information recognized. So much that was naturally *assumed* by the middle-class pupil or teacher, so much that was part of the "normal" atmosphere of growth, needed to be discovered by, or explained to, the new working-class pupil.

Together with the element of ignorance and the lack (in some) of initiative, we must add a note on financial unease. First of all some of the parents were under very real financial stress. This was especially so in the case of large families and of widows. In nine families either the mother was widowed or there were at least four children. Only an unusual degree of determination, and a trusting readiness to do without, kept these boys and girls at school. Most children who might have come under this heading had already left. Secondly, some parents whilst not under this degree of stress, were making major sacrifices of which the child was deeply aware. Chief amongst these were those homes where a mother was going out to fairly hard manual work, at an age when her energies were diminishing. Now in both cases, though money may have been just sufficient, the boy or girl felt daily that their parents' lives were being governed and narrowed by his needs. This, added to so much that had gone before, promoted the most acute sense of debt, of dependency. And this takes us to the other side. Just as the parents might hide from the child some part of their financial difficulties less the child tried to give up the educational advance; so the children turned down courses of study because of their parents' money troubles, without consulting those parents. The act of generous deprivation and concealment happened on both sides. An illustration of this would be those instances (there were some here) in which a boy or girl with a resonable chance of entry at Oxbridge never made the attempt simply because they didn't want to bring their parents to the expense of paying for the *rail fare* and the short stay necessary to cover interviews and orals. . . .

"A" LEVEL AND LEAVING SCHOOL

It was by passing their "A" level in two subjects (a fair basic standard for college or university entrance) that these boys and girls had qualified for our sample. Thirteen children now left school for work in pharmacy, the civil service, accountancy, laboratories or the forces. The rest continued their education at the college or the university.

There were interesting differences in the final choice of university or training college. . . . Over the whole sample the pattern emerged differently for boys than girls. If we except the group of boys who went to Oxbridge, then the great majority of the rest seemed to "cling" to their home area. Two-thirds entered a university not 30 miles away. Girls spread out much more widely, only a quarter of them kept within the 30 miles radius. This was no doubt partly due to the distribution of training colleges, yet added to this there seemed a distinct movement by some girls to put a distance between them and their home. . . .

Ideas about careers had now begun to precipitate more generally. Those who left school had come to some terms with the future, though often not very satisfactory ones; and of those who went to college or university a large number were thinking of teaching. The way in which the education system produces its teachers would require a special study in itself. And at this particular point we merely record the fact that it was the "drifters" who began to make up the bulk of the future teachers. We must state too—the pattern plays all through this report—that they turned to teaching not because, deep at heart, they wanted to do it—but because they did not want to move away from the academic succession (eleven plus—O level—A level—college—teacher) which had become so entwined with their very sense of who they were in society. . . .

TRAINING COLLEGE AND UNIVERSITY

Though this was a most important stage in education, we are only able to handle it very briefly here. Twenty girls and one boy went to training college; 16 girls and 38 boys went to university.

The sheer number of training colleges seemed to permit a form of social sorting-out. Many of our sample sought entry but only a few gained it, at the top-flight colleges. The ones they attended seemed to cover only a limited social class range. They generally reported colleges full of girls from upper working-class or lower middle-class homes, in training for primary school teaching. . . .

Girls emerged from training college with better accents, some new manners, fresh expectations—but with little social poise, for they led little social life, and with few friends much above their own social range.

As for the university, here the figures tell their own story, and summarize the enquiry so far. The city of Marburton with a population of

130,000 and possessing schools and teachers of more than common distinction, managed in a four-year period to send 38 working-class boys directly from grammar school to university. A mere glance through the incomplete school records shows that very many more boys from middle-class homes entered university with them. The case of girls is even more striking. In the nine years ending in 1954 the city had sent only 16 girls (but upwards of 51 girls from middle-class homes). 10 of these 16 girls came from "sunken middle-class" families. . . .

At university. . . again the beginnings were full of doubt, some had no more idea than their parents what precisely a university was and did. There were those who were dazzled by the surface sheen of the cultural life, but that soon dimmed. "When I went to read English," said Brenda Sadler, "I'd hardly read anything; I was afraid I wouldn't be able to talk about books or music, but you soon found that you don't have to know very much about anything to talk about it." And there were those who struggled again with the old problem of accent. This ranged from strident over-imitation of upper-class timbre to straightforward discussions at home in which the natural shift to a more educated accent was plainly argued out. ("Mother, I shall have to start speaking correctly. I can't lecture to them unless I speak correctly.") There were those who reported living through waves of feeling in which they spoke broader Yorkshire at home than their parents and better English at university than their lecturers. . . .

Right from their first vacations all the students worked for money. Even for the group at Oxbridge it was clear that the idea of vacations as pauses during which to store up reading that might be deployed over the coming term, was a myth. There were very often good financial grounds for this. Many of the homes were short of money, and an ageing or widowed mother might be working long hours to keep a boy at university. Some students worked in order to buy their own clothes or extras, others because they felt they had a duty to contribute to the home. . . .

Some worked to justify themselves in their parents' and neighbours' eyes as people who could not only study, but also attempt *real* work. Keith Mountain put it like this: "I got a job on the railway, and enjoyed working with my hands. I felt quite proud, and when I came home at night, since I wasn't half as tired as I thought I might be, I used to say to my parents, 'There you are, you see!' Because it's funny, my parents have a queer idea of 'work'. Reading a book, or anything like that, isn't work: only doing things with your hands. So I suppose in their eyes all the 'work' I've ever done was in those vacations. . . ."

Coming to terms with working men at their jobs proved harder than they thought. There was the feeling of remoteness as if workmen were a quite different kind of mechanism. "It was an experience, and I felt I'd got a real insight into the way those men's minds worked, quite differently." There was a revulsion from "the never-ending sexual chatter and jokes," and there was horror at the demands a life-time of hard manual work could make—"as if their whole lives were submerged in the work and they had no time for living."

Difficulties with vacation work were associated with their struggles to come to terms with their parents and their background. Resentments and irritation at the coarser streaks in working-class living, that they dare not introduce into the discussion of home problems, could be exercised on this safer ground. Some mothers and fathers found difficulty in even physically imagining a university which their children never invited them to see. "When he went to Cambridge, I thought it must be all big classrooms." or "I would dearly have liked to go there and look, but he never encouraged that. He didn't seem interested in our going there". . . .

OXFORD AND CAMBRIDGE

The group of boys who went to Oxford or Cambridge are worth describing separately, because they bring to a momentary focus many of the divergent lines. It was hard to decide whether they did represent the most gifted section of that working-class entry at the age of 11, or not. We were unable to come by measurement here, but (as a personal impression only) we were disinclined to accept this supposition. Glancing over their histories it is quite clear that there was a special impetus coming from their home background, quite independent of native intelligence; and further that for many of them their Oxbridge ambitions had come to a fierce intensity or fallen into a lucky vein, whilst they were at school. They had gone when others had not, not always because they were more intelligent, but because they were more determined, more single-minded or more fortunate. And yet this does not take us very far. A look at their degree results shows that there were no firsts here, and indeed seven of the nine took thirds or low seconds. But more remarkable is the way their results plummetted after their opening year. Henry Dibb came up with an Open Scholarship, took a first after one year, failed in his second year and ended up—working hard—with a third. Richard Beckworth also came up with an Open award, took a first in Latin and a top second in French after one year. His next year yielded only a second class, and he too ended up with a third. Ivor Gledhill similarly won an award and took his first after a year, but after three years he could only command a second, and when he stayed on for a fourth year he failed altogether.

Eric Western had taken eight distinctions in School Certificate, three at A level, and gained an Open Scholarship, yet extraordinarily hard work saw him finally through with a low second. . . .

Plainly the vagaries of the Oxbridge selection system cannot this time be held wholly responsible. There is a curious element of pattern here and this small group seems to be sensitively recording a crumbling away felt through much of the sample. . . .

The question that Eric Watson and others began to formulate— "What was it for?" It was a question born of the difficult and the obscure social rifts and struggles which for them had become part of the process of education itself. Did they, after all, want to move forward as successful middle-class citizens? Or was the temptation to try some return? Or was there a way out? The plummetting of academic results. . . seemed related at the deepest levels to a lost feeling for source, means, purpose; a loss heightened by an absence of the sustaining powers of social and family relationships. . . .

IN SUMMARY

The children who lasted the full grammar school course came largely from the upper strata of the working class. They came too from small families and lived in favorable, socially-mixed districts. A certain economic "line" was obviously still at work. Furthermore the majority had home backgrounds of no mean calibre and either one or both parents were strongly supporting the child. Many of these parents were both aspiring yet deferential—and it is perhaps not surprising to find these children to be educationally ambitious and also highly accommodating to the new worlds they meet. The majority who lasted were those who, on the one hand entwined academic ability with a positive orthodoxy and, on the other hand, had pressures behind them bearing on the school. Most accepted the new school with its different values and became some of its most hard working and worthwhile members. In turn they became its prefects and its leaders. But there was another side to the orthodoxy. At times it softened into something not simply "positive," but emollient and over-accommodating. And further it had meant a rejection at conscious or unconscious levels of the life of the "neighbourhood." This mattered less for some than others. But when the new manners, new friends, new accents, new knowledge, heightened the adolescent tensions of home life, security and sense of purpose shifted from any wide emotional life and located itself narrowly in schoolwork, in certificates, in *markability*. A minority of the survivors came from those children who had declared for the neighbourhood and against the grammar school. The detailed texture of day-to-day life was marked by local strains and conflicts which began to throw up the most radical doubts about the direction, quality and social nature of the education they were receiving.

At home the working-class parents were faced with a situation in which their children became stranger to them, and this was intensified by their lack of information about school, careers and the possible future. On the one hand were intelligent, ambitious and anxious parents; on the other capable and hard-working teachers. Yet there was little flow between the two. The difficulties promoted by this, and previous disconnections, did not break up the momentum of the higher education process; but they did much to shape the people we interviewed and—here and there, if our impressions are right—something to limit or damage them. Despite all this, the path from "A" level to college or degree was very much less treacherous than it had been up to eleven plus, or between selection and the sixth form. There was a diversion of gifted girls to the training colleges, and amongst those at university were some who were undercut by social doubts which, playing upon a sensitive or flawed personality, could have distressing results. But most of the 88 completed their education happily and successfully. There had been moments of stress, but most grew through this and accepted both the way in which they had been trained, and the world for which they were being prepared. They are now middle-class citizens.

Educational Alternatives: Reforming the School System

We have learned little more from the vast array of educational reforms instituted over the last 20 years other than the fact that educational problems are easier to identify and analyze than they are to correct. When Sputnik splashed into orbit, guidance programs and improved instructional facilities for learning foreign languages, science, and mathematics were provided for the gifted student. A few years later the disadvantaged were discovered and were provisioned with preschool centers, bilingual teachers, special reading programs, community aides, and school trips to the opera and the ballet. More recently, parents have seized onto the idea of community control, and professional educators have unionized and have become more militant.

The disappointing results, especially in the area of compensatory education, have driven many educators into cynicism and apathy. A number of educators still continue to search for solutions, however. Among those who believe that the public school can be salvaged are John Bremer, whose Parkway School in Philadelphia provides an imaginative alternative to existing models of school curricula and organization, and Judith Areen and Christopher Jencks, who believe a voucher plan will succeed where compensatory education, community control, and other recent reform efforts have failed. Of the two, Bremer's program promises a more comprehensive overhaul of the system as it places educational reform and societal reform side by side. Educational reform has little meaning unless it is somehow related to societal reform; one cannot be achieved without the other.

THE SCHOOL WITHOUT WALLS:
PHILADELPHIA'S PARKWAY PROGRAM

John Bremer and Michael von Moschzisker

The fundamental contention. . . of the Parkway Program is that no changes in an educational system will be of any significance unless the social organization of education is totally changed, that is, unless the system itself is changed. Nothing less will do, for it is the whole system that defines the nature and function of the parts. As a consequence, imaginative and fruitful ways of helping students to learn become, ultimately, only new ways of subordinating the student to the present system, only another way of keeping the student under control. New methods, new materials, and new machinery are used as new means of continuing the old pattern of fitting students into a preordained social structure.

If you ask a school or college administrator to describe the curriculum of his institution, he will probably give you a list of subjects offered together with the administrative department responsible for each one. At the college level, the catalog will list academic departments and the courses offered in them. At the school level, there is usually a detailed syllabus for each of the well-known subjects—English, mathematics, history, biology, Spanish, and so on. Schools and colleges are administratively organized in terms of these traditional subjects. In our present educational system, it is the conventional—and now outmoded—divisions of knowledge, and not the students' needs, that determine the organization of a learning institution. There is no secret about this, and, indeed, many administrators would take pride in affirming it. There is no intent to deceive when the curriculum is stated to be English, mathematics, and so on, but the motive is quite beside the point and it may well be that educational administrators do not know what they are doing. The fact is that every educational organization has one fundamental curriculum, which is never stated explicitly but which is the essential precondition of everything else. The fundamental curriculum is the social and administrative organization of the institution and the student's role in it. If the student does not learn this, then he learns nothing else that the school claims to offer.

This is particularly true of educational organizations, but it is true of every human group. The newcomer—no matter where he is to be introduced into the group, no matter what his status—has to learn the or-

Source. From *The School Without Walls: Philadelphia's Parkway Program,* by John Bremer and Michael von Moschzisker. Copyright © 1971 by Holt, Rinehart and Winston, Inc. Reprinted by permission of Holt, Rinehart and Winston, Inc.

ganization of the group and, especially, the role assigned to him. If he does not do this, the group will exert pressure upon him until he behaves properly; if he does not fall into line, he will be rejected and ejected. In educational systems this is true not only of the student but also of the superintendent. The superintendent is not expected to change the system, only to join it, and so far that is what every superintendent has done. This judgment may seem harsh, but in reality it is a tribute to the power of a group to form and mold its members. The only alternative to succumbing to this power is to educate the group so that it changes itself. For this reason the superintendent must be a master teacher.

For his part, the student must first of all learn his role in the school and the educational organization and through his proper behavior come into contact with the knowledge available in the school, particularly through its teachers. If the student cannot behave properly, that is, perform his defined role, then he is denied access to the knowledge available. It cannot be emphasized enough that behavior precedes understanding in any human group—that is, that moral education precedes intellectual education. Our major difficulty in schools is that the morality required belongs to an earlier time, a more limited view of society. It is as if schools were saying, "Adopt our life style and in exchange we will give you access to our wisdom." The hardships that this demand inflicts on all students, particularly those from minority groups, are real but easily overlooked, largely because educators take their own life style for granted.

It is easy to see how this works in practice. A student must sit at a desk, answer questions, read a book, complete an assignment, not talk to a neighbor, and so on. If he does not, he is reprimanded and his relation with the teacher becomes the focus of his attention, the problem in which he invests his energy. What happens to the subject he is supposed to be learning? It is forgotten in the face of a personal confrontation. Worse, it becomes another weapon with which the teacher attacks the student. The student responds by refusing to learn (even in the school's limited use of the word), because if he learned it would mean that he had surrendered, that he was beaten.

The moral education of the student begins, however, long before he actually enters a school or college. It begins when he applies to the institution. If he wishes to attend a college or a high school with limited enrollment, he has first to satisfy the admissions requirements; from the moment he starts to fill in the questionnaires he is programmed to think about the kind of person he is supposed to be if he is to be acceptable to the institution. Whether he is accepted or rejected, the school or college has done its work, for the student is either grateful or regretful. In either case, his role is cast as an inferior.

Most high school students, however, are simply assigned to their local school. There is no consultation, no conference, no consideration of alternatives. The morality of such a practice is totally unacceptable, and students learn more from it than educators can afford to admit. Students come to see themselves as pawns in a game of chess, to be moved at the administrator's will—the only free choice for them is to leave school altogether when the law permits. If they value their freedom and independence, this is what they often do.

It is worth considering the process by which a student enters a school simply because it structures the student's feeling about himself as a member of that school. The only way such an indelible effect can be eradicated is through a different structuring process, and that is where the Parkway Program began.

The admissions procedure for the Parkway Program was simple. First, it was open to any student in the city who was in grades nine through twelve, or who would be in those grades if he were in school. Second, the student had to apply, that is, he had to choose to come. He was self-selected. Third, he required the permission of at least one parent. Nothing else was required—no letters of recommendation, no tests, no records of behavior, no statement of aspirations or of reasons for wanting to join Parkway. All Parkway wanted was the student's signature on the completed four-line application form. . . .

When the Parkway Program began in February 1969, the plan was to admit about one hundred and twenty students, but it soon became clear that there was going to be a much larger number of applicants. In fact, there were nearly two thousand applications from city students in public schools and, in addition, about two hundred from suburban students and an additional hundred from private and parochial school students. . . .

It would have been easy at this point to have selected students who seemed able and amenable enough to learn in the program. But this approach would have been a betrayal of Parkway's mission to provide an educational program suitable for and available to anyone who wanted it. Clearly, the student body could be so selected as to ensure "success," but the victory would have been a hollow one. Rather, it was decided to have a lottery in which all applicants would have an equal chance. The absence of judgment meant that the students who did enter Parkway did not do so on the basis of being "better" or "more worthy." Institutionally, Parkway said that all students were created equal—none had preference. Under the circumstances of limited enrollment, the students themselves accepted that some were lucky and others were not. But it was only luck and not merit. . . .

Although students were admitted by lottery, it would be more accurate to say that they were admitted through one of eight lotteries.

The school district of Philadelphia was divided into eight separate school districts, each with its own district superintendent. By historical accident, presumably, these geographical districts tended to follow housing patterns and a number of them seemed to be ethnically or economically segregated. Since the media—particularly radio and television news and the newspapers—were primarily geared to the white, middle class population, it seemed probable that there would be considerably more white students applying than black. If this were so, there would be a good chance that the outcome of a general, common lottery would be a predominantly white student body.

John Bremer, the director of the Parkway Program, felt very strongly that this would be a violation of a fundamental educational principle, namely, that the learning community should be perceived by its members as a reasonable representation of the larger community in which they expected to live. If this were not so, the first thing the students would learn would be separatism, elitism, and racism. In addition, a considerable amount of energy would be diverted from learning into dealings with feelings of guilt and, more fundamentally, of fear. This is the major difficulty facing suburban school systems, and there was no need to duplicate it in the city.

As a way of reconciling the two principles of lottery and representative community, the director arranged a lottery for students from each of the eight school districts, with an equal number of places allocated to each district. By this means, the racial ratio among the city students was approximately the same as for the public school population, namely, 60 percent black and 40 percent white. . . .

The original Parkway student body was made up of one hundred and twenty students from the city public schools, twenty from the suburbs, and four from the parochial schools. This made a grand total of one hundred and forty four. Although John Bremer had originally expected only ten students from suburban and parochial schools, it seemed more than worthwhile to exploit the obvious interest of suburban students, and the total of one hundred and forty-four students was not unwieldy. It soon became apparent, however, that the size of the learning community was an important factor in the minds of the students. Time and again they expressed their dissatisfaction with their former schools in terms of the large numbers which denied them their own individuality. One student wrote:

"There is a common trust between people, a common friendship which you don't and can't find at a public school. I think that this is largely a result of the freedom, but most so because of the faculty. They make you feel human again; and that's something. At least in comparison to my old school. There, I was nothing but a computer card—my number

was 75815—my roster was made by a computer, my tests were for the most part marked by a computer and made into a report card by a computer and who knows what else was done. It knew me better than my mother, and my mother knows me pretty well. . . ."

One major purpose of the Parkway Program's social and administrative structure was to minimize anxiety by placing the responsibility for organizing his learning on the student, thus abolishing the computer; by making it possible for the student to get away from group situations that he could not handle, thus respecting individual privacy; and by keeping the learning community small, thus preserving the interdependence of its members.

After some experimentation, it seemed quite easy to work within a community of about one hundred and sixty students. This figure is not absolute, for it depends upon the structure of relations inside the community and the anxiety level of the students. But as the Parkway Program expanded, it did so simply by duplicating the original unit, slightly expanded, but with the same internal organization. Each unit was self-governing and responsible for its own day-to-day operation. . . . It has been a cardinal principle of Parkway that each community should be responsible for its own management. One important by-product of this educational principle is the lack of any large centralized administration. This both saves money and preserves flexibility, since decisions affecting the learning community can be made quickly and on the spot. . . .

When students enter the Parkway Program, they do not enter a particular building but rather join in an activity, the activity of learning. Essentially, the Parkway Program is an activity, planned and carried out by a group, with the purpose of improving the learning of the members of that group. There are no particular commitments to times and places which always seem to be the determining factors in schools; the commitment is primarily to learning and then to the means of achieving that end. . . .

The original unit of Parkway, later known as Community Alpha, had its headquarters at 1801 Market Street, four blocks from City Hall. It was photographed for *Life* magazine (May 16, 1969), which described it as follows: "Parkway has no classrooms or school building and its only facility is a rented loft where 150 students—half black, half white—have their lockers and hold a weekly meeting with the faculty."

. . . When the second unit, Community Beta, began, it had palatial quarters at 125 N. 23d Street, on the corner of 23d and Cherry streets, so that it came to be called Cherry House. Once the headquarters of an interior decorating firm, its walls were elegantly papered and the floors were carpeted. At the first parents' meeting held at Cherry House, one mother confided to the director that she thought it had been a bordello. Denying all knowledge of the subject (even academic knowledge), the director began to regret the possibilities that the name Cherry House afforded. . . .

Community Gamma, the third of the Parkway units, had a stormy career. . . . Even its baptism was by fire. The director wanted to provide a facility which would not only be a headquarters for a regular-sized Parkway unit but also provide adequate space for about a hundred and fifty elementary school children. In late spring of 1969, by a series of accidental circumstances, an appropriate building became available, at least for some time. The school district wanted to build a new complex at a site about ten blocks north of City Hall and very close to Broad Street, the main north-south thoroughfare through Philadelphia. As a preliminary step, they had purchased a number of buildings which were to be vacated and torn down. However, after the land was purchased, the bond issue supposed to provide money for the demolition and the new construction was defeated in May 1969, while the last occupiers were transferring themselves elsewhere. One of these empty buildings had housed the venerable Spring Garden Institute, a private, nonprofit school with a strong science and technology program, which had provided itself with fine new facilities in Chestnut Hill. When the Institute vacated its old building, Parkway's director looked with hungry eyes at what was available, at least until another bond issue could be promoted and passed. . . .

Toward the end of July, the bombshell came. The former Spring Garden Institute could be made legal and fit for occupancy by Philadelphia schoolchildren only at a cost of $35,000. The director protested in vain that this was absurd, that the building had been occupied by a school the previous month, that the Parkway Program could use it for only a year, and that this amount of money was simply not available. Presumably, the work allegedly required was yet another element in the continuing and unwarranted interference by the city administration in school district affairs. Why had the alleged infractions never been remedied under the previous tenant?

The facilities division promised to attempt another way of using the buildings, which might cost less; in fact, some time in August, the cost was reduced to about $20,000, but by this time the director had looked elsewhere. With some misgivings, but little choice, he decided to open an old school building which had been handed over to the Redevelopment Authority of Philadelphia, reportedly for tearing down to make room for an expressway. The Redevelopment Authority agreed to give it back to the school district for one year. The term was subsequently extended for another year.

The Parkway Program had been trying to get away from notions of school and the like, and it seemed rather dangerous to open a unit inside an old school, the Paxson School, as it was called (as a result Community Gamma was also known as the Paxson Parkway). Time was short, however, and the decision was made. The proposed elementary school program would occupy the basement and first floor levels, while the high school program used the second floor. The only other difficulty was location, for the Paxson School, now the Paxson Parkway, was in the eastern part of the city, close to the Delaware River, at 6th and Buttonwood streets. This was just one block south of Spring Garden Street, a major east-west thoroughfare, but it was nearly twenty blocks from City Hall and more than that from Community Alpha. Community Beta was eight blocks beyond Alpha. It emerged much later that Paxson was near the turf boundary of one of Philadelphia's gangs.

The director, optimistic to the last, reckoned that if Parkway would work at Paxson, it would work anywhere. And under its unit head, Cy Swartz, it worked beautifully. In any case, it was rent free and later on other organizations came to share the building. They were promptly exploited—not unwillingly—and Community Gamma was strengthened by an alliance with the Media Center, sharing the facility.

Affected no doubt by the type of building it occupied, its location, and the date of its founding, each Parkway unit developed its own style, and, as a result of its leadership, its own problems and complaints. But each had its own beauty and its own strength, unique but equal in worth. . . .

The students were not the only members of a Parkway unit. Each unit had nine or ten full-time, certified teachers, one of whom was appointed unit head by the director, in consultation with other members of the community. In addition, at least an equal number of university students, graduate and undergraduate, designated as interns, worked with each unit. They came from Antioch College, the University of Massachusetts, Penn State, the University of Pennsylvania, Oberlin College and several others. The intern's role was, perhaps, the most difficult and stressful one in the program, except possibly the director's. Young, inexperienced, and serving without pay, they were expected to share the same responsibilities and face the same problems as the regular faculty.

Finally, each unit employed someone who was skilled in office procedures and secretarial matters. Alpha had Tami Williams, an administrative officer who also did typing, Beta had Priscilla Witherspoon (later Wilmore) as secretary, and Gamma had Betty Barth as administrative officer. It was sometimes easy to forget that these people were essential members of the Parkway units. But, for example, Tami taught a course in typing and Joyce Johnson, the director's secretary, taught shorthand; they were all members of a learning community. . . .

The internal structuring of a Parkway unit is never determined by age. The program is nongraded. While it is true that students are eligible only if they are in grades nine through twelve of a conventional school, once they enter the program this fact is ignored, since it does not have any established, demonstrable connection with learning. Parkway tries to keep its priorties clear. It is a learning community, and the problem is how to provide internal structuring or grouping in such a way as to promote learning, not hamper it or simply be irrelevant to it.

The mode of admission to a Parkway Program unit and its size are of fundamental importance. Once inside the program, however, every member of the unit, student and teacher alike, belongs to a basic social group called a tutorial. Each tutorial is made up of about sixteen students, one of the full-time, certified teachers, and one of the university interns. People are assigned to a tutorial by lottery. The selection is random but compulsory. Everyone belongs, for the tutorial is the one required part of the program. In the beginning, the tutorial was scheduled to meet four times a week for two hours at a time. Later, this schedule was adapted in different ways by each of the three communities; the times and the purposes were changed, but not in any fundamental way. Since the tutorial groups are small, there is at least one place where a student or faculty member can be sure of friendly support and advice and can be certain of some interest and concern on the part of others. A visitor once remarked that the tutorial was an extended homeroom; the connotations are perhaps unfortunate, but the comment suggests one aspect of the tutorial's function.

The tutorial, since it has a small, permanent membership and meets frequently, is an ideal unit for communication and administration purposes. It is particularly valuable. . . for evaluation purposes.

Finally, the tutorial has, as its academic function, the development of the so-called basic skills. Originally, the tutorials were to focus on language and mathematics, but some units found that much time had to be spent on personal and group problems, and so while language was continued, social studies replaced mathematics. This trend was helped by the fact that many of the faculty were afraid of mathematics, or at least unskilled in it. . . . All that needs to be noted now is that the tutorials are randomly selected groups to which everybody belongs. It is the only compulsory group and every other group and activity is chosen by the students and faculty in the light of their own purposes.

The major part of every student's time is spent in regularly scheduled courses taught by the faculty, interns, businessmen, parents, students, librarians, curators, and individual volunteers. Each instructor brings to the course whatever interests him in his field of expertise. The students choose their own courses in consultation with their parents, so that the number of students in each course is highly variable. It did not matter if, in the past, some courses had only one student; if the instructor was willing, the course went on. Students' reasons for choosing their particular courses vary considerably. Sometimes the motive is interest in the subject itself, sometimes the character of the instructor, sometimes the fulfillment of a state requirement, sometimes parental insistence, sometimes to be with a friend, or a combination of any of these or other motives. Whatever the motives, they themselves became objects of inquiry, something to be understood by the students, and this is possible only because the motives are able to move the student. The administrative structure permits it—or, more correctly, requires it. After a brief settling down period, during which changes can be made, the student commits himself to a particular series of courses, and this is regarded as a kind of contract to which he and the Parkway Program are held.

In addition to taking some of the courses offered by the Parkway unit, a student can elect to spend part of his time on independent study.

Since each Parkway unit is responsible for its own day-to-day operations, special groups are set up within each unit to help members learn the necessary managerial skills and to assume responsibility for carrying out particular assignments—the most obvious one being the creation of the community's catalog of courses. These are called management groups and they are open to anyone—students, faculty and parents. They can be continuing groups—standing committees—or temporary groups set up to solve a particular problem. Time is set aside for management groups as a way of encouraging participation.

Periodically, each Parkway unit brings together all of its members in a town meeting. At the beginning of a unit's life, town meetings are held once a week (or even more frequently), but as the community develops, the business to be transacted becomes less in quantity and less urgent. Every other week seems to be the common rhythm. Although unit heads usually call town meetings, anybody can call one, and at the beginning of Parkway, Bremer, faculty members, and a small group of students all called town meetings to deal with problems that were on their minds.

Finally, groups are often set up on an *ad hoc* basis to undertake a specific task or to accomplish a particular purpose. . . .

This brings us to the aspects of Parkway's curriculum. The first aspect is freedom and responsibility. The second aspect is the social and administrative organization and more particularly the student's role, which in Parkway is seen to be as cooperator, as manager, and as artist (the third aspect). But the student as artist needs to know his material; just as the potter must know, understand, and respect his clay to see its possibilities, so the student must know, understand, and respect his material—the city. It is the city, therefore, that constitutes the fourth aspect of Parkway's curriculum. Every student must come to know the city, the complex of places, processes, and people with which he lives. He must know it for what it is, understand it in terms of what it can do, and respect it for what it could be. He must know it, respect it, and revere it simply because he is about to change it—not do it violence, not destroy it, but change it—that is, transform it in terms of the principles of its being into what, potentially, it already is. Since the Parkway Program has the city as its curriculum, it must have the city as its campus. This is the educational reason for the school without walls. To learn about the city, to let it become familiar, to see it as the earthly counterpart of the City of God, can be accomplished only in the city; only academics suppose that this is learned in a course called Urban Dwelling followed by Urban Dwelling 2. . . .

Simple city skills come hard at first, but students rapidly catch on and also acquire the courage to attempt more imaginative projects. What is public space? Who can reasonably be expected to help us? How do we ask? when? where? What organizations of men are there in the city? What do they do? why? What is a telephone for? How does a telephone directory help us? The answers to such questions may seem simple, but they are not simple, and certainly not to students—particularly to students from minority groups. They all need to acquire the skills of dealing with the city, to gain a small measure of power over it, for without this they cannot make a contribution. It would be foolish to imagine a potter with no knowledge of his clay and with his hands tied behind his back, but that is effectively the situation of students in most schools, and then there are complaints that they are idle, destructive and takers of hallucinatory drugs. They are pressured toward the psychedelic by the impossibility of achieving anything in the real world. "Mind expansion" is encouraged if there is no way of realizing ideas in the actual world. In Parkway, the taking of drugs declined markedly as the students' capacity for action increased. Instead of pressuring the student to live an inner, fantasy life, Parkway exerts pressure in the other direction by having no space of its own and by using the expertise of the citizens for educational purposes. If anything happens, it is because members of Parkway take the initiative, go out into the city, and make the city their curriculum by making it their campus. . . .

EDUCATION VOUCHERS:
A PROPOSAL FOR
DIVERSITY AND CHOICE

Judith Areen and Christopher Jencks

Ever since Adam Smith first proposed that the government finance education by giving parents money to hire teachers, the idea has enjoyed recurrent popularity. Smith's ideal of consumer sovereignty is built into a number of government programs for financing higher education, notably the G.I. Bill and the various state scholarship programs. Similarly a number of foreign countries have recognized the principle that parents who are dissatisfied with their local public school should be given money to establish alternatives. In America, however, public financing for elementary and secondary education has been largely confined to publicly managed schools. Parents who preferred a private alternative have had to pay the full cost out of their own pockets. As a result, we have almost no evidence on which to judge the merit of Smith's basic principle, namely, that if all parents are given the chance, they will look after their children's interests more effectively than will the state.

During the late 1960s, a series of developments in both public and nonpublic ecucation led to a revival of interest in this approach to financing education. In December, 1969, the United States Office of Economic Opportunity made a grant to the Center for the Study of Public Policy to support a detailed study of "education vouchers." This article will summarize the major findings of that report and outline briefly the voucher plan proposed by the Center.

THE CASE FOR CHOICE

Conservatives, liberals, and radicals all have complained at one time or another that the political mechanisms which supposedly make public schools accountable to their clients work clumsily and ineffectively. Parents who think their children are getting inferior schooling can, it is true, take their grievances to the local school board or state legislature. If legislators and school boards are unresponsive to the complaints of enough citizens, they may eventually be unseated. But mounting an effective campaign to change local public schools takes an enormous investment of time, energy, and money. Dissatisfied though they may be, few parents have the political skill or commitment to solve their problems this way. As a result, effective control over the character of the public schools is largely vested in legislators, school boards, and educators—not parents.

If parents are to take genuine responsibility for their children's education, they cannot rely exclusively on political processes. They must also be able to take individual action on behalf of their own children. At present, only relatively affluent parents retain any effective control over the education of their children. Only they are free to move to areas with "good" public schools, where housing is usually expensive (and often unavailable to black families at any price). Only they can afford nonsectarian, private schooling. The average parent has no alternative to his local public school unless he happens to belong to one of the few denominations that maintain low-tuition schools.

Not only does today's public school have a captive clientele, but it in turn has become the captive of a political process designed to protect the interests of its clientele. Because attendance at a local public school is nearly compulsory, its activities have been subjected to extremely close political control. The state, the local board, and the school administration have established regulations to ensure that no school will do anything to offend anyone of political consequence. Virtually everything of consequence is either forbidden or compulsory. By trying to please everyone, however, the schools have often ended up pleasing no one.

A voucher system seeks to free schools from the restrictions which inevitably accompany their present monopolistic privileges. The idea of the system is relatively simple. A publicly accountable agency would issue a voucher to parents. The parents could take this voucher to any school which agreed to abide by the rules of the voucher system. Each school would turn its vouchers in for cash. Thus parents would no longer be forced to send their children to the school around the corner simply because it was around the corner.

Even if no new schools were established under a voucher system, the responsiveness of existing public schools would probably increase. We believe that one of the most important advantages of a voucher system is that it would encourage diversity and choice *within the public system*. Indeed, if the public system were to begin matching students and schools on the basis of interest, rather than residence, one of the major objectives of a voucher system would be met without even involving the private sector. Popular public schools would get more applicants, and they would also have incentives to accommodate them, since extra students would bring extra funds. Unpopular schools would have few students, and would either have to change their ways or close up and reopen under new management.

As this last possibility suggests, however, there are great advantages to involving the private sector in a voucher system if it is properly regulated. Only in this way is the overall system likely to make room for fundamentally new initiatives that come from the bottom instead of the top. And only if private initiative is possible will the public sector feel real pressure to make room for kinds of education that are politically awkward but have a substantial constituency. If the private sector is involved, for example, parents can get together to create schools reflecting their special perspectives or their children's special needs. This should mean that the public schools will be more willing to do the same thing—though they will never be willing or able to accommodate *all* parental preferences. Similarly if the private sector is involved, educators with new ideas—or old ideas that are now out of fashion in the public schools—would also be able to set up their own schools. Entrepreneurs who thought they could teach children better and more inexpensively than the public schools would have an opportunity to do so. None of this ensures that every child would get the education he needs, but it would make such a result somewhat more likely than at present.

Beyond this, however, differences of opinion begin. Who would be eligible for vouchers? How would their value be determined? Would parents be allowed to supplement the vouchers from their own funds? What requirements would schools have to meet before cashing vouchers? What arrangements would be made for the children whom no school wanted to educate? Would church schools be eligible? Would schools promoting unorthodox political views be eligible? Once the advocates of vouchers begin to answer such questions, it becomes clear that the catch phrase around which they have united stands not for a single panacea, but for a multitude of controversial programs, many of which have little in common.

REVISED VOCABULARY

To understand the voucher plan recommended by the Center, it is useful to begin by reconsidering traditional notions about "public" and "private" education. Since the nineteenth century, we have classified schools as "public" if they were owned and operated by a governmental body. We go right on calling colleges "public," even when they charge tuition that many people cannot afford. We also call academically exclusive high schools "public," even if they have admissions requirements that only a handful of students can meet. We call neighborhood schools "public," despite the fact that nobody outside the neighborhood can attend them, and nobody can move into the neighborhood unless he has white skin and a down payment on a $30,000 home. And we call whole school systems "public," even though they refuse to give anyone information about what they are doing, how well they are doing it, and whether children are getting what their parents want. Conversely, we have always called schools "private" if they were owned and operated by private organizations. We have gone on calling these schools "private," even when, as sometimes happens, they are open to every applicant on a nondiscriminatory basis, charge no tuition, and make whatever information they have about themselves available to anyone who asks.

Definitions of this kind conceal as much as they reveal, for they classify schools entirely in terms of *who* runs them, not *how* they are run. If we want to describe what is really going on in education, there is much to be said for reversing this emphasis. We would then call a school "public" if it were open to everyone on a nondiscriminatory basis, if it charged no tuition, and if it provided full information about itself to anyone interested. Conversely, we would call any school "private" if it excluded applicants in a discriminatory way, charged tuition, or withheld information about itself. Admittedly, the question of who governs a school cannot be ignored entirely when categorizing the school, but it seems considerably less important than the question of how the school is governed.

Adopting this revised vocabulary, we propose a regulatory system with two underlying principles:

—*No public money should be used to support "private" schools.*
—*Any group that operates a "public" school should be eligible for public subsidies.*

THE PROPOSAL

Specifically, the Center has proposed an education voucher system (for *elementary* education) which would work in the following manner:

1. An Educational Voucher Agency (EVA) would be established to administer the vouchers. Its governing board might be elected or appointed, but in either case it should be structured so as to represent minority as well as majority interests. The EVA might be an existing local board of education, or it might be an agency with a larger or smaller geographic jurisdiction. The EVA would receive all federal, state, and local education funds for which children in its area were eligible. It would pay this money to schools only in return for vouchers. (In addition, it would pay parents for children's transportation costs to the school of their choice.)
2. The EVA would issue a voucher to every family in its district with children of elementary school age. The value of the basic voucher

would initially equal the per pupil expenditure of the public schools in the area. Schools which took children from families with below-average incomes would receive additional incentive payments. These "compensatory payments" might, for example, make the maximum payment for the poorest child worth double the basic voucher.

3. To become an "approved voucher school," eligible to cash vouchers, a school would have to:

   a. Accept each voucher as full payment for a child's education, charging no additional tuition.
   b. Accept any applicant so long as it had vacant places.
   c. If it had more applicants than places, fill at least half these places by picking applicants randomly and fill the other half in such a way as not to discriminate against ethnic minorities.
   d. Accept uniform standards established by the EVA regarding suspension and expulsion of students.
   e. Agree to make a wide variety of information about its facilities, teachers, program, and students available to the EVA and to the public.
   f. Maintain accounts of money received and disbursed in a form that would allow both parents and the EVA to determine where the money was going. Thus a school operated by the local board of education (a "public" school) would have to show how much of the money to which it was entitled on the basis of its vouchers was actually spent in that school. A school operated by a profit-making corporation would have to show how much of its income was going to the stockholders.
   g. Meet existing state requirements for *private* schools regarding curriculum, staffing, and the like. Control over policy in an approved voucher school might be vested in an existing local school board, a PTA, or any private group. Hopefully, no government restrictions would be placed on curriculum, staffing, and the like, except those already established for all private schools in a state.

4. Just as at present, the local board of education (which might or might not be the EVA) would be responsible for ensuring that there were enough places in publicly managed schools to accommodate every elementary school age child who did not want to attend a privately managed school. If a shortage of places developed for some reason, the board of education would have to open new schools or create more places in existing schools. (Alternatively, it might find ways to encourage privately managed schools to expand, presumably by getting the EVA to raise the value of the voucher.)

5. Every spring each family would submit to the EVA the name of the school to which it wanted to send each of its elementary school age children next fall. Any children already enrolled in a voucher school would be guaranteed a place, as would any sibling of a child enrolled in a voucher school. So long as it had room, a voucher school would be required to admit all students who listed it as a first choice. If it did not have room for all applicants, a school could fill half its places in whatever way it wanted, choosing among those who listed it as a first choice. It could not, however, select these applicants in such a way as to discriminate against racial minorities. It would then have to fill its remaining places by a lottery among the remaining applicants. All schools with unfilled places would report these to the EVA. All families whose children had not been admitted to their first-choice school would then choose an alternative school which still had vacancies. Vacancies would then be filled in the same manner as in the first round. This procedure would continue until every child had been admitted to a school.
6. Having enrolled their children in a school, parents would give their vouchers to the school. The school would send the vouchers to the EVA and would receive a check in return.

SOME CAVEATS

The voucher system outlined above is quite different from other systems now being advocated; it contains far more safeguards for the interests of disadvantaged children. A voucher system which does not include these or equally effective safeguards would be worse than no voucher system at all. Indeed, an unregulated voucher system could be the most serious setback for the education of disadvantaged children in the history of the United States. A properly regulated system, on the other hand, may have the potential to inaugurate a new era of innovation and reform in American schools.

One common objection to a voucher system of this kind is that many parents are too ignorant to make intelligent choices among schools. Giving parents a choice will, according to this argument, simply set in motion an educational equivalent of Gresham's Law, in which hucksterism and mediocre schooling drive out high quality institutions. This argument seems especially plausible to those who envisage the entry of large numbers of profit-oriented firms into the educational marketplace. The argument is not, however, supported by much evidence. Existing private schools are sometimes mere diploma mills, but on the average their claims about themselves seem no more misleading, and the quality of the services they offer no lower, than in the public schools. And while some private schools are run by hucksters interested only in profit, this is the exception rather than the rule. There is no obvious reason to suppose that vouchers would change all this.

A second common objection to vouchers is that they would "destroy the public schools." Again, this seems far-fetched. If you look at the educational choices made by wealthy parents who can already afford whatever schooling they want for their children, you find that most still prefer their local public schools if these are at all adequate. Furthermore, most of those who now leave the public system do so in order to attend high-cost, exclusive private schools. While some wealthy parents would doubtless continue to patronize such schools, they would receive no subsidy under the proposed system.

Nonetheless, if you are willing to call every school "public" that is ultimately responsible to a public board of education, then there is little doubt that a voucher system would result in some shrinkage of the "public" sector and some growth of the "private" sector. If, on the other hand, you confine the label "public" to schools which are equally open to everyone within commuting distance, you discover that the so-called public sector includes relatively few public schools. Instead, racially exclusive suburbs and economically exclusive neighborhoods serve to ration access to good "public" schools in precisely the same way that admissions committees and tuition charges ration access to good "private" schools. If you begin to look at the distinction between public and private schooling in these terms, emphasizing accessibility rather than control, you are likely to conclude that a voucher system, far from destroying the public sector, would greatly expand it, since it would force large numbers of schools, public and private, to open their doors to outsiders.

A third objection to vouchers is that they would be available to children attending Catholic schools. This is not, of course, a necessary feature of a voucher system. The courts, a state legislature, or a local EVA could easily restrict participation to nonsectarian schools. Indeed, some state constitutions clearly require that this be done. The federal Constitution may also require such a restriction, but neither the language of the First Amendment nor the legal precedent is clear on this issue. The First Amendment's prohibition against an "establishment of religion" can be construed as barring payments to church schools, but the "free exercise of religion" clause can also be construed as requiring the state to treat church schools in precisely the same way as other private schools. The Supreme Court has never ruled on a case of this type (e.g., G.I. Bill payments to Catholic colleges or Medicare payments to Catholic hospitals). Until it does, the issue ought to be resolved on policy grounds. And since the available evidence indicates that Catholic schools have served their children no worse than public schools, and perhaps slightly better, there seems no compelling reason to deny them the same financial support given other schools.

The most worrisome objection to a voucher system is that its success would depend on the EVA's willingness to regulate the marketplace vigorously. If vouchers were used on a large scale, state and local regulatory efforts might be uneven or even nonexistent. The regulations designed to prevent racial and economic discrimination seem especially likely to get watered down at the state and local level, or else to remain unenforced. This argument applies, however, to *any* educational reform, and it also applies to the existing system. If you assume any given EVA will be controlled by overt or covert segregationists, you must also assume that this will be true of the local board of education. A board of education that wants to keep racist parents happy hardly needs vouchers to do so. It only needs to maintain the neighborhood school system. White parents who want their children to attend white schools will then find it quite simple to move to a white neighborhood where their children will be suitably segregated. Except perhaps in the South, neither the federal government, the state government, nor the judiciary is likely to prevent this traditional practice.

If, on the other hand, you assume a board which is anxious to eliminate segregation, either for legal, financial, or political reasons, you must also assume that the EVA would be subject to the same pressures. And if an EVA is anxious to eliminate segregation, it will have no difficulty devising regulations to achieve this end. Furthermore, the legal precedents to date suggest that the federal courts will be more stringent in applying the Fourteenth Amendment to voucher systems than to neighborhood school systems. The courts have repeatedly thrown out voucher systems designed to maintain segregation, whereas they have shown no such general willingness to ban the neighborhood school. Outside the South, then, those who believe in integration may actually have an easier time achieving this goal with voucher systems than they will with the existing public school system. Certainly, the average black parent's access to integrated schools would be increased under a voucher system of the kind proposed by the Center. Black parents could apply to any school in the system, and the proportion of blacks admitted would have to be at least equal to the proportion who applied. This gives the average black parent a far better chance of having their children attend an integrated school than at present. There is, of course, no way to compel black parents to take advantage of this opportunity by actually applying to schools that enroll whites. But the opportunity would be there for all. . . .

EIGHT

Educational Alternatives: Free Schools and No Schools

How to do things differently once you understand explicitly the links between school and society? Many educators decided, during the 1960s that it was not possible to do anything radically significant within the established system of public schooling. Free schools characterized most of this alternative effort, working on the integration of intellect with the emotion so disastrously separated in public schools.

Unfortunately, most free-schoolers have tended to ignore the narrow base of their efforts. The public school—the one place where the massive needs of millions of Americans can be accommodated—is forgotten, and with it, very often, those in desperate economic need as well. This is social dynamite. Free-schoolers, along with the no-schoolers who are also represented in this chapter, must assume a greater measure of responsibility; somehow they must integrate the values, practices, and experiences that their stance rests upon into public school policy. Otherwise, despite their humane pretensions, the free-schoolers and no-schoolers will more effectively serve the forces of oppression in our society than freedom by isolating large segments of the disaffected from an active role in society. This is not to say that they cannot, with integrity, remain separate from the institution of public education but, instead, that they must involve themselves more fully in the problems that have molded public schools into objects of disdain and protest.

Kozol and Dennison present persuasive record and analysis of the free-schoolers stance at its best; while Goodman and Illich provide two equally compelling views on the limitations of the school setting itself as a framework for a humane, individually sensitive, as well as a democratic, education.

157

FREE SCHOOLS

Jonathan Kozol

The term free school is used very often, in a cheerful but unthinking way, to mean entirely different kinds of things and to define the dreams and yearnings of entirely disparate and even antagonistic individuals and groups. It is honest, then, to say, right from the start, that I am speaking mainly of one type of Free School and that many of the ventures which go under the name of Free School will not be likely to find much of their own experience reflected here.

At one end of the spectrum, there is the large, public-school-connected, neighborhood-created and politically controversial operation best exemplified perhaps by I.S. 201, in its initial phase, or later by Ocean Hill—Brownsville in New York. Somewhat smaller, but still involving some of the same factors, and still tied in with the public education apparatus, is the Morgan School in Washington, D.C. At the opposite extreme is a rather familiar type of relatively isolated, politically non-controversial and generally all-white rural Free School. This kind of school is often tied in with a commune or with what is described as an "intentional community," attracts people frequently who, if not rich themselves, have parents who are wealthy, and is often associated with a certain kind of media-promoted counter-culture.

Neither of the two descriptions just preceding would apply directly to the kind of Free School I have tended to be most intensively involved with, though certainly I have been a great deal closer to the first than to the second. There is also a considerable difference in the way I feel about the two. The large, political and public-school-associated ventures like Ocean Hill—Brownsville are, in my opinion, brave, significant and in many ways heroic struggles for survival on the part of those who constitute the most despised and brutalized and properly embittered victims of North American racism and class-exploitation. While these are not the kinds of schools that I am writing about here, they seem to me to be of vast importance and I look upon the people who are active in them with immense respect.

The other end of the spectrum does not seem to me to be especially courageous or heroic. In certain ways, it appears to me to be a dangerous and disheartening phenomenon. I know, of course, that very persuasive arguments can be presented for the idea of escaping from the turmoil and the human desperation of the cities, and for finding a place of physical isolation in the mountains of Vermont or in the hills

Source. Excerpted from *Free Schools,* by Jonathan Kozol. Copyright © 1972 by Jonathan Kozol. Reprinted by permission of Houghton Mifflin Company.

of Southern California. Like many people here in Boston and New York, I have often felt the urge to run away, especially when I see a picture or read something in a magazine about these pastoral and isolated Free Schools in their gentle and attractive settings of hillside, farmland and warm country-meadow. When I am the most weary, the inclination to escape is almost overwhelming.

Despite this inclination, which I feel so often, I believe we have an obligation to stay here and fight these battles and work out these problems in the cities where there is the greatest need and where, moreover, we cannot so easily be led into a mood of falsified euphoria. If a man should feel, as many people do, that whites should not be working in black neighborhoods, then there are plenty of poor-white neighborhoods in major cities, or neighborhoods of the marginal lower-middle-class along the edges of the major cities, in which we might establish roots and settle down to try to build our Free Schools and to develop those communities of struggle which so frequently grow up around them. I know it is very appealing and, for people who are weary from a long, long period of fruitless struggle and rebellion, it is almost irrestible to get away from everything. I don't believe, however, that we should give in to this yearning, even if it is very appealing and even if we are very, very weary. . . .

There is one point about the exodus to the woods and hills which is, to me, particularly disturbing. Some of the most conscientious and reflective of the people in the country Free Schools will seek to justify their manner of escape by pointing out that they, and their young children with them, have in a sense "retired" from the North American system as a whole, and especially from its agencies of devastation, power and oppression. Though earnestly presented, this argument does not seem honest. Whether they like it or not, or whether they wish to speak of it or not, the beautiful children of the rich and powerful within this nation are going to be condemned to wield that power also. This power, which will be theirs if they are cognizant of it and even if they aren't, will be the power to affect the lives of millions of poor men and women in this nation, to do so often in the gravest ways, often indeed to grant or to deny life to these people. It will be the power, as well, to influence the lives of several hundred million people who are now subject to North American domination in far-distant lands. Even in the idealistic ritual of formal abdication of that power, as for example, by going out into the isolated hills of Western Massachusetts or into the mountains of Vermont to start a Free School, they will still be profiting from the consequences of that power and from the direct profits and extractions of a structure of oppression.

Free Schools, then, cannot with sanity, with candor or with truth, endeavor to exist within a moral vacuum. However far the journey and however many turnpike tolls we pay, however high the spruce or pine that grow around the sunny meadows in which we live and dream and seek to educate our children, it is still one nation. It is not one thing in Lebanon, New Hampshire, one thing in the heart of Harlem. No more is it one thing in Roxbury or Watts, one thing in Williamsburg or Sausalito, California. The passive, tranquil and protected lives white people lead depend on strongly armed police, well-demarcated ghettos. While children starve and others walk the city streets in fear on Monday afternoon, the privileged young people in the Free Schools of Vermont shuttle their handlooms back and forth and speak of love and of "organic processes." They do "their thing." Their thing is sun and good food and fresh water and good doctors and delightful, old and battered eighteenth-century houses, and a box of baby turtles; somebody else's thing may be starvation, broken glass, unheated rooms and rats inside the bed with newborn children. The beautiful children do not *wish* cold rooms or broken glass, starvation, rats or fear for anybody; nor will they stake their lives, or put their bodies on the line, or interrupt one hour of the sunlit morning, or sacrifice one moment of the golden afternoon, to take a hand in altering the unjust terms of a society in which these things are possible.

I know that I will antagonize many people by the tenor of these statements; yet I believe them deeply and cannot keep faith with the people I respect, and who show loyalty to me, if I put forward a piece of writing of this kind and do not say these things. In my belief, an isolated upper-class rural Free School for the children of the white and rich within a land like the United States and in a time of torment such as 1972, is a great deal too much like a sandbox for the children of the SS Guards at Auschwitz. If today in our history books, or in our common conversation, we were to hear of a network of exquisite, idealistic little country-schools operated with a large degree of personal freedom, but within the bounds of ideological isolation, in the beautiful sloping woodlands outside of Munich and Berlin in 1939 or 1940, and if we were to read or to be told that those who ran these schools were operating by all innovative methods and enlightened notions and that they had above their desks or on their walls large poster-photographs of people like Maria Montessori and Tolstoi and Gandhi, and that they somehow kept beyond the notice of the Nazi government and of the military and of the police and SS Guards, but kept right on somehow throughout the war with no experience of rage or need for intervention in the lives of those defined by the German press and media as less than human, but kept right on with waterplay and innovative games while smoke rose over Dachau... I think that we would look upon those people now as some very fine and terrifying breed of alienated human beings.

It is not a handsome or a comfortable parallel; yet, in my judgment it is not entirely different from the situation of a number of the country communes and the rural Free Schools that we now see in some sections of this nation. At best, in my belief, these schools are obviating pain and etherizing evil; at worst, they constitute a registered escape-valve for political rebellion. Lease conscionable is when the people who are laboring and living in these schools describe themselves as revolutionaries. If this is revolution, then the men who have elected Richard Nixon do not have a lot to fear. They would do well in fact to subsidize these schools and to covertly channel resources to their benefactors and supporters, for they are an ideal drain on activism and the perfect way to sidetrack ethical men from dangerous behavior.

The direct opposite of the all-white rural Free Schools may logically appear to be the large, political, public-school-affiliated venture such as I.S. 201 or Ocean Hill—Brownsville. These schools, for certain, have been two of the most important prototypes of strong and serious urban struggle in the Eastern section of the nation in the past ten years. They also are two centers—or "complexes"— in which some of the most productive work has taken place in the creation and the evolution of a deep sense of black consciousness, of neighborhood participation and of neighborhood control. It is, above all, in the reconstruction of the metaphor and symbolism of the *school itself* as something other than a walled and formidable bunker of archaic data and depersonalized people in the midst of living truth—it is, above all, in the labor of creative repossession of the "marketplace" by its own clientele—that many of us now view ourselves as the direct inheritors of men like Preston Wilcox and Charles Wilson.

There are, however, a number of important reasons for which I feel the need to draw a clear and definite line of demarcation between large ventures of this shape and character and those within which I have tried to take my place and to invest my energies. It seems—to begin with—more than obvious by now that in such areas as New York, Washington, Cleveland, Boston or St. Louis there cannot be much serious role for white men and white women in the genesis of these operations. They constitute, in almost every situation, an important portion of the black and Spanish process of self-liberation and of self-determination. Their function is as much political as pedagogic. They are enormously significant in community organization. They are not, however, a sound or reasonable context for active and conspicuous participation on the part of white men.

There is a second reason why I have not chosen to participate in—or write about—these large, political "sub-systems." The kinds of public-school-affiliated operations I now have in mind, no matter how inventive or how passionate or how immediately provocative, constitute nonetheless a basic extension of the ideology of public school. They cannot, for reasons of immediate operation, finance and survival, raise serious doubts about the indoctrinational and custodial function of the public education apparatus. No matter how sophisticated or how inventive these "alternatives within the system" may contrive to be, they nonetheless must continue to provide, within a single package: custodial functions, indoctrinational functions, credentializing, labeling and grading services, along with more purely educational functions such as skill-training. The public-school-affiliated ventures such as those that I have named above, or such as Parkway School in Philadelphia or Morgan School in Washington, D.C., may constantly run skirmishes on the edges of the functions and priorities of domestication; in the long run, however, they cannot undermine them. The school that flies the flag is, in the long run, no matter what the handsome community leader in the startling Afro likes to say, *accountable to that flag* and to the power and to the values which it represents. This is, and must remain, the ultimate hang-up of all ventures which aspire to constitute, in one way or another, a radical alternative "within the system."

There is a third reason, also, why I am not involved with public-school-associated ventures. This reason has to do with size. It has been my experience that something bad happens often to good people when they go into programs that involve large numbers of young people and a correspondingly extended political constituency. The most gentle and least manipulative of people often prove to be intolerable "operators" once they are faced with something like two thousand children and four thousand angry parents. Even those people who care the most about the personal well-being of young children turn easily into political performers once they are confronted with the possibilities for political machination that are created by a venture that involves so many people and so much publicity. There are those, I think, who have been able to resist it to a large degree. Kenneth Haskins is one of several important leaders in the Washington and New York area who seem to have been able to maintain a comfortable balance between politics and education in the face of formidable odds. The point, however, is that those odds are *there*—and they are very much against us.

Then, too, and possibly the most important, the likelihood of going through deep transformations and significant alterations of our own original ideas (by this I mean the possibilities for growth and for upheaval in our consciousness of what "school" is about) is seriously circumscribed when we become accountable to fifteen city blocks and to ten thousand human beings. This is perhaps a somewhat impractical position. I just think many more remarkable things can happen to good people if they happen in small places and in a multiple of good ways. Even a school of five hundred children and two thousand parents, friends and teachers, hangers-on and teacher-aides, seems much too large. The Free Schools that seem to have the greatest chance of real success, not just in terms of publishable statistics, but in deep human terms as well, are those in which there are not more than eighty to one hundred children.

It may be I am only justifying my own inclinations. I know that I feel far more comfortable and can be in better touch with my own instincts and with my own sense of justice in a Free School that remains as small, non-formidable and non-spectacular as possible. When I first read Paul Goodman's essay about "mini-schools," I felt it sounded coy and unrealistic. Today I believe that Goodman is correct in arguing for a limited size and for a modest scale of operations. It is not easy in this nation to resist the emphasis on bigness, growth, constant expansion. It is, however, something well worth fighting to resist, if it is in our power to do so.

I am, then, speaking for the most part about Free Schools (1) outside the public education apparatus, (2) outside the white man's counter-culture, (3) inside the cities, (4) in direct contact with the needs and urgencies of those among the poor, the black, the dispossessed, who have been the most clearly victimized by public education, (5) as small, "decentralized" and "localized" as we can manage, (6) as little publicized as possible. . . .

THE LIVES OF CHILDREN, THE STORY OF THE FIRST STREET SCHOOL

George Dennison

There is no need to add to the criticism of our public schools. The critique is extensive and can hardly be improved on. The processes of learning and teaching, too, have been exhaustively studied. One thinks of the books of Paul Goodman, John Holt, Greene and Ryan, Nat

Source. From *The Lives of Children, The Story of the First Street School* by George Dennison. Copyright © 1969 by George Dennison. Reprinted by permission of Random House, Inc.

Hentoff, James Herndon, Jonathan Kozol, Herbert Kohl; and of such researches as those of Bruner and Piaget; and of Joseph Featherstone's important *Report*. The question now is what to do. In the pages that follow, I would like to describe one unfamiliar approach to the problems which by now have become familiar. And since "the crisis of the schools" consists in reality of a great many crises in the lives of children, I shall try to make the children of the First Street School the real subject of this book. There were twenty-three blacks, whites, and Puerto Ricans in almost equal proportions, all from low-income families in New York's Lower East Side. About half were on welfare. About half, too, had come to us from the public schools with severe learning and behavior problems.

Four things about the First Street School were unusual: first, its small size and low teacher/pupil ratio; second, the fact that this luxurious intimacy, which is ordinarily very expensive, cost about the same per child as the $850 annual operating costs of the public schools; third, our reversal of conventional structure, for where the public school conceives of itself merely as a place of instruction, and puts severe restraints on the relationships between persons, we conceived of ourselves as an environment for growth, and accepted the relationships between the children and ourselves as being the very heart of the school; and fourth, the kind of freedom experienced by teachers and pupils alike. . . .

We had no administrators. We were small and didn't need them. The parents found that, after all, they approved of this. They themselves could judge the competence of the teachers, and so could their children—by the specific act of learning. The parents' past experience of administrators had been uniformly upsetting—and the proof, of course, was in the pudding: the children were happier and *were* learning. As for the children, they never missed them.

We did not give report cards. We knew each child, knew his capacities and his problems, and the vagaries of his growth. This knowledge could not be recorded on little cards. The parents found—again—that they approved of this. It diminished the blind anxieties of life, for grades had never meant much to them anyway except some dim sense of *problem*, or some dim reassurance that things were all right. When they wanted to know how their children were doing, they simply asked the teachers.

We didn't give tests, at least not of the competitive kind. It was important to be aware of what the children knew, but more important to be aware of *how* each child knew what he knew. We could learn nothing about Maxine by testing Eléna. And so there was no comparative testing at all. The children never missed those invidious comparisons, and the teachers were spared the absurdity of ranking dozens of personalities on one uniform scale.

Our housing was modest. The children came to school in play-torn clothes. Their families were poor. A torn dress, torn pants, frequent cleanings—there were expenses they could not afford. Yet how can children play without getting dirty? Our uncleanliness standard was just right. It looked awful and suited everyone.

We treated the children with consideration and justice. I don't mean that we never got angry and never yelled at them (nor they at us). I mean that we took seriously the pride of life that belongs to the young—even to the very young. We did not coerce them in violation of their proper independence. Parents and children both found that they approved very much of this.

Now I would like to describe the school, or more correctly, the children and teachers. I shall try to bring out in detail three important things:

1. That the proper concern of a primary school is not education in a narrow sense, and still less preparation for later life, but the present lives of the children—a point made repeatedly by John Dewey, and very poorly understood by many of his followers.

2. That when the conventional routines of a school are abolished (the military discipline, the schedules, the punishments and rewards, the standardization), what arises is neither a vacuum nor chaos, but rather a new order, based first on relationships between adults and children, and children and their peers, but based ultimately on such truths of the human condition as these: that the mind does not function separately from the emotions, but thought partakes of feeling and feeling of thought; that there is no such thing as knowledge *per se*, knowledge in a vacuum, but rather all knowledge is possessed and must be expressed by individuals; that the human voices preserved in books belong to the real features of the world, and that children are so powerfully attracted to this world that the very motion of their curiosity comes through to us as a form of love; that an active moral life cannot be evolved except where people are free to express their feelings and act upon insights of conscience.

3. That running a primary school-*provided it be small*—is an extremely simple thing. It goes without saying that the teachers must be competent (which does not necessarily mean passing courses in a teacher's college). Given this *sine qua non*, there is nothing mysterious. The present quagmire of public education is entirely the result of unworkable centralization and the lust for control that permeates every bureaucratic institution.

In saying this, I do not mean that the work in a free school is easy. On the contrary, teachers find it taxing. But they find it rewarding, too—quite unlike the endless round of frustrations experienced by those at work in the present system. . . .

For the twenty-three children there were three full-time teachers, one part-time (myself), and several others who came at scheduled periods for singing, dancing, and music.

Public school teachers, with their 30 to 1 ratios, will be aware that we have entered the realm of sheer luxury. One of the things that will bear repeating, however, is that this luxury was purchased at a cost per child a good bit lower than that of the public system, for the similarity of operating costs does not reflect the huge capital investment of the public schools or the great difference in the quality of service. Not that our families paid tuition (hardly anyone did); I mean simply that our money was not drained away by vast administrative costs, book-keeping, elaborate buildings, maintenance, enforcement personnel, and vandalism (to say nothing of the costs hidden in those institutions which in a larger sense must be seen as adjuncts to the schools: houses of correction, prisons, narcotic wards, and welfare).

Our teacher/pupil ratio varied according to need. Gloria handled up to eleven children, ages five to eight. At least half of her children were just starting school, and were beautifully "motivated," as the educationists say. Motivated, of course, means eager, alive, curious, responsive, trusting, persistent; and it is not as good a word as any of these. They were capable of forming relationships and of pursuing real interests. Every child who came to us after several years in the public schools came with problems.

Susan Goodman, who taught the next group, ages eight to ten, usually had six or seven in her room. Two of these were difficult and required a great deal of attention. They got the attention, and they were the two (Maxine and Eléna) who of all the children in the school made the most spectacular progress academically. In a year and a half, Eléna, who was ten, went from first-grade work to advanced fourth; and let me hasten to say that Susan, like the other teachers, followed Rousseau's old policy of *losing time*. ("The most useful rule of education is this: do not save time, but lose it.") Eléna's lessons were very brief and were often skipped.

The remaining children, boys to the age of thirteen, had come to us in serious trouble of one kind or another. Several carried knives, all had been truants, José could not read, Willard was scheduled for a 600 school, Stanley was a vandal and thief and was on his way to Youth House. They were characterized, one and all, by an anxiety that amounted to desperation. It became clear to us very quickly to what an extent they had been formed by abuse and neglect. Family life was a factor for several, but all had had disastrous experiences in school, and with authorities outside of school, and with the racism of our society as a whole, and with poverty and the routine violence of violent streets. They were destined for environments of maximum control—prison in one form or another. How they fared in our setting of freedom may be interesting.

Some pupils, as Dr. Elliott Shapiro points out (Nat Hentoff's *Our Children Are Dying* is about Elliott Shapiro and the children of Harlem), require a one-to-one relationship. I worked with José on just that basis. At other times I took the boys in a group, or Mabel Chrystie (now Dennison) did, or they were divided between the two of us. . . .

Perhaps I can give the reader some feeling of the atmosphere of the school by describing a fairly typical morning. I mean the very beginning of the day. (And I should start by being more honest: the morning I have in mind was unusually pleasant. What was typical was the simplicity of our routines and the fact that the persons themselves were, by and large, the real business of the day.) I would like to contrast this description with its parallel period in the public schools, as reconstructed by Greene and Ryan in *The Schoolchildren*. My purpose is not to heap criticism on the public schools, but to show what it means to children to begin the day relating on the one hand to institutional routines, and on the other hand to persons they already know and trust. . . .

Our own school day began with a companionable milling around in one room, students and teachers still shaking off sleep and exchanging gossip of the night before. Often Gloria and Susan arrived with containers of coffee and that look around the eyes which one inspects so as to guess at the state of the soul. Some few of the children always came to school hungry, and they seized the sandwiches meant for lunch. Munching these, they would talk with other children, or roughhouse, or cluster around the teachers' chairs and reenact television episodes of the night before, or talk of family and neighborhood events. I liked these morning interludes. They were courteous and companionable, and sometimes actually warm. In the description below only a few children are mentioned, but their numbers varied up to twenty-three. I cannot remember that the room became too crowded. They kept running back and forth into the hallway and into the adjacent room. The paragraph is taken from my journal of events at school.

"In the morning, as school begins, we tend to sit around for a while in the front room while the kids hang up their coats, all greeting each

other and chatting with whomever they please. Tom Gomez has just delivered Maxine and is still outside in the truck he uses for his painting business. José and Eléna, who sometimes ride with him, stand on the window sill and open the top of the window and yell down to him. I join them for a moment and yell down to Tom, who is leaning out from the driver's seat. I kid him about all the breakdowns last Friday when he helped transport us to a picnic. He grins and shouts something back. I can't understand him because of all the yelling in the room, but José, who is used to yelling, interprets for me. A few minutes later I sit down to smoke a cigarette, and five-year-old Laura (almost six) comes over with a roll of masking tape. 'Look what I have.' She peels a little strip and asks me to break it off for her, which I do. She says, 'How come you can break it and I can't?' I say, 'Because I have nice big fingernails,' meaning the big nail on my thumb, which is the only one I don't bite . . . and I take her hand and look at her fingernails, all bitten to the quick. She laughs and hides her hands. Then I look at the gap in her teeth and ask her if the new teeth are on their way yet, and she shrugs and says, 'I don't know,' and puts her fingers on another front tooth and wiggles it. 'See!' She draws a clockface, almost correctly, on the strip of masking tape and pastes it on my wrist like a wristwatch, saying nothing as she does this. Gloria and I exchange a few words about the Ellison novel she loaned me. At the other end of the room Mabel is opening the lunch provisions because Julio is hungry. She helps him make a sandwich. Vicente asks for a sandwich, too. He usually comes to school without breakfast because his mother works and the older sister who's left in charge either won't or can't make breakfast. Stanley and Willard have asked Mabel if they can make one telephone call, and they are busy doing this. Laura has asked me to tear off several more pieces of masking tape. She draws circles on one of them and holds it up, saying, 'What's this?' I say that I don't know, and she informs me that those are peanuts. Gloria says that Susan is home sick, and so she'll take Susan's kids for the day. Eléna complains that there won't be anyone to help her with her arithmetic. I tell her that either Mabel or I will help her. José is strutting and acting tough. He makes a swipe at my head, saying, 'Come on, man, you think you tough. Come on, man,' and in the very next breath says, 'Come on, George, we gonna have the most terrific lesson in the world.' Willard has been tinkering with the typewriter. I put some paper in for him and stand there a while. Then I ask him for the typewriter, since it's essential in the lessons with José. He gives it up readily and I promise to return it as soon as we're through."

The milling around usually lasted about twenty minutes and gave way almost imperceptibly to the first activities of the day.

I would like to make clear that in contrasting our own procedures with those of the public schools, I am not trying to criticize the teachers who find themselves embattled in the institutional setting and overburdened to the point of madness. The staggering defeat of teachers as well as children is one of the things made clear in Greene and Ryan's vividly descriptive book. My point is precisely that the intimacy and small scale of our school should be imitated widely, since these things alone make possible the human contact capable of curing the diseases we have been naming with such frequency for the last ten years. . . .

THE PRESENT MOMENT
IN EDUCATION

Paul Goodman

It is possible that the chief problem in the coming generation will be survival, whether from nuclear bombs, genocide, ecological disaster, or mass starvation and endless wars. If so, this is the present task of pedagogy. There already exist wilderness schools for self-reliance and it has been proposed to train guerrillas in schools in Harlem. The delicately interlocking technologies of the world indeed seem to be overextended and terribly vulnerable, and the breakdown could be pretty total. But let us fantasize that this view is not realistic.

My own thinking is that:

1. Incidental education, taking part in the on-going activities of society, should be the chief means of learning.
2. Most high schools should be eliminated, with other kinds of communities of youth taking over their sociable functions.
3. College training should generally follow, not precede, entry into the professions.
4. The chief task of educators is to see to it that the activities of society provide incidental education, if necessary inventing new useful activities offering new educational opportunities.
5. The purpose of elementary pedagogy, through age twelve, is to protect children's free growth, since our community and families both pressure them too much and do not attend to them enough.

Let me review the arguments for this program. We must drastically cut back the schooling because the present extended tutelage is against nature and arrests growth. The effort to channel growing up according to a preconceived curriculum and method discourages and wastes many of the best human powers to learn and cope. Schooling does not prepare for real performance; it is largely carried on for its own sake. Only a small fraction, the "academically talented"—between 10 and 15 percent according to Conant—thrive in this useless activity without being bored or harmed by it. It isolates the young from the older generation and alienates them.

On the other hand, it makes no sense for many of the brightest and most sensitive young simply to drop out or confront society with hostility. This cannot lead to social reconstruction. The complicated and confusing conditions of modern times need knowledge and fresh thought, and therefore long acquaintance and participation precisely by the young. Young radicals seem to think that mere political change will solve the chief problems, or that they will solve themselves after political change, but this is a delusion. The problems of urbanization, technology, and ecology have not been faced by any political group. The educational systems of other advanced countries are no better than ours, and the young are equally dissenting. Finally, it has been my Calvinistic, and Aristotelian, experience that most people cannot organize their lives without productive activity (though, of course, not necessarily paid activity); and the actual professions, services, industries, arts and sciences are the arena in which they should be working. Radical politics and doing one's thing are careers for very few.

As it is, however, the actual activities of American society either exclude the young, or corrupt them, or exploit them. Here is the task for educators. We must make the rules of licensing and hiring realistic to the actual work and get rid of mandarin requirements.

We must design apprenticeships that are not exploitative. Society desperately needs much work that is not now done, both intellectual and manual, in urban renewal, ecology, communications, and the arts, and all these could make use of young people. Many such enterprises are best organized by young people themselves, like most of the community development and community action Vocations for Social Change. Little think tanks, like the Oceanic Institute at Makapuu Point or the Institute for Policy Studies in Washington, which are not fussy about diplomas, have provided excellent spots for the young. Our aim should be to multiply the paths of growing up, with opportunity to start again, cross over, take a moratorium, travel, work on one's own. To insure freedom of option and that the young can maintain and express their critical attitude, all adolescents should be guaranteed a living. (The present cost of high schooling would almost provide this.)

The advantage of making education less academic has, of course, occurred to many school people. There are a myriad of programs to open
the school to the world by (1) importing outside professionals, artists in
residence, gurus, mothers, dropouts as teachers' aides; and (2) giving
academic credit for work-study, community action, writing novels,
service in mental hospitals, junior year abroad, and other kinds of
released time. Naturally I am enthusiastic for this development and
only want it to go the small further step of abolishing the present school
establishment instead of aggrandizing it.

Conversely, there is a movement in the United States, as in China
and Cuba, for adolescent years to be devoted to public service, and this
is fine if the service is not compulsory and regimenting.

It is possible for every education to be tailor-made according to each
youth's developing interest and choice. Choices along the way will be
very often ill-conceived and wasteful, but they will express desire and
immediately meet reality, and therefore they should converge to
finding the right vocation more quickly than by any other course.
Vocation is what one is good at and can do, what uses a reasonable
amount of one's powers, and gives one a useful occupation in a community that is one's own. The right use of the majority of people would
make a stable society far more efficient than our own. And those who
have peculiar excellences are more likely to find their own further way
when they have entry by doing something they can do and being accepted.

Academic schooling can be chosen by those with academic talents,
and such schools are better off unencumbered by sullen uninterested
bodies. But the main use of academic teaching is for those already busy
in sciences and professions, who need academic courses along the way.
Cooper Union in New York City used to fulfill this function very well.
And in this context of need, there can finally be the proper use of new
pedagogic technology, as a means of learning at one's own time,
whereas at present this technology makes the school experience still
more rigid and impersonal.

Of course, in this set-up employers would themselves provide
ancillary academic training, especially if they had to pay for it anyway,
instead of using parents' and taxpayers' money. In my opinion, this
ancillary rather than prior schooling would do more than any other
single thing to give black, rural, and other "culturally deprived" youth
a fairer entry and chance for advancement, since what is to be learned
is objective and functional and does not depend on the abstract school
style. As we have seen, *on the job* there is no correlation between
competence and years of prior schooling.

But this leads to another problem. Educationally, schooling on the
job is usually superior, but the political and moral consequences of

such a system are ambiguous and need more analysis than I can give them here. At present, a youth is hired for actual credentials, if not actual skill; this is alienating to him as a person, but it also allows a measure of free-market democracy. If he is to be schooled on the job, however, he must be hired for his promise and attended to as a person; this is less alienating, but it can lead to company paternalism, like Japanese captialism, or like Fidel Castro's Marxist vision of farm and factory-based schools (recently reported in *New Left Notes*). On the other hand, *if the young have options and can organize and criticize*, on-the-job education is the quickest way to workers' management which, in my opinion, is the only effective democracy.

University education—liberal arts and the principles of the professions—is for adults who already know something, who have something to philosophize. Otherwise, as Plato pointed out, it is just verbalizing.

To provide a protective and life-nourishing environment for children up through twelve, Summerhill is an adequate model. I think it can be easily adapted to urban conditions if we include houses of refuge for children to resort to, when necessary, to escape parental and neighborhood tyranny or terror. Probably an even better model would be the Athenian pedagogue, touring the city with his charges; but for this the streets and working-places of the city must be made safer and more available than is likely. (The pre-requisite of city-planning is for the children to be able to use the city, for no city is governable if it does not grow citizens who feel it is theirs.) The goal of elementary pedagogy is a very modest one: it is for a small child, under his own steam, to poke interestedly into whatever goes on and to be able, by observation, questions, and practical imitation, to get something out of it in his own terms. In our society this happens pretty well at home up to age four, but after that it becomes forbiddingly difficult.

I have often spelled out this program of incidental education, and found no takers. Curiously, I get the most respectful if wistful attention at teachers' colleges, even though what I propose is quite impossible under present administration. Teachers know how much they are wasting the children's time of life, and they understand that my proposals are fairly conservative, whereas our present schooling is a new mushroom. In general audiences, the response is incredulity. Against all evidence, people are convinced that what we do must make sense, or is inevitable. It does not help if I point out that in dollars and cents it might be cheaper, and it would certainly be more productive in tangible goods and services, to eliminate most schools and make the community and the work that goes in it more educational. Yet the majority in a general audience are willing to say that they themselves got very little out of *their* school years. Occasionally an old reactionary businessman agrees with me enthusiastically, that book-learning isn't worth a penny; or an old socialist agrees, because he thinks you have to get your books the hard way.

Among radical students, I am met by a sullen silence. They want Student Power and are unwilling to answer whether they are authentically students at all. That's not where it's at. (I think they're brainwashed.) Instead of "Student Power," however, what they should be demanding is a more open entry into society, spending the education money more usefully, licensing and hiring without irrelevant diplomas, and so forth. And there *is* an authentic demand for Young People's Power, their right to take part in initiating and deciding the functions of society that concern them—as well, of course, as governing their own lives, which are nobody else's business. Bear in mind that we are speaking of ages seventeen to twenty-five, when at all other times the young would already have been launched in the real world. The young have the right to power because they are numerous and are directly affected by what goes on, but especially because their new point of view is indispensable to cope with changing conditions, they themselves being part of the changing conditions. This is why Jefferson urged us to adopt a new constitution every generation.

Perhaps the chief advantage of incidental education rather than schooling is that the young can then carry on their movement informed and programmatic, grounded in experience and competence, whereas "Student Power," grounded in a phony situation, is usually symbolic and often mere spite.

AFTER DESCHOOLING, WHAT?

Ivan Illich

Schools are in crisis, and so are the people who attend them. The former is a crisis in a political institution; the latter is a crisis of political attitudes. This second crisis, the crisis of personal growth, can be dealt with only if understood as distinct from, though related to, the crisis of the school.

Source. "After Deschooling, What?" by Ivan Illich. From *Social Policy,* September/October 1971, pages 5–13. Copyright © 1971 Social Policy Corporation. Reprinted by permission of the Social Policy Corporation, New York, New York 10010.

Schools have lost their unquestioned claim to educational legitimacy. Most of their critics still demand a painful and radical reform of the school, but a quickly expanding minority will not stand for anything short of the prohibition of compulsory attendance and the disqualification of academic certificates. Controversy between partisans of renewal and partisans of disestablishment will soon come to a head.

As attention focuses on the school, however, we can be easily distracted from a much deeper concern: the manner in which learning is to be viewed. Will people continue to treat learning as a commodity—a commodity that could be more efficiently produced and consumed by greater numbers of people if new institutional arrangements were established? Or shall we set up only those institutional arrangements that protect the autonomy of the learner—his private initiative to decide what he will learn and his inalienable right to learn what he likes rather than what is useful to somebody else? We must choose between more efficient education of people fit for an increasingly efficient society and a new society in which education ceases to be the task of some special agency.

SCHOOLS REPRODUCE SOCIETY

All over the world schools are organized enterprises designed to reproduce the established order, whether this order is called revolutionary, conservative, or evolutionary. Everywhere the loss of pedagogical credibility and the resistance to schools provide a fundamental option: shall this crisis be dealt with as a problem that can, and must, be solved by substituting new devices for school and readjusting the existing power structure to fit these devices? Or shall this crisis force a society to face the structural contradictions inherent in the politics and economics of any society that reproduces itself through the industrial process?

In the United States and Canada huge investments in schooling only serve to make institutional contradictions more evident. Experts warn us: Charles Silberman's report to the Carnegie Commission, published as *Crisis in the Classroom*, has become a best seller. It appeals to a large public because of its well-documented indictment of the system— in the light of which his attempts to save the school by patching up its most obvious faults pall into insignificance. The Wright Commission, in Ontario, had to report to its government sponsors that postsecondary education is inevitably and without remedy taxing the poor disproportionately for an education that will always be enjoyed mainly by the rich. Experience confirms these warnings: Students and teachers drop out; free schools come and go. Political control of schools replaces bond issues on the platforms of school board candidates, and—as recently happened in Berkeley—advocates of grassroots control are elected to the board.

On March 8, 1971, Chief Justice Warren E. Burger delivered the unanimous opinion of the court in the case of *Griggs v. Duke Power Co.* Interpreting the intent of Congress in the equal opportunities section of the 1964 Civil Rights Act, the Burger Court ruled that any school degree or any test given prospective employees must "measure the man for the job," not "the man in the abstract." The burden for proving that educational requirements are a "reasonable measure of job performance" rests with the employer. In this decision, the court ruled only on the use of tests and diplomas as means of racial discrimination, but the logic of the Chief Justice's argument applies to any use of an educational pedigree as a prerequisite for employment. "The Great Training Robbery" so effectively exposed by Ivar Berg must now face challenge from congeries of pupils, employers, and taxpayers.

In poor countries schools rationalize economic lag. The majority of citizens are excluded from the scarce modern means of production and consumption, but long to enter the economy by way of the school door. And the liberal institution of compulsory schooling permits the well-schooled to impute to the lagging consumer of knowledge the guilt for holding a certificate of lower denomination, thereby rationalizing through a rhetorical populism that is becoming increasingly hard to square with the facts. . . .

The crisis is epochal. We are witnessing the end of the age of schooling. School has lost the power, which reigned supreme during the first half of this century, to blind its participants to the divergence between the egalitarian myth its rhetoric serves and the rationalization of a stratified society its certificates produce. The loss of legitimacy of the schooling process as a means of determining competence, as a measure of social value, and as an agent of equality threatens all political systems that rely on schools as the means of reproducing themselves.

School is the initiation ritual to a society oriented toward the progressive consumption of increasingly less tangible and more expensive services, a society that relies on worldwide standards, large-scale and long-term planning, constant obsolescence through the built-in ethos of never-ending improvements: the constant translation of new needs into specific demands for the consumption of new satisfactions. This society is proving itself unworkable.

SUPERFICIAL SOLUTIONS

Since the crisis in schooling is symptomatic of a deeper crisis of modern industrial society, it is important that the critics of schooling avoid superficial solutions. Inadequate analysis of the nature of schooling only postpones the facing of deeper issues. But most criticism of the schools is pedagogical, political, or technological. The criticism of the educator is leveled at what is taught and how it is taught. The curriculum is outdated, so we have courses on African culture, on North American imperialism, on Women's Liberation, on food and nutrition. Passive learning is old-fashioned, so we have increased student participation, both in the classroom and in the planning of curriculum. School buildings are ugly, so we have new learning environments. There is concern for the development of human sensitivity, so group therapy methods are imported into the classroom.

Another important set of critics is involved with the politics of urban school administration. They feel that the poor could run their schools better than a centralized bureaucracy that is oblivious to the problems of the dispossessed. Black parents are enlisted to replace white teachers in the motivation of their children to make time and find the will to learn.

Still other critics emphasize that schools make inefficient use of modern technology. They would either electrify the classroom or replace schools with computerized learning centers. If they follow McLuhan, they would replace blackboards and textbooks with multimedia happenings; if they follow Skinner, they would compete with the classical teacher and sell economy packages of measurable behavioral modifications to cost-conscious school boards.

I belive all these critics miss the point, because they fail to attend to what I have elsewhere called the ritual aspects of schooling—what I here propose to call the "hidden curriculum," the structure underlying what has been called the certification effect. Others have used this phrase to refer to the environmental curriculum of the ghetto street or the suburban lawn, which the teacher's curriculum either reinforces or vainly attempts to replace. I am using the term "hidden curriculum" to refer to the structure of schooling as opposed to what happens in school, in the same way that linguists distinguish between the structure of a language and the use the speaker makes of it.

THE REAL HIDDEN CURRICULUM

The traditional hidden curriculum of school demands that people of a certain age assemble in groups of about thirty under the authority of a professional teacher for from five hundred to a thousand times a year. It does not matter if the teacher is authoritarian so long as it is the teacher's authority that counts; it does not matter if all meetings occur in the same place so long as they are somehow understood as attendance. The hidden curriculum of school requires—whether by law or by fact—that a citizen accumulate a minimum quantum of school years in order to obtain his civil rights.

The hidden curriculum of school has been legislated in all the united nations from Afghanistan to Zambia. It is common to the United States and the Soviet Union, to rich nations and poor, to electoral and dictatorial regimes. Whatever the ideologies and techniques explicitly transmitted in their school systems, all these nations assume that political and economic development depend on further investment in schooling.

The hidden curriculum teaches all children that economically valuable knowledge is the result of professional teaching and that social entitlements depend on the rank achieved in a bureaucratic process. The hidden curriculum transforms the explicit curriculum into a commodity and makes its acquisition the securest form of wealth. Knowledge certificates—unlike property rights, corporate stock, or family inheritance—are free from challenge. They withstand sudden changes of fortune. They convert into guaranteed privilege. That high accumulation of knowledge should convert to high personal consumption might be challenged in North Vietnam or Cuba, but school is universally accepted as the avenue to greater power, to increased legitimacy as a producer, and to further learning resources.

For all its vices, school cannot be simply and rashly eliminated; in the present situation it performs certain important negative functions. The hidden curriculum, unconsciously accepted by the liberal pedagogue, frustrates his conscious liberal aims, because it is inherently inconsistent with them. But, on the other hand, it also prevents the takeover of education by the programmed instruction of behavioral technologists. While the hidden curriculum makes social role depend on the process of acquiring knowledge, thus legitimizing stratification, it also ties the learning process to full-time attendance, thus illegitimizing the educational entrepreneur. If the school continues to lose its educational and political legitimacy, while knowledge is still conceived as a commodity, we will certainly face the emergence of a therapeutic Big Brother.

The translation of the need for learning into the demand for schooling and the conversion of the quality of growing up into the price tag of a professional treatment changes the meaning of "knowledge" from a term that designates intimacy, intercourse, and life experience into one that designates professionally packaged products, marketable entitlements, and abstract values. Schools have helped to foster this translation.

Of course, schools are by no means the only institutions that pretend to translate knowledge, understanding, and wisdom into behavioral traits, the measurement of which is the key to prestige and power. Nor are schools the first institution used to convert knowledge to power. But it is in large measure the public school that has parlayed the consumption of knowledge into the exercise of privilege and power in a society in which this function coincided with the legitimate aspirations of those members of the lower middle classes for whom schools provided access to the professions.

EXPANDING THE CONCEPT OF ALIENATION

Since the nineteenth century, we have become accustomed to the claim that man in a capitalist economy is alienated from his labor, that he cannot enjoy it, and that he is deprived of its fruits by those who own the tools of production. Most countries that officially subscribe to Marxist ideology have had only limited success in changing this exploitation, and then usually by shifting its benefits from the owners to the New Class and from the living generation to the members of the future nation-state.

The concept of alienation cannot help us understand the present crisis unless it is applied not only to the purposeful and productive use of human endeavor but also to the use made of men as the recipients of professional treatments. An expanded understanding of alienation would enable us to see that in a service-centered economy man is estranged from what he can "do" as well as from what he can "make," that he has delivered his mind and heart over to therapeutic treatment even more completely than he has sold the fruits of his labor.

Schools have alienated man from his learning. He does not enjoy going to school. If he is poor he does not get the reputed benefits; if he does all that is asked of him, he finds his security constantly threatened by more recent graduates; if he is sensitive, he feels deep conflicts between what is and what is supposed to be. He does not trust his own judgment, and even if he resents the judgment of the educator, he is condemned to accept it and to believe that he cannot change reality. The converging crisis of ritual schooling and of acquisitive knowledge raises the deeper issue of the tolerability of life in an alienated society. If we formulate principles for alternative institutional arrangements and an alternative emphasis in the conception of learning, we will also be suggesting principles for a radically alternative political and economic organization.

Just as the structure of one's native language can be grasped only after he has begun to feel at ease in another tongue, so the fact that the hidden curriculum of schooling has moved out of the blind spot of social analysis indicates that alternative forms of social initiation are beginning to emerge and are permitting some of us to see things from a new perspective. Today it is relatively easy to get wide agreement on the fact that gratuitous, compulsory schooling is contrary to the political self-interest of an enlightened majority. School has become pedagogically indefensible as an instrument of universal education. It no longer even fits the needs of the seductive salesman of programmed learning. Proponents of recorded, filmed, and computerized instruction used to court the schoolmen as business prospects; now they are itching to do the job on their own.

As more and more sectors of society become dissatisfied with school and conscious of its hidden curriculum, increasingly large concessions are made to translate their demands into needs that can be served by the system—and thus disarm their dissent. As the hidden curriculum moves out of the darkness and into the twilight of our awareness, phrases such as the "deschooling of society" and the "disestablishment of schools" become instant slogans. I do not think these phrases were used before last year. This year they have become, in some circles, the badge and criterion of the new orthodoxy. Recently I talked by amplified telephone to students in a seminar on deschooling at the Ohio State University College of Education. Everett Reimer's book on deschooling became a popular college text even before it was commercially published. But this is urgently important: Unless the radical critics of school are not only ready to embrace the deschooling slogan but also prepared to reject the current view that learning and growing up can be adequately explained as a process of programming, and the current vision of social justice based on it—more obligatory consumption for everybody—we may face the charge of having provoked the last of the missed revolutions.

SCHOOLS ARE TOO EASY TARGETS

The current crisis has made it easy to attack schools. Schools, after all, are authoritarian and rigid; they do produce both conformity and conflict; they do discriminate against the poor and disengage the privileged. These are not new facts, but it used to be a mark of some boldness to point them out. Now it takes a good deal of courage to defend schools. It has become fashionable to poke fun at alma mater, to take a potshot at the former sacred cow.

Once the vulnerability of schools has been exposed, it becomes easy to suggest remedies for the most outrageous abuses. The authoritarian rule of the classroom is not intrinsic to the notion of an extended confinement of children in schools. Free schools are practical alternatives; they can often be run more cheaply than ordinary schools. Since accountability already belongs to educational rhetoric, community control and performance contracting have become attractive and respectable political goals. Everyone wants education to be relevant to real life, so critics talk freely about pushing back the classroom walls to the borders of our culture. Not only are alternatives more widely advocated, they are often at least partially implemented: experimental schools are financed by school boards; the hiring of certified teachers is decentralized; high school credit is given for apprenticeship and college credit, for travel; computer games are given a trial run.

Most of the changes have some good effects: the experimental schools have fewer truants; parents have a greater feeling of participation in the decentralized districts; children who have been introduced to real jobs do turn out more competent. Yet all these alternatives operate within predictable limits, since they leave the hidden structure of schools intact. Free schools, which lead to further free schools in an unbroken chain of attendance, produce the mirage of freedom. Attendance as the result of seduction inculcates the need for specialized treatment more persuasively than reluctant attendance enforced by truant officers. Free school graduates are easily rendered impotent for life in a society that bears little resemblance to the protected gardens in which they have been cultivated. Community control of the lower levels of a system turns local school board members into pimps for the professional hookers who control the upper levels. Learning by doing is not worth much if doing has to be defined, by professional educators or by law, as socially valuable learning. The global village will be a global schoolhouse if teachers hold all the strings. It would be distinguishable in name only from a global madhouse run by social therapists or a global prison run by corporation wardens.

In a general way I have pointed out the dangers of a rash, uncritical disestablishment of school. More concretely, these dangers are exemplified by various kinds of co-option that change the hidden curriculum without changing the basic concepts of learning and of knowledge and their relationship to the freedom of the individual in society.

BENIGN INEQUALITY

The rash and uncritical disestablishment of school could lead to a free-for-all in the production and consumption of more vulgar learning, acquired for immediate utility or eventual prestige. The discrediting of school-produced, complex, curricular packages would be an empty victory if there were no simultaneous disavowal of the very idea that knowledge is more valuable because it comes in certified packages and is acquired from some mythological knowledge-stock controlled by professional guardians. I believe that only actual participation constitutes socially valuable learning, a participation by the learner in every stage of the learning process, including not only a free choice of what is to be learned and how it is to be learned but also a free determination by each learner of his own reason for living and learning—the part that his knowledge is to play in his life.

Social control in an apparently deschooled society could be more subtle and more numbing than in the present society, in which many people at least experience a feeling of release on the last day of school. More intimate forms of manipulation are already common, as the amount learned through the media exceeds the amount learned through personal contact in and out of school. Learning from programmed information always hides reality behind a screen.

Let me illustrate the paralyzing effects of programmed information by a perhaps shocking example. The tolerance of the American people to United States atrocities in Vietnam is much higher than the tolerance of the German people to German atrocities on the front, in occupied territories, and in extermination camps during World War II. It was a political crime for Germans to discuss the atrocities committed by Germans. The presentation of U.S. atrocities on network television is considered an educational service. Certainly the population of the United States is much better informed about the crimes committed by its troops in a colonial war than were the Germans about the crimes committed by its SS within the territory of the Reich. To get information on atrocities in Germany meant that one had to take a great risk; in the United States the same information is channeled into one's living room. This does not mean, however, that the Germans were any less aware that their government was engaged in cruel and massive crime than are contemporary Americans. In fact, it can be argued that the Germans were *more* aware precisely because they were not physically overwhelmed with packaged information about killing and torture, because they were not drugged into accepting that everything is possible, because they were not vaccinated against reality by having it fed to them as decomposed "bits" on a screen.

The consumer of precooked knowledge learns to react to knowledge he has acquired rather than to the reality from which a team of experts has abstracted it. If access to reality is always controlled by a therapist and if the learner accepts this control as natural, his entire worldview becomes hygienic and neutral; he becomes politically impotent. He becomes impotent to know in the sense of the Hebrew world *jdh*, which means intercourse penetrating the nakedness of being and reality, because the reality for which he can accept responsibility is hidden from him under the scales of assorted information he has accumulated.

The uncritical disestablishment of school could also lead to new performance criteria for preferential employment and promotion and, most importantly, for privileged access to tools. Our present scale of "general" ability, competence, and trustworthiness for role assignment is calibrated by tolerance to high doses of schooling. It is established by teachers and accepted by many as rational and benevolent. New devices could be developed, and new rationales found, both more insidious than school grading and equally effective in justifying social stratification and the accumulation of privilege and power.

Participation in military, bureaucratic, or political activities or status in a party could provide a pedigree just as transferable to other institutions as the pedigree of grandparents in an aristocratic society, standing within the Church in medieval society, or age at graduation in a schooled society. General tests of attitudes, intelligence, or mechanical ability could be standardized according to criteria other than those of the schoolmaster. They could reflect the ideal levels of professional treatment espoused by psychiatrist, ideologue, or bureaucrat. Academic criteria are already suspect. The Center for Urban Studies of Columbia University has shown that there is less correlation between specialized education and job performance in specialized fields than there is between specialized education and the resulting income, prestige, and administrative power. Nonacademic criteria are already proposed. From the urban ghetto in the United States to the villages of China, revolutionary groups try to prove that ideology and militancy are types of "learning" that convert more suitably into political and economic power than scholastic curricula. Unless we guarantee that job relevance is the only acceptable criterion for employment, promotion, or access to tools, thus ruling out not only schools but all other ritual screening, then deschooling means driving out the devil with Beelzebub. . . .

THREE RADICAL DEMANDS

Any dialogue about knowledge is really a dialogue about the individual in society. An analysis of the present crisis of school leads one, then, to talk about the social structure necessary to facilitate learning, to encourage independence and interrelationship, and to overcome alienation. This kind of discourse is outside the usual range of educational concern. It leads, in fact, to the enunciation of specific political goals. These goals can be most sharply defined by distinguishing three general types of "intercourse" in which a person must engage if he would grow up.

Get at the facts, get access to the tools, and bear the responsibility for the limits within which either can be used. If a person is to grow up, he needs, in the first place, access to things, places, processes, events, and records. To guarantee such access is primarily a matter of unlocking the privileged storerooms to which they are presently consigned.

The poor child and the rich child are different partly because what is a secret for one is patent to the other. By turning knowledge into a commodity, we have learned to deal with it as with private property. The principle of private property is now used as the major rationale for declaring certain facts off limits to people without the proper pedigree. The first goal of a political program aimed at rendering the world educational is the abolition of the right to restrict access to teaching or learning. The right of private preserve is now claimed by individuals, but it is most effectively exercised and protected by corporations, bureaucracies, and nation-states. In fact, the abolition of this right is not consistent with the continuation of either the political or the professional structure of any modern nation. This means more than merely improving the distribution of teaching materials or providing financial entitlements for the purchase of educational objects. The abolition of secrets clearly transcends conventional proposals for educational reform, yet it is precisely from an educational point of view that the necessity of stating this broad—and perhaps unattainable political goal is most clearly seen.

The learner also needs access to persons who can teach him the tricks of their trades or the rudiments of their skills. For the interested learner, it does not take much time to learn how to perform most skills or to play most roles. The best teacher of a skill is usually someone who is engaged in its useful exercise. We tend to forget these things in a society in which professional teachers monopolize initiation into all fields and disqualify unauthorized teaching in the community. An important political goal, then, is to provide incentives for the sharing of acquired skills.

The demand that skills be shared implies, of course, a much more radical vision of a desirable future. Access to skills is restricted not just by the monopoly of schools and unions over licensing: there is also the fact that the exercise of skills is tied to the use of scarce tools. Scientific knowledge is overwhelmingly incorporated into tools that are highly specialized and that must be used within complex structures set up for the "efficient" production of goods and services for which demand becomes general while supply remains scarce. Only a privileged few get the results of sophisticated medical research, and only a privileged few get to be doctors. A relatively small minority will travel on supersonic airplanes, and only a few pilots will know how to fly them.

The simplest way to state the alternatives to this trend toward specialization of needs and their satisfaction is in educational terms. It is a question of the desirable use of scientific knowledge. In order to facilitate more equal access to the benefits of science and to decrease alienation and unemployment, we must favor the incorporation of scientific knowledge into tools or components within the reach of a great majority of people.

Insight into the conditions necessary for the wider acquisition and use of skills permits us to define a fundamental characteristic of post-industrial socialism. It is of no use—indeed it is fraudulent—to promote public ownership of the tools of production in an industrial, bureaucratic society. Factories, highways, and heavy-duty trucks can be symbolically "owned" by all the people, as the Gross National Product and the Gross National Education are pursued in their name. But the specialized means of producing scarce goods and services cannot be used by the majority of people. Only tools that are cheap and simple enough to be accessible and usable by all people, tools that permit temporary association of those who want to use them for a specific occasion, tools that allow specific goals to emerge during their use—only such tools foster the recuperation of work and leisure now alienated through an industrial mode of production.

To recognize, from an educational point of view, the priority of guaranteeing access to tools and components whose simplicity and durability permit their use in a wide variety of creative enterprises is simultaneously to indicate the solution to the problem of unemployment. In an industrial society, unemployment is experienced as the sad inactivity of a man for whom there is nothing to make and who has "unlearned" what to do. Since there is little really useful work, the problem is usually "solved" by creating more jobs in service industries like the military, public administration, education, or social work. Educational considerations oblige me to recommend the substitution of the present mode of industrial production, which depends on a growing market for increasingly complex and obsolescent goods, by a mode of postindustrial production that depends on the demand for tools or components that are labor intensive and repair intensive, and whose complexity is strictly limited.

Science will be kept artificially arcane so long as its results are incorporated into technology at the service of professionals. If it were used to render possible a style of life in which each man could enjoy housing, healing, educating, moving, and entertaining himself, then scientists would try much harder to retranslate the discoveries made in a secret language into the normal language of everyday life.

SELF-EVIDENT EDUCATIONAL FREEDOMS

The level of education in any society can be gauged by the degree of effective access each of the members has to the facts and tools that—within this society—affect his life. We have seen that such access requires a radical denial of the right to secrecy of facts and complexity of tools on which contemporary technocracies found their privilege, which they, in turn, render immune by interpreting its use as a service to the majority. A satisfactory level of education in a technological society imposes important constraints on the use to which scientific knowledge is put. In fact, a technological society that provides conditions for men to recuperate personally (and not institutionally) the sense of potency to learn and to produce, which gives meaning to life, depends on restrictions that must be imposed on the technocrat who now controls both services and manufacture. Only an enlightened and powerful majority can impose such constraints.

If access to facts and use of tools constitute the two most obvious freedoms needed to provide educational opportunity, the ability to convoke peers to a meeting constitutes the one through which the learning by an individual is translated into political process—and political process, in turn, becomes conscious personal growth. Data and skills an individual might have acquired shape into exploratory, creative, open-ended, and personal meaning only when they are used in dialectic encounter. And this requires the guranteed freedom for every individual to state, each day, the class of issue which he wants to discuss, the class of creative use of a skill in which he seeks a match—to make this bid known—and, within reason, to find the circumstances to meet with peers who join his class. The rights of free speech, free press, and free assembly have traditionally meant this freedom. Modern electronics, photo-offset, and computer techniques in principle have provided the hardware that can provide this freedom with a range undreamt of in the century of enlightenment. Unfortunately, the scientific know-how has been used mainly to increase the power and decrease the number of funnels through which the bureaucrats of education, politics, and information channel their quick-frozen TV dinners. But the same technology could be used to make peer-matching, meeting, and printing as available as the private conversation over the telephone is now.

On the other hand, those who are both dispossessed and disabused of the dream of joy via constantly increasing quanta of consumption need to define what constitues a desirable society. Only then can the inversion of institutional arrangement here drafted be put into effect—and with it a technological society that values occupation, intensive work, and leisure over alienation through goods and services.

Educational Alternatives: A Postscript

A POSTSCRIPT: SOCIAL REFORM AS EDUCATIONAL POLICY

James J. Shields, Jr.

The diverse and often antagonistic education reforms initiated in the 1960s follow very definite and historically well-established lines. They continue reform patterns set by the Romantics, who focus on freedom in learning; the structuralists, who deal with school services, organization, and control; and the Social Reformers, who are interested in the ways that education can be used to improve society.

THE ROMANTICS

Much of the discussion of contemporary education reform centers on the romantics or, as Van Til calls them, "the compassionate critics." Over the last decade radical thinking in education for most people has meant the work of A.S. Neill, Carl Rogers, and George Leonard, just to mention some of the leading lights in the movement. Edgar Frieden-berg, Jonathan Kozol, George Dennison, James Herndon, and Paul Goodman also belong in this list even though they are somewhat of a breed apart. While, indeed, they are Romantics, theirs is a romanticism that is charged with more social realism than the others.

Paul Goodman conveys the sense of what the Romantics are about in the comments he made on A.S. Neill's *Summerhill*. He said, "... our recent form of progressive education has been a reaction to social engineering, the trend of 1984, as Orwell came to call it: obedience to authoritarian rules, organizational role playing instead of being,

Source. "The New Critics in Education," by James J. Shields, Jr. From Intellect, October 1973. Copyright © 1973 by *Society for the Advancement of Education.* Also published in James J. Shields, Jr., The Crisis in Education is Outside the Classroom, Fastback Series, Bloomington, Indiana, Phi Delta Kappa, 1973.

destruction of community by competition and grade-getting, objective knowledge without personal meaning."

The Romantics are in reaction to the way the individual is treated in school. They argue that in our society the individual is undervalued and that objects and institutions are overvalued. Schools, the Romantics hold, reflect this trend in that they imbue in students the sense that they are worthless, that their individuality is to be despised, and that their true importance rests in their ability to serve the purposes of the school, the state, and the economy.

Human beings are not carbon copies of each other, yet schools treat them as if they are. Each individual has a unique nervous system that picks up distinctive impulses and, as a result each individual interprets the world in a distinctive manner and learns different things. Romantics want educators to give more thought to inborn individuality and to build educational programs that will enable each child to discover himself and pursue his particular interests in his own special way.

Generally, Romantics feel that incidental education—that is, educational experience centered in the ongoing activities of society—is better suited to learning than direct teaching. In fact, much of what goes on in the name of teaching is thought to arrest human growth. One critic in response to the question: Is teaching possible? answered, ". . .my bias is that teaching is largely a delusion."

Some Romantics have moved away from the concept of public education entirely to the notion of a deschooled society. They argue that schooling is wasteful of human energy and intelligence, and that formal education should be replaced with a network of opportunities for incidental education. Basically, they want to multiply the variety of experiences under which youth can learn and grow into adulthood.

The interest in deschooling is a predictable reaction to the tight grip the public school has on our society. In 1968, educational services comprised 50 percent of state and local governmental activities, and, since then, education has been the area of fastest growth in the country. As schooling absorbs more and more of our lives, it is difficult to recall that less than a century ago the majority of children had no direct school experiences, and that less than 25 years ago only 35 percent of all pupils completed high school.

Schooling has become a major condition for entry into society. Earlier in the century jobs that provided a foothold on the occupational ladder were available for young people who wished to drop out of school. Today, almost all positions are reserved for those who have had at least 12 years of schooling.

Like Mandarin China, we have locked ourselves into a system of school degrees and certificates. This is unfortunate because, as Berg has shown, not only is there no correlation but in most cases there is an inverse correlation between educational achievement and subsequent proficiency on the job.

The deschooling advocates have made a significant contribution by publicizing the dangers involved in using school certificates as a condition of employment. They have made a clear case that the use of school credentials in this way is a violation of basic civil liberties. Just as the use of race, sex, color or age as a condition for employment is a violation of civil liberties, so, too, is the use of school certificates.

Countless millions of students are forced to sit in classrooms five and six hours a day because they want a job as a supermarket clerk or an assembly worker in an automotive plant. They do not want to be in those classrooms, and they are understandably angry. But what can they do? If they complain or resist they are threatened with expulsion from school and denied access to employment; they know failure in school means failure in life.

It is not just the threat of failure in life that keeps children in school, it is also the threat of being jailed as a truant. Educators in the deschooling movement propose that along with doing away with the use of school diplomas and credentials as requirements for employment, compulsory education laws should be repealed. As long as compulsory education laws exist, and school certificates are required for employment, people will go to schools whether they want to or not, or whether they learn anything or not.

Much of what the Romantics have to say makes natural good sense and is usually apparent to sensitive educators. However, there are definite limits to the value of their proposals. For example, if the deschooling advocates studied the historical record they would find that education can be, at least, as restrictive under a format of incidental learning as under one of formal learning.

Many of the teachers who have tried to put the ideas of the Romantic critics into practice in their classrooms have been ineffective, frustrated, and even defeated. A number of books have begun to appear discussing this failure. In the first part of *Freedom and Beyond,* John Holt accepts as a given the importance of freedom in learning and moves the reader to a forthright analysis of some of the difficulties and tensions that are created when learners are free to learn on their own terms. Although *Freedom and Beyond* is one of the best of the new works that agonize over the frustration that is in store for the educator who structures freedom into his classroom, it offers little that is really helpful in averting these problems.

THE STRUCTURALISTS

The best-organized and most fully financed efforts to reform education can be seen in the work of the Structuralists. This branch of the reform movement is represented in the drive for school integration, the provision for compensatory educational assistance for the poor, plans for community control of schools, and the voucher system.

Between 1965 and 1968 over $3 billion was spent in compensatory education programs to offset the disadvantages that the poor brought to schools. Yet little in the way of academic gains were made by the children in these programs. Study after study confirmed what James Coleman reported in 1966, that increased school spending does not in and of itself improve pupil achievement on standardized tests.

Critics casting around for explanations for the failure settled on the claim that educational problems would not be resolved until school control was taken away from professional educators and placed in the hands of those in local communities. Unfortunately, the experiments that came into national view in 1968 proved to be a disaster, and little has happened since then to give any indication that community control will fulfill the promises of its proponents. For all intents and purposes, community control has joined integration and compensatory education as still another reform that has turned out to be longer on promise than on results.

The failure of efforts to place educational control in the hands of those in local communities has stimulated interest in proposals for voucher plans that give considerable power over education to parents. The federal government is experimenting with a voucher system in scattered localities around the country. Christopher Jencks, the primary author of the government's plan, has worked out a procedure to give parents educational vouchers with which they might buy whatever kind of eduction they want for their children, either at a neighborhood school or elsewhere.

The rallying cry of advocates of the voucher system is that public schools must become more truly public. Actually, as Areen and Jencks point out, there is little that is public about our public schools; the word "public" is a misnomer. Exclusive suburban neighborhoods restrict access to good public schools in precisely the same way admissions committees and tuition charges operate to limit access to good private schools. Academically exclusive urban high schools have admission standards only a few can meet. And even though we call our school systems "public," they refuse to give anyone information about what they are doing, how well they are doing it, and whether children are getting what parents want.

Milton Friedman at the University of Chicago was an early pioneer of the voucher system. He held that the poor would have far better opportunities in a school system open to the competition of the market than they do in our current closed and more paternalistic system. Under the Friedman plan, each school-age child would be granted a voucher good for a sum of money, probably equal to the average per capita cost of public education, that could be used either at a public or at a private school. The result, he predicted, would be the destruction of professional educators' monopoly over schooling, more power for parents and students, and higher-quality education.

Educational programs in the majority of private schools in America provide a strong counter argument against the claim that a voucher plan would effect widespread experimentation. Private schools have to compete for students, yet have not done a great deal more experimentation than public schools.

Actually, the secondary school curriculum in most private schools is interchangeable and similar to the curriculum of most public high schools. This is not an accident any more than it is the fact that widely divergent public schools serving greatly different constituencies reach, basically, the same decisions about their curriculum. All secondary schools, public and private, conform to schooling practices called "standards" set by nongovernmental national and regional accrediting bodies. Also, all schools feel compelled to shape their programs to reflect what the Educational Testing Service and the elite colleges define as education.

The reality is that professional educators, whether in public or private schools, do not initiate critical educational policy decisions; they respond to societal forces shaped by the requirements of our industrial system and mediated by groups that are national in scope. Professional educators do little more than administer their own dependency. There is nothing in voucher system plans that will change this. In fact, there is every likelihood that the voucher system will provide universities and private industry with an important vehicle for participating in the educational marketplace in a more significant way, thereby accelerating the nationalization of the decision-making process.

THE SOCIAL REFORMERS

Voucher plans, along with programs to introduce freer learning in schools, the deschooling of society, integration, compensatory education, and community control, are doomed to failure because their perspective on the problem of change is so limited. Unless educational change is integrated with societal change, there is little chance for success.

In *Pedagogy of the Oppressed,* a work which is giving new fire to the social reform movement in education, Freire tells us that the process of full human education rests at the crosspoint of action and the reflection of men upon their world in order to change it; for Freire, education takes place when men are engaged in inquiry and the creative transformation of the world.

Instead of teaching students to come to terms with society, Freire proposes that students be taught to question and change it. It is a problem-posing method that starts with the present, concrete world in which the learner lives. Freire believes that knowledge cannot be acquired apart from an individual's knowledge of himself and his position in the world.

Problem-posing education strives for the emergence of social conscience. Underlying the process is the assumption that an individual's conscience conditions his attitudes and ways of behaving, and that until an individual perceives and works to resolve social, political, and economic contradictions, he will be mastered by them. It is a form of social psychoanalysis. At its best, psychoanalysis is a cooperative project in which individuals try to learn why they are suffering and how they can become whole. It is a process of discovery in which the hidden wellsprings of behavior are found that provide clues as to how change can be realized. In problem-solving education, the roots of behavior are analyzed in much the same way that personal roots of behavior are analyzed in traditional psychoanalytical practice.

C.Wright Mills, an ideological ancestor of Freire, also was a proponent of problem-posing education. He wanted schools to provide training in skills and an education in values that would enable individuals to acquire those cultural, political, and technical sensibilities that would help them turn personal troubles into public issues and public issues into personal action.

Mills and Freire believe that true education is a process of drawing action out of thinking. As they see it, problem-posing education involves critical intervention in the world. Problem-posing education does more than prepare men for action; it engages them in action within the structure of the entire society.

In Freire's world, politics and education are not separated; teacher, student and politician are one. The myth is that education and politics are separate. The fact is, education and politics never have been separate and are not separate now. Our schools require daily flag salutes, the singing of the national anthem, teacher loyalty oaths, the removal of "un-American books" from libraries, the dismissal of teachers for holding views incompatible with community prejudice, and the use of educational material produced and distributed nationally by oil companies. What Freire does is to ask educators to face up to this reality and institute a politics of liberation in the place of the politics of oppression that are now practiced in schools.

Freire's ideas sound radical; actually, they are not. He simply asks that we educate for citizenship. One of the reasons our cities are ungovernable, Goodman points out, is that there are not enough citizens; no city is governable that does not educate citizens who feel it is theirs. The beginning of meaningful city planning rests nowhere else except in the provision of educational experiences that engage individuals in the invention and the reinvention of the cities in which they live. Freire calls for the provision of educational experiences that present the city, indeed the world, as a problem to be solved; basically, that is what education for citizenship is.

In the final analysis, unless societal change is built into education reform activities, the efforts are much like flapping arms in the breeze and expecting to fly. Not only are the efforts useless, they are damaging as well. They continue a long tradition in American educational reform of form without substance, a tradition that has led to crippling cynicism and, unnecessarily, has dampened real hope regarding the possibilities for significant educational reform.

There are forces outside education that must be confronted if true reform is to take place. The words of a student, who wrote to me at the end of the first term in which I attempted to create a free-learning environment in my college classes, captures the sense of these forces quite well. She wrote:

"We spent the majority of the time getting acquainted with each other and taking advantage of our freedom away from lectures and required readings. In the beginning, our group behaved very much like the students of Summerhill who stayed away from classes on their arrival because they did not know how to handle freedom. This was because freedom and democracy require both responsibility and participation—two elements which are never asked of students. Dewey's idea of learning by doing is easier said than done.

"I do not think the fault lies merely with the students; the fault lies in our authoritarian society that addicts you to consumption and indentures you to a corporation to pay off your addiction. It is a society in which if you don't dominate, you are dominated. Unfortunately, most students spent the semester keeping up with the authoritarians in society, that is doing things that would give them a position of authority *in society. The students, myself included, neglected those things they would have liked to do in your course.*

"No changes in your course, indeed in the entire university, will have any meaning unless that big world beyond your course and the university changes. For this reason, I suggest that in the future you and your students apply your energies to the world rather than to the course."

Obviously, the crisis in education begins outside the classroom and a whole new approach to educational reform is required if education is to succeed. This approach would bring teachers and students together to identify societal problems they consider important and to work together to resolve them. Of necessity, this will bring them in touch with doctors, engineers, politicians, and lawyers because teachers have only limited usefulness as agents of change. Also, it will bring them out of the schools and into the towns and into the cities, towns, and villages because the classroom is too small and too simple a place to achieve much in the way of reform.

At this juncture, it is difficult to visualize the full shape this approach to educational reform will take. Few if any precedents are available for guidance. There are a few places in the traditional school, however, where social reform activities could be started immediately. For instance, they could be placed in social studies courses in junior and senior high schools, in political science and sociology courses in liberal arts programs, and in the social foundations of education courses required in teacher-education programs.

In addition, school and college clubs could be established along the lines of Common Cause and Ralph Nader's Center for the Study of Responsive Law on Food Safety and Chemical Harvest. These represent but initial steps in infusing education with activities organized to raise social consciousness and to involve students in effective social reform. Nonetheless, because they can be implemented immediately, they represent important steps in shifting the function of education from the mass production of individuals who are helpless in the face of problems that threaten to destroy them to the cultivation of individuals who feel responsible to work daily for a better and more equitable world.

Unfortunately, the awareness that, in the final analysis, the key to improving education is in societal reform (that a fundamental task of educators, indeed of all professionals, is to work for social change) generates no magic. My own efforts to design courses around personal growth and social change attest to this. Ours is not an ideal world populated by ideal men. And fears by conservative elders aside, youth tend to be cast pretty much in the mold of their parents. Their experiences in their families and in their schools have successfully kept them from developing the independence of spirit, the self-awareness, and the sensitivity toward others that effective social-reform activities require. Another more difficult problem is the determination of those who have a vested interest in endless economic growth and in the way wealth is distributed to keep things as they are.

It is easy to despair of structuring social reform into the educational process; however, to do so is to despair of true educational reform. School problems have and will continue to resist conventional in-school answers. The solution lies in the interaction of the classroom with the source of the crisis outside the classroom. Therefore, a primary task for the reformer is to help educators realize that there is no middle ground; either they work to make education, schooling, and social reform one, or they function as agents of a vastly inequitable and repressive society.

bibliography

THE FUNCTIONS AND PURPOSES OF SCHOOLS: PHILOSOPHICAL
FOUNDATIONS

Farber, Jerry. *The Student as Nigger*. North Hollywood, California: Contact Books, 1969.

Freire, Paolo. *Pedagogy of the Oppressed*. New York: Herder and Herder, 1972.

Friedenberg, Edgar. *Coming of Age in America: Growth and Acquiescence*. New York: Random House, 1965.

Gattegno, Caleb. *What We Owe Children: The Subordination of Teaching to Learning*. New York: Outerbridge and Dienstfrey, 1970.

Goodman, Paul. *Compulsory Miseducation*. New York: Horizon Press, 1964.

———. *Growing Up Absurd*. New York: Random House, 1956.

Greene, Mary F. and Orlette Ryan. *The Schoolchildren Growing Up in the Slums*. New York: Pantheon Books, 1965.

Greer, Colin. *Cobweb Attitudes*. New York: Teachers College Press, 1970.

Hentoff, Nat. *Our Children Are Dying*. New York: Viking Press, 1966.

Herndon, James. *How to Survive in Your Native Land*. New York: Simon and Schuster, 1971.

———. *The Way It Spozed to Be*. New York: Simon and Schuster, 1969.

Holt, John. *How Children Fail*. New York: Pitman, 1964.

Kaufman, Bel. *Up the Downstaircase*. Englewood Cliffs, New Jersey: Prentice-Hall, 1964.

Kohl, Herbert. *36 Children*. New York: New American Library, 1967.

Kozol, Jonathan. *Death at an Early Age. The Destruction of Hearts and Minds of Negro Children in Public Schools*. Boston: Houghton Mifflin, 1967.

Nordstrom, Carl, et al. *Society's Children. A Study of Resentment in Secondary School Education*. New York: Random House, 1967.

Silberman, Charles E. *Crisis in the Classroom*. New York: Random House, 1970.

A HISTORICAL PERSPECTIVE ON THE FUNCTIONS AND PURPOSES
OF SCHOOLS

Bailyn, Bernard. *Education in the Forming of American Society*. New York: Vintage Books, 1965.

Callahan, Raymond E. *Education and the Cult of Efficiency: A Study of the Social Forces That Have Shaped the Administration of the Public Schools*. Chicago: University of Chicago Press, 1962.

Curti, Merle. *The Social Ideas of American Educators*. Toronto: Littlefield, Adams, 1961.

Greene, Maxine. *The Public School and the Private Vision*. New York: Random House, 1965.

Greer, Colin. *The Great School Legend: A Revisionist Interpretation of American Public Education*. New York: Basic Books, 1972.

Karier, Clarence, *et al. Roots of Crisis: American Education For the Twentieth Century*. Chicago: Rand McNally & Co., 1973.

Katz, Michael B. *The Irony of Early School Reform: Educational Innovation in Mid-Nineteenth Century Massachusetts*. Cambridge: Harvard University Press, 1968.

Spring, Joel. *Education and the Rise of the Corporate State*. Boston: Beacon Press, 1972.

THE SOCIAL AND CULTURAL DIMENSION: FAMILY BACKGROUND AND EDUCATIONAL OPPORTUNITY.

Birley, Derek and Ann Dufton. *An Equal Chance: Equalities and Inequalities in Educational Opportunity*. New York: Fernhill, 1971.

Bronfenbrenner, Urie and John C. Condry, Jr. *Two Worlds of Childhood*. New York: Russell Sage, 1970.

Carnoy, Martin, ed. *Schooling in a Corporate Society: The Political Economy of Education in America*. New York: David McKay, 1972.

Carter, Thomas P. *Mexican Americans in School: A History of Educational Neglect*. Princeton, N. J.: College Entrance Examination Board, 1970.

Coleman, James, *et al. Equality of Educational Opportunity*. Washington, D.C.: U.S. Government Printing Office, 1966.

Conant, James B. *Slums and Suburbs*. New York: McGraw-Hill, 1961.

Craft, Maurice, ed. *Family, Class, and Education: A Reader*. New York: Fernhill, 1970.

Crossland, Fred E. *Minority Access To College*. New York: Schocken Books, 1971.

Davis, Allison. *Social Class Influences upon Learning*. Cambridge: Harvard University Press, 1948.

Fuchs, Estelle. *Teachers Talk: Views from Inside City Schools*. New York: Doubleday, 1969.

Guthrie, James W., *et al. Schools and Inequality*. Cambridge: MIT Press, 1971.

Havighurst, Robert J. and Daniel U. Levine. *Education in Metropolitan Areas*. Second edition. Boston: Allyn and Bacon, 1971.

Havighurst, Robert J., *et al. Growing up in River City*. New York: John Wiley, 1962.

Herriott, Robert E. and Nancy H. St. John. *Social Class and the Urban School*. New York: Wiley, 1966.

Hollingshead, A. B. *Elmstown's Youth: The Impact of Social Classes on Adolescents.* New York: Wiley, 1949.

Jackson, Brian and Denis Marsden. *Education and the Working Class.* London: Routledge and Kegan Paul, 1962.

Jencks, Christopher, *et al. Inequality: A Reassessment of the Effects of Family and Schooling in America.* New York: Basic Books, 1972.

Leacock, Eleanor Burke. *Teaching and Learning in City Schools.* New York: Basic Books, 1969.

Levy, Gerald E. *Ghetto School: Class Warfare in an Elementary School.* New York: Pegasus, 1970.

Miller, Gordon W. *Educational Opportunities and the Home.* New York: Humanities Press, 1971.

Miller, Harry L. and Roger R. Woock. *Social Foundations of Urban Education.* Hinsdale, Illinois: Dryden Press, 1970.

Passow, Harry, *et al. Education of the Disadvantaged.* New York: Holt, Rinehart, and Winston, 1967.

Roberts, Joan I. *Scene of the Battle: Group Behavior in the Urban Classroom.* New York: Doubleday, 1970.

Rosenthal, Robert and Leonore Jacobs. *Pygmalion in the Classroom: Teacher Expectation and Pupil Intellectual Development.* New York: Holt, Rinehart, and Winston, 1968.

Schoolboys of Barbiana. *Letters to a Teacher.* New York: Random House, 1970.

Sexton, Patricia. *Education and Income.* New York: Viking Press, 1961.

Young, Michael. *The Rise of Meritocracy, 1870–2033: An Essay on Education and Equality.* New York: Random House, 1959.

HOW SCHOOLS ARE FINANCED: THE ECONOMIC FOUNDATIONS OF EDUCATION.

Coons, John E., William H. Clune, and Stephen Sugarman. *Private Wealth and Public Education.* Cambridge: Harvard University Press, 1970.

New York State Commission on the Quality Cost and Financing of Elementary and Secondary Education. *Report.* Albany, New York: The Commission, 1972.

Wise, Arthur E. *Rich Schools, Poor Schools: The Promise of Equal Educational Opportunity.* Chicago: University of Chicago Press, 1968.

WHO CONTROLS EDUCATION: THE POLITICS OF EDUCATION.

Agger, Robert E. and Marshall N. Goldstein. *Who Will Rule the Schools: A Cultural Class Crisis.* Belmont, Calif.: Wadsworth Publishing Company, 1971.

Anderson, James G. *Bureacuracy in Education.* Baltimore: Johns Hopkins Press, 1969.

Berube, Maurice R. and Marilyn Gittell. *Confrontation at Ocean Hill Brownsville.* New York: Praeger, 1969.

Corwin, Ronald G. *Militant Professionalism: A Study of Organizational Conflict in High School.* New York: Appleton-Century-Crofts, 1970.

Crain, Robert L., et al. *The Politics of School Desegregation: Comparative Case Studies of Community Structure and Policy Making.* Chicago: Aldine, 1968.

Gans, Herbert. *The Levitttowners: How People Live and Politic in Suburbia.* New York: Pantheon Books, 1967.

Gittell, Marilyn. *Participants and Participation: A Study of School Policy in New York.* New York: Praeger, 1967.

Fischer, Louis and David Schimmel. *The Civil Rights of Teachers.* New York: Harper and Row, 1973.

Mayer, Martin. *The Teacher Strike: New York 1968.* New York: Harper and Row, 1969.

Mills, C. Wright. *The Power Elite.* New York: Oxford University Press, 1956.

Ridgeway, James. *The Closed Corporation: American Universities in Crisis.* New York: Random House, 1969.

Rogers, David. *110 Livingston Street: Politics and Bureaucracy in New York City Schools.* New York: Random House, 1968.

Rosenthal, Alan, ed. *Governing Education: A Reader on Politics, Power, and Public School Policy.* Garden City, N.Y.: Doubleday, 1969.

Schrag, Peter. *The Village School Downtown: Politics and Education, A Boston Report.* Boston: Beacon Press, 1967.

Swanson, Bert E. *The Struggle for Equality: School Integration Controversy in New York.* New York: Hobbs, Dorman, 1966.

Wasserman, Miriam. *The School Fix: NYC, USA.* New York: Outerbridge and Deinstfrey, 1970.

EDUCATIONAL ALTERNATIVES: REFORM WITHIN THE SCHOOL SYSTEM.

Ashton-Warner, Sylvia. *Teacher.* New York: Simon and Schuster, 1963.

Bremer, John and Michael von Moschzisker. *The School Without Walls: Philadelphia's Parkway Program.* New York: Holt, Rinehart, and Winston, 1971.

Brown, George I. *Human Teaching for Human Learning: An Introduction to Confluent Education.* New York: Viking Press, 1971.

Counts, George S. *Dare the Schools Change the Social Order.* New York: John Day, 1932.

Fantini, Mario and Gerald Weinstein. *Making Urban Schools Work.* New York: Holt, Rinehart and Winston, 1968.

Gartner, Alan, Mary Kohler, and Frank Riessman. *Children Teach Children.* New York: Harper and Row, 1971.

Gordon, Edmund W. and Doxey A. Wilkerson. *Compensatory Education for the Disadvantaged.* Princeton, N.J.: College Entrance Examination Board, 1966.

Guthrie, James W. and Edward Wynne. *New Models for American Education.* Englewood Cliffs, N.J.: Prentice-Hall, 1971.

Hassett, Joseph H. and Arlene Weisberg. *Open Education: Alternatives Within Our Tradition.* Englewood Cliffs, N.J.: Prentice-Hall, 1971.

Havighurst, Robert J., ed. *Metropolitanism: Its Challenge to Education.* The 67th Yearbook of the National Society for the Study of Education. Chicago: University of Chicago Press, 1968.

Holt, John. *How Children Learn.* New York: Pitman, 1967.

———. *What Do I Do on Monday Morning.* New York: Dutton, 1970.

Kohl, Herbert. *The Open Classroom.* New York: New York Review of Books, 1970.

Leonard, George. *Education and Ecstasy.* New York: Delacorte Press, 1968.

Levin, Henry M., ed. *Community Control of Schools.* Washington, D.C.: Brookings Institution, 1970.

Lurie, Ellen. *How to Change the Schools: A Parent's Action Handbook on How to Fight the System.* New York: Vintage Books, 1970.

Miller, S. M. *Breaking the Credentials Barrier.* New York: Ford Foundation, n.d.

Murrow, Casey and Liza. *Children Come First.* New York: Harper and Row, 1971.

Nader, Ralph. *Action For a Change: A Student's Manual for Public Interest Organizing.* New York: Grossman Publishers, 1972.

Passow, Harry, ed. *Developing Programs for the Disadvantaged.* New York: Teachers College Press, 1968.

Postman, Neil and Charles Weingartner. *The Soft Revolution: A Student Handbook for Turning Schools Around.* New York: Dell, 1971.

———. *Teaching as a Subversive Activity.* New York: Delacorte Press, 1969.

Rogers, Carl. *Freedom to Learn.* Columbus, Ohio: Charles Merrill, 1969.

Taba, Hilda and Deborah Elkins. *Teaching Strategies for the Culturally Disadvantaged.* Stokie, Illinois: Rand McNally, 1966.

Weber, Lillian. *The English Infant School and Informal Education.* Englewood Cliffs, N.J.: Prentice-Hall, 1971.

Weinberg, Meyer. *Integrated Education.* Beverly Hills, Calif.: Glencoe Press, 1968.

EDUCATIONAL ALTERNATIVES: FREE SCHOOL AND NO SCHOOLS

Bhaerman, Steve and Joel Denker. *No Particular Place to Go: The Making of a Free High School.* New York: Simon and Schuster, 1972.

Dennison, George. *The Lives of Children, The Story of the First Street School.* New York, Random House, 1969.

Graubard, Allen. *Free the Children.* New York: Pantheon Books, 1972.

Gross, Ronald and Beatrice. *Radical School Reform.* New York: Simon and Schuster, 1971.

Holt, John. *Freedom and Beyond.* New York: Dutton, 1972.

Illich, Ivan. *Deschooling Society.* New York: Harper and Row, 1971.

Illich, Ivan, et al. *After Deschooling, What?* New York: Harper and Row, 1973.

Kozol, Jonathan. *Free Schools.* Boston: Houghton, Mifflin, 1972.

Neill, A. S. *Summerhill.* New York: Hart, 1960.

O'Gorman, Ned. *The Storefront.* New York: Harper/Colophon, 1970.

Reimer, Everett. *School Is Dead: Alternatives in Education.* Garden City, N.Y.: Doubleday, 1971.

Snitzer, Herb. *Living at Summerhill.* New York: Macmillan, 1968. *Summerhill: For and Against.* New York: Hart, 1970.